COACHES CLINICS

INSTANT REVIEW

BASKETBALL NOTEBOOK

VOLUME 5

©1999 Coaches Choice Books. All rights reserved. Printed in the United States.

No part of this book may be reproduced, stored in a retrieval system, or transmitted, in any form or by any means, electronic, mechanical, photocopying, recording, or otherwise, without the prior permission of Sagamore Publishing, Inc.

ISBN: 157167-375-X
Library of Congress Catalog Card Number: 97-81339

Book Layout and Diagrams : Ryan Gray and Janet Wahlfeldt
Cover Design: Britt Johnson
Cover Photos: Photos courtesy of: The University of Arkansas and the University of North Carolina
Editor: Bob Murrey

Coaches Choice Books is a division of: Sagamore Publishing, Inc.
P.O. Box 647
Champaign, IL 61824-0647
Web Site: http://www.sagamorepub.com

1994 CHAMPIONS

NCAA

MEN'S	WOMEN'S
DIVISION I	
ARKANSAS	NORTH CAROLINA
NOLAN RICHARDSON	SYLVIA HATCHELL
DIVISION II	
CAL STATE-BAKERSFIELD	NORTH DAKOTA STATE
PAT DOUGLASS	AMY RULEY
DIVISION III	
LEBANON VALLEY	CAPITAL UNIVERSITY
PAT FLANNERY	DIXIE JEFFERS

NAIA

DIVISION I	
OKLAHOMA CITY	SO. NAZARENE
WIN CASE	JERRY FIENKBEINER
DIVISION II	
EUREKA	NO. STATE-SD
DAVE DARNALL	AMY RULEY

NJCAA

DIVISION I	
HUTCHINSON	TRINITY VALLEY
C. DAVID FARRAR	JOE CURL
DIVISION II	
JOLIET	SW MICHIGAN
PAT KLINGER	TOM BARNES
DIVISION III	
GLOUCESTER COUNTY	ANOKA-RAMSEY
STEPHEN SOLOMONE	DON MIELKE

CONTENTS

1994 CHAMPIONS 3

PREFACE 5

QUICK CLIP BIOS 6

DIAGRAM LEGEND 8

COACH	TOPIC	PAGE
MURRY BARTOW	HIGH-POST OFFENSE	9
GEORGE BLANEY	DRILLS FOR THE PRESSING GAME	16
JOAN BONVICINI	TRANSITION BASKETBALL	21
DALE BROWN	HOW TO MOTIVATE YOURSELF AND OTHERS	28
JOE CIAMPI	THE MATCH-UP DEFENSE	32
JANE ALBRIGHT-DIETERLE	HALF-COURT OFFENSE	43
JIM FOSTER	COMMODORE OFFENSE	50
CRAIG HARTMAN	MOTION OFFENSE	59
DEBBIE HOLLEY	HOW TO BLOW OFF STEAM...	69
STU JACKSON	FULL-COURT PRESSURE	74
	SKILL DEVELOPMENT	80
MIKE JARVIS	PHILOSOPHY AND SECONDARY OFFENSE	84
TANYA JOHNSON	SUMMER PROGRAM: MAKE USE OF WHAT YOU HAVE	88
LON KRUGER	EXPECTATIONS FOR PLAYERS/COACHES	92
	OUT-OF-BOUNDS UNDERNEATH	94
THE LEGENDS	A PANEL DISCUSSION	102
BRIAN MAHONEY	TEACHING MAN-TO-MAN DEFENSE	108
	1-4 PRESS OFFENSE	110
MUFFET McGRAW	OFFENSIVE DRILLS	114
	IRISH OFFENSE	119
JOE McKEOWN	BLIZZARD DEFENSE	125
	DEVELOPING POST PLAYERS	131
BILLIE MOORE	TEACHING FUNDAMENTALS	137
	SPECIAL SITUATIONS, TIME, AND SCORE	140
DANNY NEE	THE NEBRASKA OFFENSE	144
TOM PENDERS	GUARD PLAY	153
DAWSON PIKEY	A FAST BREAK FOR ALL PEOPLE	156
RENE PORTLAND	CHANGING DEFENSES	166
	EFFECTIVE PRESSES	171
GEORGE RAVELING	CREATING BETTER PLAYER/COACH RELATIONSHIPS	175
MEL ROUSTIO	COACHING BEYOND THE X'S AND O'S	183
JO ANN RUTHERFORD	TIGER FAST BREAK	189
	REBOUNDING	193
SONNY SMITH	TWELVE RULES FOR A ZONE OFFENSE	197
	THE ZONE OFFENSE	202
	SHOOTING	206
BOB SUNDVOLD	PRACTICE PREPARATION	209
	A ZONE DEFENSE FOR A MAN-TO-MAN COACH	211
ROY WILLIAMS	TEACHING THE "3"	219
	FIELD GOAL PERCENTAGE DEFENSE	224

PREFACE

The 1994 season couldn't have closed on a more exciting note. In the men's championship game, Arkansas narrowly defeated Duke 76-72, and in the women's championship game, North Carolina defeated Louisiana Tech 60-59 on a three-point basket in the last .7 seconds.

USA Coaches Clinics is proud to present Volume 5 of the Instant Review Notebook Series. This 31st annual edition includes presentations covering nearly every phase of basketball including practice sessions, player relationships, individual and team drills, plus lots of offenses and defenses. You will find in-depth presentations that will help as you prepare for the season.

A special thank-you is extended to Tom Desotell, Burt Droste, Patrick Gifford, Mary Jane Grellner, and Mike Kunstadt for the many hours they spent compiling this notebook.

We hope you enjoy this edition of the Instant Review Notebook and remind you USA Coaches Clinics offers nearly 1,100 book and video titles in many sports. If you would like to be added to our mailing list, please call us for a free catalog at 1-800-COACH-13.

We look forward to meeting you at future clinics.

Sincerely,

Bob Murrey
President and Editor

1993-1994

MURRY BARTOW - UAB
This bright young coach is in his fifth year as an assistant at UAB. He will be a head coach in another year. Works with the defense. Spent the '86-'87 season at Indiana and two years as an assistant at William and Mary.

GEORGE BLANEY - Holy Cross
He is the veteran coach in the Patriot League with 22 years as the head coach at Holy Cross. During that time, the Crusaders have won over 355 games (430 in a 26-year career). Served as President of the NABC in 1993-94.

JOAN BONVICINI - Arizona (Women's)
Third year at Arizona. Had 12 consecutive winning seasons at Long Beach State. Has young club with outstanding shooting ability. She has the unique ability to communicate and get players to play above their talents.

DALE BROWN - LSU
The second-winningest coach in SEC history. 22 years at LSU with 12 NCAA and two NIT appearances. Considered one of the best motivators in the game. Recruited and coached Shaquille O'Neal.

JOE CIAMPI - Auburn
He has masterfully developed a program based on defense, rebounding and winning. In 16 years at Auburn (350-9 1) his teams have made 10 NCAA appearances, reaching the Final Four three times. 68-game winning streak at home 1986-91.

JANE ALBRIGHT-DIETERLE - Northern Illinois
Tenth year at NU (164-104). She helped coach the USA Women's 1992 Jr. National team to a silver medal in the World Championship Tournament in Mexico. Recently moved to the University of Wisconsin.

JIM FOSTER - Vanderbilt (Women's)
His team was ranked #1 until a recent clash with Tennessee. Second year at Vanderbilt. Final 8 last year. Assistant U.S. Olympic Coach in 1992.

"BIGHOUSE" GAINES - Winston-Salem
Over 40 years at the same school. His teams have won 822 games, second only to Adolph Rupp. Very active on NABC Board. In Naismith Hall of Fame. Retired in April '93.

CRAIG HARTMAN - Indiana
The 26-year-old Hartman has been involved in the Indiana program for eight years, four as a manager. He is currently an Administrative Assistant in the program and is considered an astute young coach with a bright future.

ERNIE HOBBIE - The Shot Doctor
He has spent a lifetime teaching shooting and has the rare ability to take poor shooters and make them great. The Shot Doctor teaches simple techniques to young kids, as well as stars in the NBA. He is a retired elementary principal.

DEBBIE HOLLEY - Communications Specialist
Do you ever get angry with your players? Her experience in business, as a mother, and now as a youth coach enables her to show you how anger can be made a positive point. A popular clinic speaker.

STU JACKSON - Wisconsin
Second year at Wisconsin and is picked to contend for the Big 10 title. His first recruiting class had an instant impact. He brought the up-tempo style with him from the NBA. Head coach of the Knicks 1989-91.

MIKE JARVIS - George Washington
Last year he led the Colonials (21-9) to the school's 1st NCAA tournament in 32 years and its first Sweet 16 appearance. Eight consecutive winning seasons in Division 1. Coached at Boston U. and Cambridge and Latin (Patrick Ewing).

TANYA JOHNSON - Northfield Marillac H.S. (IL)
She has been there 10 years, and recently her team (19-4) won its 200th game of her career. This Class AA all Catholic girls' school competes with the best in Chicago, even though it is the smallest school in this class.

LON KRUGER - Florida
At Florida four years and has gained national respect for his ability to run an impeccable program. The Gators are now contenders for a divisional title in the SEC. Coached and played at Kansas State (11 years, 179-148-55).

QUICK CLIP BIOS

BRIAN MAHONEY - St. John's
His first year as the head coach. He succeeded the legendary Lou Carnesecca after 16 years as his assistant. His team is in the race for the title.

MUFFET McGRAW - Notre Dame
In the six years at ND, her teams have won the conference championship four years. She was the head coach at Lehigh for five years (88-4 1). In 11 seasons her teams have never had a losing season. Coached two years in high school (50-3).

JOE McKEOWN - George Washington (Women's)
Four years at George Washington, where he rebuilt the program in two years. Has coached at New Mexico State. Career record shows 73% win-loss ratio.

BILLIE MOORE - UCLA (Women's)
23 years as a head coach. Ranks eighth on list of winningest coaches (423). Two NCAA Championships—one at Cal State-Fullerton and one at UCLA.

DANNY NEE - Nebraska
Eighth year at NU. Since 1990, the Cornhuskers own the Big 8's best record at 65-29 (700). Three straight NCAA Tournament bids plus two NIT bids. His teams have won over 250 games in 15 years at Nebraska and Ohio U.

TOM PENDERS - Texas
Likes to play an aggressive and quick press and run style. His backcourt is ranked as in the country. Had outstanding success at Rhode Island. His teams have won 376 games in 22 years as a head coach.

DAWSON PIKEY - Clayton H. S. (MO)
He has coached both boys and girls very successfully for 20 years. His teams have played in the state Final Four. Also coached a women's junior college team to a state title.

RENE PORTLAND - Penn State (Women's)
1991 USBWA Coach of the Year. 11 years at Penn State, all winning seasons. Postseason bids 10 of 11 years.

GEORGE RAVELING - USC
He's developed fine programs at Washington State, Iowa and now USC. One of the top recruiters in the business. A member of the NABC Board of Directors. Highly respected by his peers.

MEL ROUSTIO - Jacksonville H.S. (IL)
30th year in high school coaching. He is the winningest coach (17 years) in JHS history. His teams have won over 450 games and he ranks high on the list of winningest coaches in Illinois. Very active in community affairs.

JO ANN RUTHERFORD - Missouri (Women's)
Has won over 350 games in 17 years at Mizzou. Big 8 Coach of the Year three times. Active in USA Basketball as a coach in Olympic sports festivals.

RALPH SAMPSON - Former NBA Player
After an outstanding career at Virginia, Sampson played in the NBA for 10 years. He is the only player to be named Associated Press Player of the Year three times (1981, '82, '83).

SONNY SMITH - Virginia Commonwealth
Five years at VCU. You will like his presentations. Humorous and effective. He has good information on zone offense for high school. Had an outstanding program at Auburn, where he coached for 17 years.

BOB SUNDVOLD - Central Missouri State
After a successful career as a high school coach, he assistanted at Missouri under Norm Stewart. Sundvold worked one year with Charlie Spoonhour at Southwest Missouri State prior to becoming the head coach at CEMO in 1992.

JERRY TARKANIAN - Former UNLV Coach
He is the winningest collegiate coach in the history of the game (winning percentage). Successful at every level from high school to junior college to Division I. He led UNLV to the 1990 Division I Championship.

ROY WILLIAMS - Kansas
His teams play a swarming, tenacious man-to-man defense, and they run at every opportunity. Two trips to the FINAL FOUR in the last three years. Kansas has been ranked in the Top 20 every year. Assistant coach at North Carolina for 10 years.

DIAGRAM LEGEND

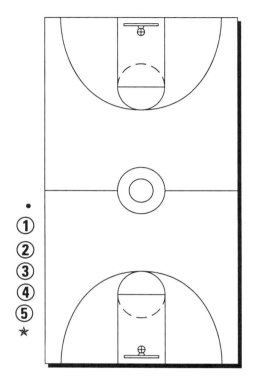

◯ = Offense

X = Defense

◐ = Player with the Ball

— — → = Direct Pass

———⊣ = Screen

∽∽∽→ = Dribble

———→ = Cut of Player without Ball

⊢⊢⊢⊢⊢→ = Shot

MURRY BARTOW

High-Post Offense

Some key thoughts:

- Good spacing is critical-we want to have good floor balance at all times.
- Timing is very important, and we like to use a "guard interchange" to help with the flow and timing of these sets.
- Read the defense. These high-post sets are structured but we want our players to play the game-to see the game-and take what the defense gives them.
- Set good, solid, legal screens. We don't want to get called for setting illegal screens, but we do want to nail people and get our shooters open looks at the basket.
- Good movement without the ball is vital. Players have to use the V-cut and have to learn how to work "up and out" in order to be open to receive the pass on the wing. Players have to be taught how to get open, so the offense can flow smoothly.
- Make hard, sharp cuts. Pass the ball crisply-be sharp-and make hard cuts.
- Shot selection is very important. We want our best shooters taking the most shots and we want these to be high-percentage shots.
- When feeding the post, we want our post feeders to drive the ball down toward the baseline and make sure they have a good angle to feed the post.
- We want our post players just above the block in a strong post-up position. We don't want them to be pushed way out off the block.
- Don't over-use the dribble. Use the dribble to:
  - Improve a passing angle.
  - Get dribble penetration.
  - Take the ball to the basket, etc. Don't dribble just for the sake of dribbling. Make your dribble take you somewhere.
- Versus hard overplay, look for guard and forward backdoors. This has to be worked on and executed, so it can be done instinctively.
- As in any set, execution is critical. You have to work on these sets daily (5-on-0 dry run and 5-on-5) to get the timing down and to perfect the execution of these sets.

High-Post Offensive Sets

- Straight Cuts. Excellent set to get the ball to block the four-man or five-man.

(Diagram 1) Guard interchange—can start to either side.

Diagram 1

(Diagram 2) Straight cut-off, 3's screen.

(Diagram 3) Pass to 3 and make a solid down-screen for 1.

(Diagram 4) Best look: 1 improves angle and feeds 5 on the block.

- Straight Cuts-Backdoor-The high-post offense gives you the needed floor balance to look for guard and forward backdoors.

MURRY BARTOW

Diagram 2

Diagram 3

Diagram 4

(Diagram 5 & 6) Forward Backdoor. If 4 is overplayed and the pass is made to 3, 4 immediately looks to backcut.

Diagram 5

Diagram 6

(Diagram 7 & 8) Guard Backdoor. The first look is to 2 on the backcut, then to 1 on hand-off or 2 cutting off double-screen.

Diagram 7

MURRY BARTOW

Diagram 8

Diagram 10

- Straight Cuts-Lob. This is an excellent quick-hitter for an athletic guard. Will catch the defense off-guard if you've run straight cuts two-three times prior to running this and looking for the lob.

(Diagram 9 & 10) Main look: lob to 2. Great Quick-hitter, after you've run straight cuts several times.

Diagram 11

Diagram 9

Diagram 12

- Double. This is a good set to get your best shooter an open shot cutting off a double-screen.

(Diagram 11)   Guard interchange.

(Diagram 12)   Straight cuts action.

(Diagram 13)   Main look: 2 cuts off double-screen, looking for the "3."

- Go-Pattern-Pass to corner. Great opportunity for an open 3 on top for a shooter cutting off a double-screen.

MURRY BARTOW

Diagram 13

(Diagram 14)   Pass from 1 to 3.

Diagram 14

(Diagram 15)   First look: lob from 3 to 1.

Diagram 15

(Diagram 16 & 17)   On the pass from 3 to 2, there is a two-man between 2 and 4, and the primary look is to 1 on top.

Diagram 16

Diagram 17

- Go-Pattern-Pass to top-Shuffle cut to three-man is the first main look-then look for shooter on top off staggered double-screen.

(Diagram 18)   Pass from 1 to 3.

(Diagram 19)   First look: lob to 1.

(Diagram 20)   On the pass to the top, we look for the shuffle cut by 3.

(Diagram 21)   Next look: is to 2 on top cutting off double-screen.

MURRY BARTOW

Diagram 18

Diagram 19

Diagram 20

Diagram 21

- Go-Pattern-2-Man Game.

(Diagram 22 & 23)   Two-Man game between 1 and 5.

Diagram 22

Diagram 23

MURRY BARTOW

- Handoff. Get a great look to post player on the block-then screen on the ball and nice action off the dribble to a shaping-up post player or to a spot-up shooter off dribble penetration.

(Diagram 24) V-cuts, then takes a handoff from 4.

Diagram 26

Diagram 24

(Diagram 25) Main look: 5 on block-then to 4 on lob.

(Diagram 27 & 28) Power-oriented set, looking to pound the ball in to 4 or 5. When 4 receives the ball at the high post, his first look is to 5. Stepping up and his second look is to 3 (who is a shooter) on the opposite wing.

Diagram 27

Diagram 25

(Diagram 26) Screen on the ball. 1 looks for 4 coming up the lane, then to 2 for a spot-up three-pointer.

- Power-Power-oriented set, working high-low between the 4 and 5.

Diagram 28

- Forward Reverse. Good set to run when you've got a size mismatch on your 2, 3, or 4 man.

(Diagram 29)   1 dribbles; 3 cuts out.

Diagram 29

(Diagram 30)   First look: 3 on block.

Diagram 30

(Diagram 31)   Second look: 3 cutting off double-screen.

Diagram 31

Drills for the Pressing Game

The actual press itself is not as important as how you teach the way to press. One thing I want to stress to you is to coach to your personality. You can't mimic someone else. You cannot do exactly what someone else does offensively or defensively.

When Al McGuire was at Marquette, he would press defensively and then come back on offense and literally hold the ball for two or three minutes. He did this because he was looking for three or four "runs" defensively to take command of the game. The most difficult team I faced as a player was a team that pressured. This defense made it very hard for me to pass, shoot, or dribble.

Forcing me to take the ball out of the center of my body and move it to the side made it difficult for me to do many things. As I built our program at Holy Cross, we started from the defensive end, deciding that we were going to pressure the ball, force turnovers, and score quickly.

Offensively, we wanted to be patient and look for the good shots. This required our players learning to play at two tempos. The player, himself, must be unselfish, self-disciplined, and team-oriented.

Why should you employ the press?

- Most teams you press, won't press you. We played 30 games this year, and we only had three or four teams press us.

- Keeps constant pressure on the opponent.

- Forces your opponent out of its offensive patterns. The more disciplined, and better coached teams are pattern-oriented.

- Forces forwards and centers to come out from the basket so it negates size.

- Allows for steals and a chance to score.

- Picks the tempo of the game. You can speed up or slow down the tempo of the pressing.

- You can hide your weaknesses in the press.

- Pressure defense requires your players to play hard. If they do this, they know there is something good that can happen for them.

- It allows you to blow the game up or to catch up when behind. Players have to worry less about falling behind because they know the press gives them the chance to catch up quickly.

When will you press?

This is a philosophical question you have to answer early. If you are going to press all the time, you are making an unbelievable, total commitment. We did this for quite a few years and then changed our philosophy a little bit by pressing full-court 80% of the time. We did this because teams seemed to be better prepared to handle full-court pressure, so we did more three-quarter court and half-court pressing.

Drills we use to teach our pressing game are:

Take It to the Line
(Diagram 1)   The offensive player attempts to take the ball toward the baseline, but isn't looking to score. The defense attempts to force the offense to pick up the ball and then pressures him. When this occurs, the offensive player throws the ball back to the next person in line and assumes the defensive role. The man who was on defense goes to the back of the opposite line. You should stress to your players keeping their head in the middle of their body and staying balanced.

GEORGE BLANEY

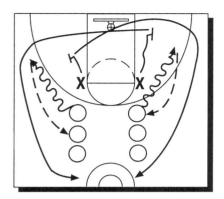

Diagram 1

Box Drill
(Diagram 2) This is a 1-on-2 drill with the offensive player starting in the center of the foul circle and the two defensive players starting on the elbows.

The offensive player tries to get the ball to the opposite end of the floor. We tell our defensive players that if the offensive man dribbles at you, you're to pressure the ball and the opposite defender is to come over and form the trap.

Diagram 2

2-on-1 Drill
(Diagram 3) Here we have two offensive players and one defensive player. The defense; starts between the ball and the offensive player that is inbounds. The offensive player lines up outside the three-point line, and he has to move outside the three-point line to get open. We run this drill to teach our players how hard they have to work to keep their man from getting the ball.

Diagram 3

Zig-Zag Drill
We run this drill everyday. At the end of each zig-zag, we do rim touches, sit-ups, or pushups. We run these drills early in practice, and we never spend more than five minutes on each.

Next, we set up our whole press and show our players what is expected of each. We place two men on offense, and their job is to inbound the ball if possible.

(Diagram 4) We tape a square on the area indicated with our defensive men in their respective positions. We tell X2 that he is to stop his man from getting the ball inside the box except when his man is cutting to the corner. If X2 forces his man to go outside the square to get the ball, we stop the drill and tell our defender what a great job he's done. If the offense gets the ball inbounds, we attempt to trap and cover.

Our positions are set up as such: X1 - our best athlete, big player, "hungry to score": lines up on the ball. X2 - our quickest small forward: lines up on the ball side below the foul. X3 - our second guard: lines up away from the ball below the foul line. X4 - our point guard: lines up away from the ball at half-court. X5 - our center: lines up on the ball side at half-court.

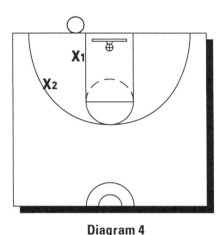

Diagram 4

3-on-3 Press Drill

(Diagram 5) We set up the front of our press against three offensive players. If the ball goes to X2's man, he must play his man straight up and not allow him to dribble to the middle.

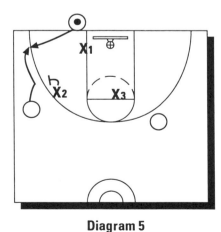

Diagram 5

(Diagram 6) If X2 allows anything, he allows a dribble up the sideline. X1 is to come over and help form the "L" trap if the ball is inbounded below the foul line extended. X3 moves to stop the return pass to the inbounder.

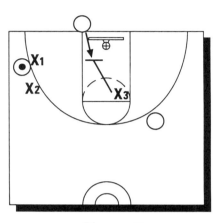

Diagram 6

(Diagram 7) Anything below the top of the key, X1 and X2 and are to trap. Once the ball crosses the top of the key, X1 moves to cover the middle. You can add your X5 man to this drill and tell him that if the ball is forced up the sideline by X2, he is to move to trap with X2 once the ball reaches the old 28-foot hash mark.

Diagram 7

(Diagram 8) This drill teaches our players to force the ball up the sideline. We have a player on offense start below the foul line extended. Our defense starts at half-court with a basketball. He is to roll the ball to the offensive player and then run to pick up the offense and force him to the sideline.

Another drill we use to teach pressing fundamentals is called the Drill. The defense is outside the three-point line in the corner and passes to the offensive player who is in the opposite corner.

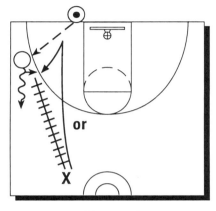

Diagram 8

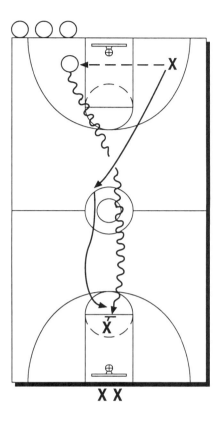

Diagram 9

(Diagram 9) The offense takes off dribbling up the court, and the defense attempts to come up behind and tap the ball away from the offense. If the defense can't tap the ball away, he tries to trap with his defensive partner who started in the lane on the opposite end. If the defense is able to steal the ball, they are to come back up the court playing 2-on-1. Looking at our press as a whole, we start in a 1-2-2 set and we man-to-man the ball before the first pass.

(Diagram 10) We always have our players go to their specific positions and look up to pick the man that is closest to them. Try to deny all inbound passes. X1 has to try real hard to make the pass go to the side closest to him. If 1 is successful in forcing the ball to the sideline, then we look to trap with X1 and X2. X3 moves to cover the inbounder.

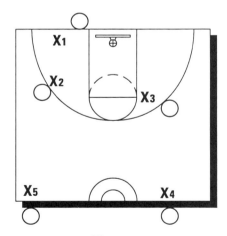

Diagram 10

X4 moves to cover the middle and looks to pick anyone up cutting into this area. X4 must have good judgment and never goes for the steal unless he is 85% certain he'll get the ball. X5 moves back to cover the area behind the trap.

(Diagram 11) If the ball goes beyond our front three defenders, we hustle back to play the half-court defense.

Some of you are asking how we would defend the 1-4 set against our press because of Brian Mahoney's talk on the 1-4 press offense. We can do this several ways:

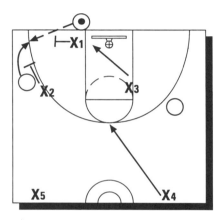

Diagram 11

(Diagram 12) Option 1: We have X1 shade the ball to the short corner, X2 and X3 are to face deny, and X4 and X5 are to deny the sidelines. If X5's man moves up to catch the inbound pass, X2 and X5 switch defensive responsibilities.

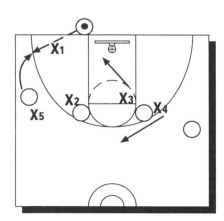

Diagram 12

(Diagram 13) Option 2: We take X1 off the ball and have him play back similar to a free safety.

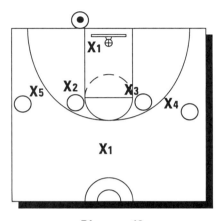

Diagram 13

(Diagram 14) Option 3: We put X5 back and we play X2, X3, and X4 between the four men across.

Diagram 14

We have had great success with pressure during our years at Holy Cross, and I think it can reap you great rewards. Good Luck!

JOAN BONVICINI

Transition Basketball

I'm here to talk about transition basketball, and some things that I do to organize our program. One of the first things I do is to set up goals for the team. I have 10 offensive and 10 defensive goals. You will have to adjust them to the level of your program.

OFFENSIVE TEAM GOALS PER GAME

- Shoot 51% as a team from the floor.
- Take a minimum of 70 shots.
- Shoot 70% from the free-throw line.
- Shoot 20 free throws.
- Get eight fast-break baskets.
- Get 12 offensive rebounds
- Get 20 assists.
- No more than 17 turnovers.
- Have no 30-second violations.
- Score at least 85 points.

DEFENSIVE TEAM GOALS PER GAME

- Hold opponents to 42% field goal percentage.
- Allow a maximum of 60 shots.
- Allow a maximum of 15 free throws.
- Out rebound my opponent by five or more.
- Allow a maximum of 12 assists.
- Force a minimum of 20 turnovers.
- Force one 30-second violation.
- Take two charges.
- Get at least eight steals.
- Allow no more than 70 points.

I give these goals to each player, and they put them in their notebook.

Obviously, if we are going to play a tough opponent, I will adjust them before the game. We will put these on the board at halftime. Your goals must be realistic so you must adjust them to fit your level, but maybe as the season progresses, you can increase them. It makes a big difference if you put them down as team goals as opposed to individual goals.

Something else I did. Coach John Wooden had a Pyramid of Success. I made a little pyramid, too. At the bottom, I put all of our non-conference opponents and I listed them. Then, at the next level, I listed all the conference opponents. Above that, I put in the conference tournament and each level of the play-offs. The players really liked that. They would put up the pyramid in the locker room before a game, with the goals listed. This also went into the notebooks. Before the season starts, I make a chart of what I must cover for the season, and then break it down into week by week prior to the first game. Because of the shortening of our preseason, I tried to put in too much too soon. I learned a good lesson. We needed more fundamental teaching. So, keep it simple and then build on it as the season progresses.

Before the season starts, I put out a master plan and discuss it with the staff. This includes all the things that I want to teach for that particular year. I list conditioning and fundamentals. Under fundamentals, I list individual offense and individual defense. Then, I

JOAN BONVICINI

list the team offenses and defenses, transition game, jump-ball offense, free-throw situations, out-of-bounds plays, and presses. Then these must be put in week-by-week prior to the start of the season.

My main topic is transition. I always considered myself a fast-break coach; I was averaging about 80 points per game. When I put this in, we went to 90 points per game. What happened is that our pace is very difficult to defend. It's not like Westhead when he was at Loyola Marymount. We worked at defense, too. Let's start at the beginning, the way I do it.

(Diagram 1) 5 takes it out-of-bounds. 5 must get the ball out of the net before it hits the floor, steps out-of-bounds and throws the baseball pass. 1, the point guard, starts about the free-throw line extended. The further you start the guard from the baseline, the faster she will get down the floor.

1 is in the middle of the court. 1 will make one or two dribbles and make a chest pass on the run to either 2 or 3. You don't necessarily use your best ballhandler here because she is only going to make one or two dribbles. But, she must be able to make the chest pass on the run. 2 is on the left side of the court; 3 on the right. No matter where they are when the ball is shot, 2 will always go on the left, 3 on the right. They must be able to catch the ball on the run and should be good perimeter shooters. 4 is generally the big forward. As soon as the basket is made, 4 runs the middle of the floor and goes midpost ball side. 4 will then reverse pivot.

(Diagram 2) 3 has the ball; 4 is on the block; 2 is in the corner; 1 went opposite and is spotting up on the weakside. 5 is the trailer. 3 can pass to 2 or 4, but in this case, reverses to 5 who passes to flashes toward 5 as 5 has the ball. 5 can shoot the 3 as an option. After 5 passes to 1, 5 cuts to the block. 4 fills the high post.

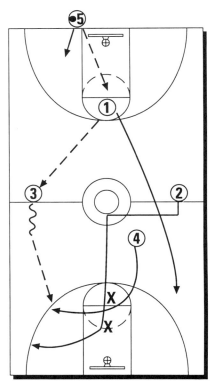

Diagram 1

Diagram 2

(Diagram 3) 5 inbounds to 1 and 1 passes ahead to 2. 4 goes down the middle and posts up strongside block. 1 goes away. 3 cuts to the middle. 2 dribbles down the side. When 3 fills the middle, the cut to the ball must be a direct cut. Do not cut on a diagonal. Make an "L" cut. 3 then goes to the corner. If 2 and 3 can't handle the ball, have 1 dribble down the middle until 2 and 3 spot up.

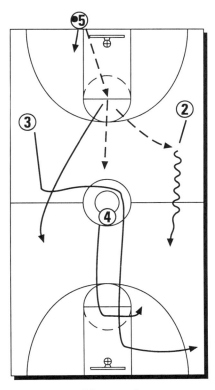

Diagram 3

(Diagram 5) 3 passes to 1 to 5 to 2. 5 cuts to the low post; 4 comes high. The person on the block is the number one option. We want her to get the ball as often as possible. That's why the strong reverse pivot. Some years I made 4 and 5 interchangeable.

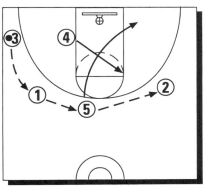

Diagram 5

(Diagram 4) 3 is in the corner and you have a triangle with 2, 3, and 4. 2 passes to 3 in the corner. The defense must make a decision to guard either the corner or the post. 2 interchanges with 1. This keeps 2's defense from double-teaming in the corner.

(Diagram 6) Let's say that 1 is guarded. 1 runs a circle route to try to get the ball. 3 and 2 have started to run, but it is important that they are not more than 15 feet from 1. When 2 and 3 see 1 being guarded, they come back. Suppose this time, 5 passes to 3. 3 takes the ball on the dribble; 1 goes opposite; 2 goes middle. 4 posts up on the strongside block. If 5 has a strong arm, she can pass the ball to half-court to 2 or 3. When you run this system, your opponents will be so conscious of this that instead of sending 4 players to the offensive boards, they will send 3.

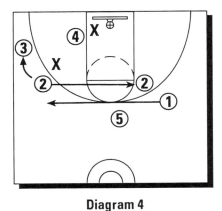

Diagram 4

JOAN BONVICINI

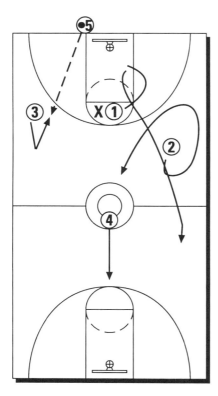

Diagram 6

(Diagram 7) Skip-passes. 3 has the ball; 2 runs the turnout; 4 is on the block. Instead of passing to 5, 3 skip-passes to 1. If 1 has the three-point shot, she shoots it. 5 cuts to the block; 4 flashes high. 3 fills at the point. You must teach your team when this transition ends and when we start our regular offense. It ends when we have a reversal and get nothing out of it.

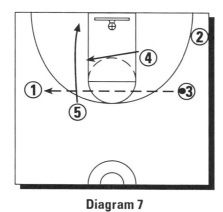

Diagram 7

(Diagram 8) Assume that 2 and 3 are not open. 1 declares a side. 2 will remain opposite. 5 will come down and set a screen.

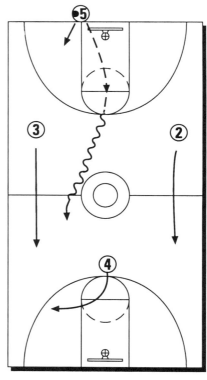

Diagram 8

(Diagram 9) 1 has kept the dribble. 5 sets a screen for 1 near the top of the circle and goes to the block. 1 could have the jump shot, or 1 can pass to 2 for the shot. 5 can also step back and get the pass back from 1. 4 then goes to the high post.

Diagram 9

(Diagram 10) This is how opponents try to stop this. They allow the point guard to get the ball and they defend 2 and 3 and 4. It is very important that 1 declares a side and stays on that side. This makes the screen by 5 very important.

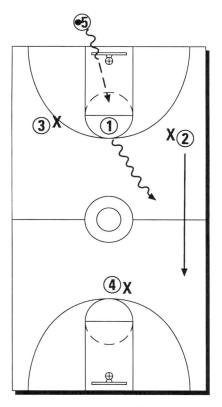

Diagram 10

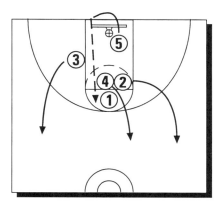

Diagram 11

(Diagram 11) This is the way we practice it starting on the first day of practice. Prior to going out on the floor, I tell each person their position. Then I diagram and go through the simple options in the beginning. Then we will walk through it stressing the importance of how 5 takes the ball out of the net. The point guard must start in the middle of the court. If 1 goes on the side, she takes away the option to the wing. I do 5 on 0 every single day. All five players are in the key. 5 puts the ball in the basket and we break. I will give them options, no defense, rebound all missed shots.

(Diagram 12) Then we do 5 on. We have a coach near mid-court with five defensive players. She will send out three players, or four players or all five. They could be trapping, could be challenging the point guard. We spend 10 to 15 minutes a day on this. When don't we run transition? On a dead ball, if it's a crucial part of the game, or at the end of a close game.

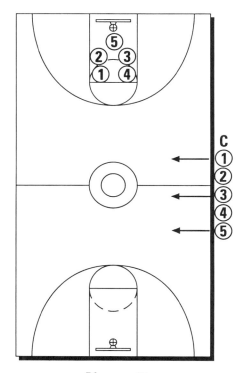

Diagram 12

(Diagram 13) After a missed basket, we do the same thing. Suppose 4 rebounds and outlets to 1. 1 fills the middle and 2 and 3 run wide. The player who didn't get the rebound, (5), goes to the block on the ball side. I like the fast break. It's fun to play and fun to watch. More kids are going to play, and they must be in shape.

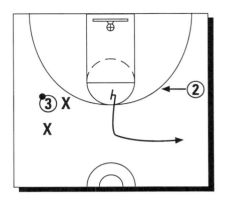

Diagram 14

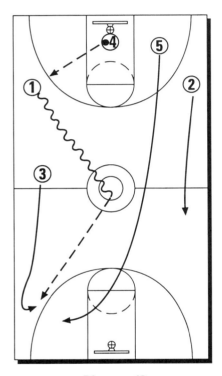

Diagram 13

(Diagram 14) If you are being pressed and the ball is inbounded to 3, 1 goes away and 2 replaces.

(Diagram 15) With this system, people are afraid to press you. But, let's say that they do press with a 2-2-1. 1 must come up to get the ball. 1 gets trapped. 5 does a semicircle, and I promise you, 5 will be open for the pass from 1. 2 and 3 are now open for the pass from 5. I don't let 5 dribble. 5 catches, jumpstops, and passes to 2 or 3.

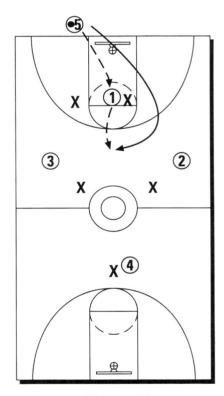

Diagram 15

(Diagram 16) 3 dribbles down; 2 does a turnout; 4 is on the block, and we are in the offense. I don't believe that you can run an offense like ours and then sit in a 2-3 zone on defense. I have always liked to switch defenses.

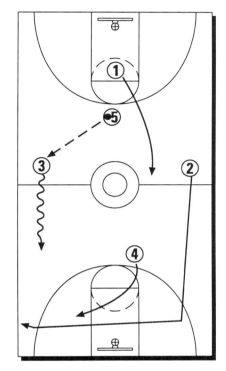

Diagram 16

DALE BROWN

How to Motivate Yourself and Others

You don't have to listen to me to be able to do something that I'm going to talk to you about. When I got the job at LSU, I wanted to learn from the experts, so I wrote letters to the most successful people in their areas. I didn't want to take just coaching, I wanted all areas. At the time, the two most successful people in entertainment were Bob Hope and Lawrence Welk. The two most successful coaches in the history of the game were John Wooden and Adolph Rupp. Who's the father of positive thinking? Norman Vincent Peale. I reached the president of General Motors.

I spent a minimum of forty-eight hours with each of them, a week with Coach Wooden. The common denominator among all of them was their unique ability to lift others and make them feel good about themselves and have a good self-image. I visited with their office help, people who answered phones, custodians; I went to the whole works, not just their right-handed men and women. All of them had the unique ability to lift others and make them feel good about themselves, a good self-image. They were hard workers and they were great persevering—type people.

I'm going to talk about the one that is very important. By the time that you are 18 years old, you are told 180,000 times "no." I believe that Moses came down with 10 commandments and written on the back of those commandments is "what thou shall do," and those are the most important. I want to share with you what I think is the singularly most important ingredient. You don't have to be a Rhodes Scholar to coach, but if you have the technique and the ability to lift others, you can coach. I'm not talking about false evangelism.

What does it take to lift a team? The kind of team you don't want to play is a team that has a spirit about them. They believe they can do anything. It is how we look at life that determines whether we are ever going to find that elusive thing we are all looking for—peace, love, happiness and success. It starts with something very simple. It is how you look at things, what you fix in your mind that actually happens. In this age of negativism, cynicism, sensationalism, who lifts you? Where do you get a positive uplift? You must do it yourself. Some people will call it spiritualism. I think it comes from within. William James, the philosopher, was asked, "If you were talking to the world, in one paragraph, what would you tell the world to make it a better place?" He said, "The greatest revolution in the history of the world is the discovery that human beings, by changing the inner attitude of their minds, can change the outer aspects of their lives forever, and live with success and happiness."

Let's talk about that. A father and son go fishing. They run out of gas and have to jog a mile for gas. They get to the lake, and it rains for 12 solid hours. They catch no fish and go home. Dad goes in and says that it was the worst day of his life. His son comes in and says, "Today was the greatest day of my life. We had to jog; first time we ever worked out together. Then we spent 12 hours talking. I didn't know you met Dad in high school, etc." Why is it that two people can have a different outlook? It is what you fix in your mind that you become.

Several major factors that destroy men, organizations, teams, what kills a person's spirit are basically three things. One, they are worried about criticism. You must teach teams this. Secondly, this is our job. Many kids come from poor neighborhoods and they see the pimp, the drug dealer, and the guy who just got six months for rape back on the street. They are seeing money coming in by illegal means; you don't have to work hard. We have gone through probably the most unmotivated period in the history of America in the last two decades, and we have lost a lot of our power. It is our job to be able to

DALE BROWN

teach them these things. Some lose confidence, become embarrassed; they toss it in; they take drugs; they blame someone else, they become comfortable, and what you get is a lesson in mediocrity. That is what happened in the athletic scene. This is the last bastion of discipline. Some teams don't have any spirit, and then there is a selfishness. We all preach team above self.

There is a poem:

> I'd rather see a lesson than hear one any day.
>
> I'd rather you walk with me than to merely show the way.
>
> The eye is a better teacher and more willing than the ear.
>
> The counsel is confusing but examples are always clear.
>
> But best of all the teachers are the ones who live the creed.
>
> To see "good" put into action is what everybody needs.
>
> I soon can learn to do it if you let me see it done.
>
> I can see your hand in action, but your tongue too fast may run.
>
> And the counsel you are giving may be very fine and true.
>
> But I'd rather get my lesson by observing what you do.

What are the prerequisites for going to the top? They don't change for any of us. These four things never change. I call them Life's Four Hurdles.

- You must eliminate from people's vocabulary and mentality the "I can't do something." Kids come from homes where they have been beaten down. They begin to think they can't do anything.

- Teach people not to be afraid to fail, particularly the youngsters of today. It embarrasses them. It is not your IQ, it's your FQ, your failure quotient. Kids don't want to fail. Some kids don't try hard because they are afraid to fail.

- Handicap. We are in the age of excuses. I'm too slow; I'm too black; I'm too female; I'm too skinny, etc.

- Who am I? Where am I going? What do I want out of life?

Let's go back to number one. Physiologists, sociologists and psychologists have told us for centuries that they have proven without a doubt that men and women don't get 20% of their physical and mental abilities out of their bodies. When Johnny Weismuller swam in the Olympics, he held 67 world records. They said no one would break them. Today young teenagers are breaking his records. Whatever you fix in your mind, you can become. The kids who are breaking records have someone to reinforce them.

Psychologists have proven that motivation is the key. Let's say that Bob doesn't rebound. Instead of berating him in front of the team, you call him over and tell him he isn't doing the job, but that he has done it in the past and you know he can do it. Most of the "I can'ts" come from the subconscious.

I read this poem before the start of every season.

> If you think you're beaten, you are.
>
> If you think you dare not, you don't.
>
> If you like to win, but think you can't, it's almost a cinch you won't.

If you think you'll lose, you lost for out in the world success begins with a fellow's will. It's all in the state of mind.

If you think you're outclassed, you are.

You've got to be sure of yourself before you can ever win a prize.

Life's battles don't always go to the stronger or faster men, but sooner or later the man who wins is the man who thinks he can.

Hurdle Two, "Afraid to Fail." I grew up in a poverty situation and I had an inferiority complex. I thought people built success on success. Success is not built on success. Almost every great thing that has ever happened, great inventions, come from failure. So when you fail, welcome to the world. Don't be afraid to fail. It's not your IQ, it's your FQ. How much failure can you take? In their biographies, both de Vinci and Einstein stated that 90 percent of their solutions were incorrect. But they had the guts to hang in. You must learn how to accept failure and not lose faith in yourself, nor give up.

The Third Hurdle is that you must teach people to eliminate excuses. How many of you got away with excuses? I did. Any teacher I could con, I didn't respect. Here is an example of someone with a handicap who did not give up. I gave a talk at a children's home and a blind boy told me that he was going to LSU and major in music. I was concerned that I gave someone false hope. LSU is a 3,000-acre campus, 30,000 students and many buildings. How is he going to find the classrooms?

School started in the fall and my secretary said that he was here to see me. The athletic building is built like a saucer; the hall obviously isn't straight, and my office is the fifth door on the left, so he isn't going to be able to find it. As I went to open the office door, I heard a shrill clicking noise. Here was the boy, no seeing eye dog, no cane, and nobody with him. The first thing he said was, "Coach Brown, it's good to see you again." He came in, and sat in a chair. He said that after my talk, he was in a science class with bats as the topic. Bats can't see so they have a type of sonar system; they send out sounds and determine how far away things are by the echo. He set up things in the kitchen and made the clicking noises and listened how they echoed. He developed a system that he can send out a sound, and it helps him navigate. That boy graduated in four years with a major in music.

One week before graduation, he was the fourth blind person to skydive out of a plane. And he landed exactly where he was supposed to. Am I going to land where I am supposed to land? Are you going to land where you are supposed to land? These are not stories to motivate you momentarily. Anyone can be motivated for 48 hours. These stories are about people like us who have overcome these handicaps.

Now the Fourth Hurdle. This is the most noble and perfect victory of all. It is the triumph over yourself. You can have all this other stuff, and you can still miss peace, love, and happiness. You can have success but it ends in tragedy. Some of the top people have overdosed. Why? Because they didn't understand that life is a race, and you must negotiate these hurdles.

The fourth one, "Know yourself, who am I, where am I going, what do I want out of life......" Listen to The Man in the Glass.

> When you get what you want and your struggle for self and the world makes you king or queen for a day,
>
> Just go to the mirror and look at yourself and see what that person has to say.
>
> For it isn't your father or mother, wife or sweetheart, your boss whose judgment upon you has passed.

DALE BROWN

The fellow whose verdict counts most in your life is the one staring back from the glass.

Yes, you may be like Jack Horner and chisel the plum and think you are a wonderful guy,

But, the man in the glass says you are only a bum if you can't look him straight in the eye.

He's the fellow to please, never mind all the rest for he's with you clear to the end.

You've passed your most dangerous and difficult test when the man in the glass is your friend.

You may fool the whole world on the pathway years and get pats on the back as you pass,

But, your final reward will be heartache and tears if you cheat on the man in the glass.

My mother had an eighth grade education. She was abandoned when I was three days old in the hospital by my father. She was on welfare. She was a domestic. I'd sit on the fire escape at night. One night she asked me what I thought of out there. I said that I think about three things; the mountains, travel, and I want to learn. She said, "When you sit out there, that is your true character." She used to look up big words and try to use them with the people she worked for. She said, "Son, don't ever do that. If you spend too much time polishing your image, you will eventually tarnish your own character." Now, you have to be real to teach that to youngsters. You don't have to be Christian to believe this philosophy. Buddha said, "Before man and woman can ever capture happiness, they must know themselves." One of the finest philosophers, Socrates, said, "Know Thyself." Knowing yourself is called Spiritualism. If you can radiate that, miracles can happen, just like you can have the best team and not win.

Finally, when I look back in my career, the people who touched me were my coaches. Your job is far more important than you realize. The greatest motivators on earth right now are coaches.

The Match-Up Defense

When you design a game-like drill, you can't stop them every 10 seconds, you don't correct every 10 seconds, etc. You set a time limit and you have winners and losers. You discuss why they won, and you reward them in some way.

We use three picture words in every one of our defensive drills: delay, disrupt, and deflect. We want to delay the dribbler anywhere on the floor. We want to be able to deflect every pass to the inside. We want to disrupt the shot.

Some people say "contest the shot." We want to disrupt the shot and disrupt the offensive pattern. I must get my players to understand the concepts. I want my players, to create the action, rather than be reactors, so we run a lot of traps. We run traps off the dribble or off the pass. Don't react, create. Trap the ball, overplay. When we trap, two people will be trappers; two people will be stealers, and one person will be the safety.

(Diagram 1)   The ball is passed from A to B. X2 is on the ball. On the pass, X1 and X2 will trap; X3 and X4 become stealers; X5 is the safety. The only thing we are giving you is the cross-court pass. If B would start dribbling, X1 and X2 stay with the dribbler. X3 and X4 will adjust, and X5 will stay in the lane. The trap is a basic part of the match-up. So, how do we work on that?

(Diagram 2)   A is near center court. X1 and X2 are in a position to trap. A has 10 seconds in which to handle the ball and can go anywhere she wants. X1 and X2 will work on the trap, containment. When I say, "Time," A passes to B; X1 and X2 will react and run to the center of the floor, and B will try to dribble in the other direction vs X1 and X2. If A picks up the dribble, X1 and X2 try to take away the high-post pass. Just what is the match-up?

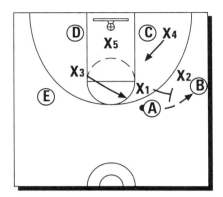

Diagram 1

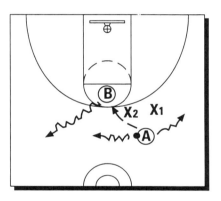

Diagram 2

We want to obtain more rebounds than our opponents, that's the key. Shooting percentage is a big thing to us. Match-up is ball pressure and four people taking away inside passes. Everyone is not a great shooter. We give certain people shots.

(Diagram 3)   This is the area where the least amount of shots are taken against us. We very seldom defend that area after the entry.

(Diagram 4)   The ball is at the wing and the ball is passed to the corner. We have a "cut-off situation." When the ball goes to the corner, X4 attacks the ball. X2 makes a backslide and covers the block. When the pass comes back from C to B, X2 covers the wing rather than chasing out to the point. We are more concerned with the pass going inside than the person at the top. We have a rotating zone with man-to-man goals.

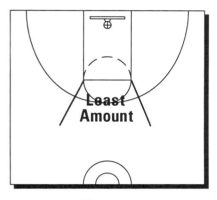

Diagram 3

Diagram 4

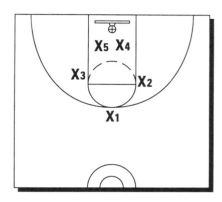

Diagram 5

(Diagram 6)   You can also do a 1-1-3 set by moving X3 back and X2 over.

(Diagram 7)   You can go 2-3 by moving X1 to the other elbow.

Diagram 6

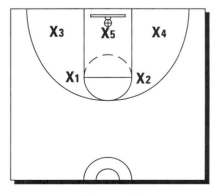

Diagram 7

(Diagram 5)   We like to show a 1-2-2 set. X1 has her heels on the top of the key. X2 is the other guard. X3 is two steps below the elbow. Eighty percent of the time the ball will go to the right side, and her move is to cover the weakside block. X4 is the top inside player and should be able to be replaced. Or else you should play your top inside player in the X3 position. X5 must play a lot of hard-nosed defense on the inside. I do not play my top inside scorer at the X5 position.

(Diagram 8) If we are in a 1-1-3, on a pass to the wing, X2 takes the first pass to either side. If you run the guards in tandem, it takes away the pass to the high post. It is also a great trapping defense.

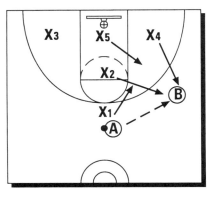

Diagram 8

(Diagram 9) Let's get back to the 1-2-2 and discuss X1, X2, and X3. The ball goes from A to B. X2's job is to delay the pass from B into the block area. You just can't say take away the inside. We want them to delay that pass. If they make a bounce pass or a lob pass, you have done your job. X2's first rule is that she cannot take more than three slides. She must not overextend. She cannot go beyond the three-point line. When X2 is out there, X2 must have her head on the ball shoulder.

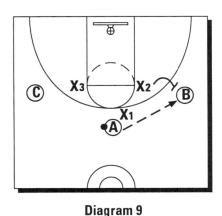

Diagram 9

(Diagram 10) If the ball is at the top of the key, X2 and X3 must take away the inside passing lanes. The inside arm, closest to the lane, must be out at shoulder level. When the ball goes from A to B, X2 should be on B when the ball is caught. X1 will be at ball elbow, and X3 will be in line with the ball and the opposite corner, one foot in the lane.

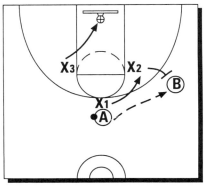

Diagram 10

(Diagram 11) When B has the ball, X2 is on the ball shoulder; X1 at ball elbow, and X3 on that line with one foot in the lane. If the pass were made to the other wing, that situation would be mirrored. When the ball goes from point to wing, X2 pivots and then "push and glide." If B dribbles instead of passing, we have a cut-off step. If B dribbles, the first step of our defensive player is back. Push off with the front foot. The defensive player must make some room so the dribbler can be stopped without committing the foul. So, one step back, two over, and on the second step, the defensive player should make contact.

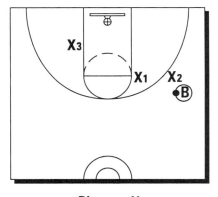

Diagram 11

(Diagram 12) X Out Series. This is a two-part drill. A and B both have their outside foot on the block. C and D are off the court waiting. A rolls the ball to the foul line. A picks it up with her back to the basket. B makes a lateral slide across the lane and then approaches A. A pivots and B plays defense. A shoots; B contests the shot, boxes out, and goes to the ball. We do that for two minutes. If A gets the rebound, she continues to shoot; if B gets the rebound the drill is over.

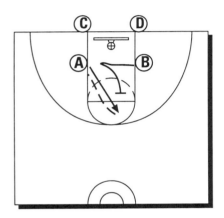

Diagram 12

(Diagram 13) "Combo." A gets no more than two dribbles. We tell A which way we want her to go. Same rules as on the last one. When A dribbles, B takes the cut-off step, and two steps over. Don't block the shot; let A shoot the ball. B blocks out. We work on cutting off, contesting the shot. If A makes the shot, B has five pushups; if B gets the rebound, A has five pushups.

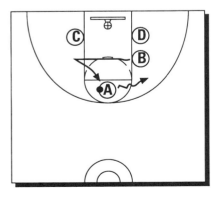

Diagram 13

Spend more time praising the good performer rather than the poor performer. I once had a player who was a good defensive player and never made a mistake. I praised her and said, "She's a pirate." I said that she is the only one on the team who can steal the ball well. Another player came to me and asked what she had to do to become a pirate. From that instance, I have given permission to certain players to go after the ballhandler.

In the X-Out Series, we are working on shot contesting, rebounding, don't foul the jump shooter outside of the paint.

(Diagram 14) For the post people, A is under the basket and B is directly behind him. A has the ball. A will toss the ball out and run out and catch the ball with her back to the basket. B will come out right behind and "belly up" to A. We want B to make contact with her upper legs. A pivots; B slides and keeps her verticality. When A shoots, B contests the shot, then boxes out. In the paint, we hit and hold. Outside the paint we hit and go to the ball.

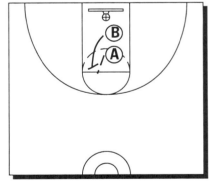

Diagram 14

(Diagram 15) At another basket, we will have the wing people either tossing the ball out or rolling the ball to the three-point line and playing one-on-one. This is a two-minute drill. Remember, from our match-up, we want to rebound, take away the inside, and contest every shot.

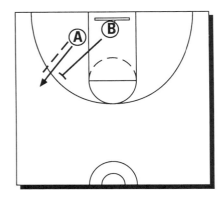

Diagram 15

(Diagram 16)   We have seven offensive people. We want to put pressure on the ball and take away the inside. A has the ball. X1 has her heels at the top of the key. X1's job is to get the ball to the side and delay the pass down the middle. X2 is at the elbow with her inside hand and arm at shoulder level. X3 is two steps below the elbow with her inside arm at shoulder level. X4 and X5 are inside in the lane. X4 and X5 are a step above F and G and sideguarding them. We want to show the offense that we are not playing a zone. So, X4 and X5 will have the foot and arm closest to the ball in front of F and G.

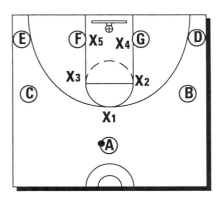

Diagram 16

(Diagram 17)   A passes to B. We should be in another position. No more than three slides. Don't overextend. We are taking away the inside. Overplay the best shooters. When B catches the ball, X2 is there, one foot on the three-point line with her head on the ball side. X4 moves halfway to the corner by going above G. X4 steps in front of G and opens up. X5 replaces X4. X5 must be in line with the ball and the basket. X3 is in line with the ball and the opposite corner, one foot in the paint. X1 drops to the ball-side elbow.

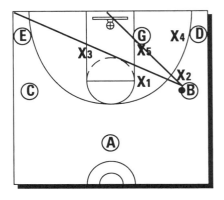

Diagram 17

(Diagram 18)   This is mirrored on the other side of the floor.

Diagram 18

(Diagram 19)   C passes to D in the corner. We call this "Fire." We create the action. X4 takes the ball; X2 fronts the post; X5 drops to the middle even with the basket; X1 denies the return pass, and X3 is in the lane weakside. We want that to be wide open; X3 can deflect the pass and score.

(Diagram 20)   If D passes to B and B passes back to the middle, by that time, X2 comes up in the middle and she becomes the point.

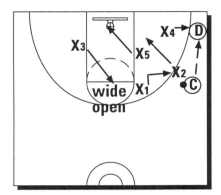

Diagram 19

Diagram 20

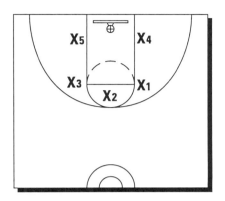

Diagram 21

Diagram 22

(Diagram 21)   This puts us in our basic match-up. When the ball goes from the wing to the corner, we create the action. We are going to play five defensive people against three offensive people and rebound five people. We let one of the offensive players shoot the ball from the outside, then take away your inside and your best shooter on the outside.

(Diagram 22)   Suppose the offense has a high post and a low post. A, B, and C are on the perimeter. A has passed to B. X2 has her head on the ball side of B. X4 is halfway to the corner, but if no one is in the corner, she steps back in. X5 is on a line between the ball and the basket, and X3 is on the line between the ball and the corner. X1 fronts the high post. We won't play the high post with X5 unless she catches the ball.

(Diagram 23)   If we see you strictly going high-low, we use "21 tandem." We match-up and play you man-to-man on the high-low and everyone else plays the zone. We like it when you take your post people away from the basket.

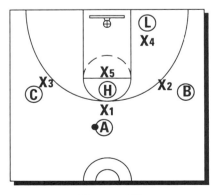

Diagram 23

(Diagram 24) If B passes to D and then cuts through, we let you go if you are going away from the ball. X2 will drop two steps and then take the person who is replacing B.

Diagram 24

(Diagram 25) We can also use "crush." This means that on the B to D pass, X2 will trap with X4. Crush means that the person on the ball goes with the pass.

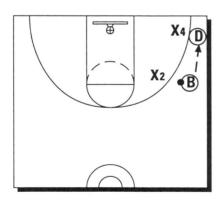

Diagram 25

(Diagram 26) This can also occur when the pass goes from the point to the wing. We trap the first pass with X1 and X2. You must get your kids to believe what we have defensively will create opportunities for us.

The drills should be time-related, and goal-related. When we leave the locker room, the last thing that they will see are three statements. Ball pressure. We want the ball pressured at all times. Take away the inside. Take away the inside with the arms first. X2 and X3 will have the inside arms shoulder high in the lane. X4 and X5 will have both arms shoulder high. Take away the passing lanes with your arms; you take away the dribble penetration with the body. Rebound. We want you to rebound the blocks.

Diagram 26

(Diagram 27) When the ball is passed from A to B, move when the ball moves. X3 slides to the three-point line. X5 goes halfway to the corner. X4 will be in line with the ball and the basket. X2 will be in line with the ball and the corner. X1 will take ball-side elbow. X3 exerts ball pressure. X3's head is on the ball shoulder. If B switches the ball from one shoulder to the other, X3 doesn't step over. She switches hands and mirrors the ball.

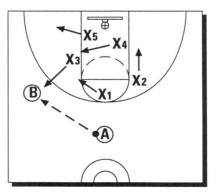

Diagram 27

(Diagram 28)   30-second drill. A and B are 15' apart. C is in the middle. Hold the ball for a two-count. C mirrors the ball. No lob passes.

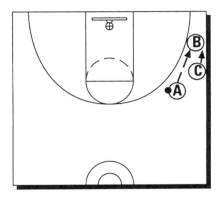

Diagram 28

(Diagram 29)   On the dribble, X3 makes a cut-off step and slides over.

Diagram 29

(Diagram 30)   When the ball is passed from the point to the wing to the corner, you can play it different ways. You can play it "normal."

(Diagram 31)   You can "Fire." X2 replaces X5, and X5 drops across the lane; X3 goes to the ball-side elbow; X1 denies the return pass. X5 is in a position to rebound, and X2 fronts the high post.

(Diagram 32)   X4 must have the inside arm up shoulder level to take away the inside. When the pass is made, X4 must move on the pass. When X4 comes out, she has her hands above her head. X4 runs two thirds of the way, and then comes under control and closes out.

Diagram 30

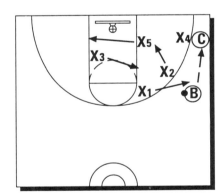

Diagram 31

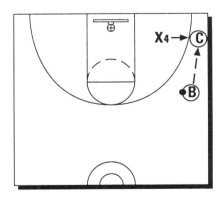

Diagram 32

JOE CIAMPI

We are really playing a sagging man-to-man. She's taking away the passing lane and the shot. If C is a good shooter, close in. Stop the shot. If she goes baseline, we are going to try to jam you on the baseline. X4's job is to stop the shot first. X4 gets help on the dribble. Close in on great shooters. Make them put the ball on the floor.

(Diagram 33)   The players run back to their original positions. Now the drill is run on the other side. The same rules apply. If X3 shoots a three-point shot and makes it, her team gets three points. The scoring is three points for a three-point shot, two points for a two, two points for a rebound and three points for a putback.

Diagram 33

(Diagram 34)   X3 shoots and misses and X2 gets the rebound. Someone must play the ball. C will take X3 and they will play 3-on-3.

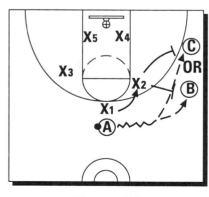

Diagram 34

(Diagram 35)   When these six players finish, the next six are up.

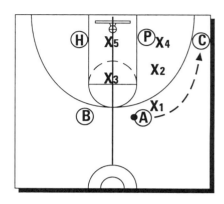

Diagram 35

(Diagram 36)   Now we do the drill with a shot from the wing.

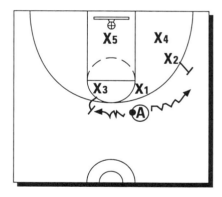

Diagram 36

(Diagram 37)   When the ball is in the corner, the back leg of X2 should be even with the hip of B. Be aggressive. How many ways can you play the post? You front, play behind, and sideguard. When do you keep the post away from the basket? When you play behind. Do it the way you feel you can do the best. Now for the close-out. When the ball is passed to C, X2 must sprint 2/3 of the way, get under control the last 1/3 and contest the shot. X3 will sprint and front the block from the baseline side. X1 takes A. The coach makes a soft pass to give them time to get there.

Diagram 37

(Diagram 38) We allow B to turn and try to screen X2 as X2 closes out on C.

Diagram 38

(Diagram 39) Who's going to rebound weakside? X1 has the weakside all by herself. X3 boxes B. C passes to A or to B; they must shoot. There is only one pass and the shot. In the third phase, C dribbles the ball.

(Diagram 40) Then we do it on the other side. Don't do it longer than six minutes because fatigue becomes a factor.

Diagram 39

Diagram 40

(Diagram 41) When the shot goes up, both A and X1 go to the weakside. C boxes X2; B hits and goes. If the shot is made and the ball is passed back to the coach, the players run back to the position.

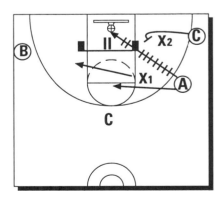

Diagram 41

(Diagram 42) Now the shot is taken from the wing and on the pass, X1 will close-out on C and X3 sideguards A. X2 sideguards highside on B. Move when the ball moves. On this high-low drill, don't put the dribble in too early. You will have too many breakdowns. Allow two dribbles.

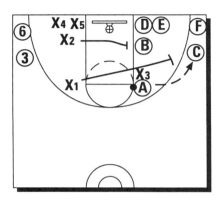

Diagram 42

(Diagram 43) We do this drill when we warm up. We go at 3/4 speed full court. Slide and run at the same head level, not bouncing up and down. If you get down too low, you have to stand to run. Just flex the knees. Slide, run, slide. A is facing the baseline. A slides left, runs right. The coach makes a pass to another coach. A will try to deflect the pass.

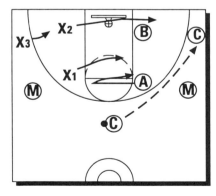

Diagram 43

(Diagram 44) "ROPS." Rebound, outlet, post-up, score. The coach shoots and misses. B rebounds and outlets to A. B posts up; X2 plays behind. A passes to B. B shoots. X1 boxes out. Whoever gets the ball, passes out.

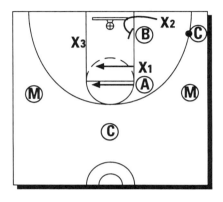

Diagram 44

There are four basic elements for success: discipline, strength, endurance and speed. How many of you have a strength program? How many do pushups every day? We do 15 of these every day. Lay back on your elbows with your hands by your hips. Come up on your hands and bring your knees to your chest. Don't let your feet hit the floor. The toughest drill we do is called "sidelines." We run the width of the floor eight reps in 58 seconds. Over and back is one rep. We start with four reps and build. We go from side to side because there are more stops and turns. Basketball is stops and turns.

Half-Court Offense

GENERAL COMMENTS

Before we get into the X's and O's, I want to tell you some things that have worked for us. The bottom line is that you want to win the game, but we will break things down. My first year of coaching, we were 3 and 17 and we had to make a lot of little goals. The score was irrelevant to us. We would pick about five goals for each game. Now, we have 10 things that we try to do every game. You can adjust these numbers to fit your situation.

TEN GOALS

- We want to shoot 50%. That's extremely high. We only hit that figure seven times this year.
- We want to commit under 16 turnovers.
- From the foul line, we want to shoot 75%. We really emphasize this.
- We want to score 18 points or more in transition.
- We want to score first in each half.
- We want to force 22 turnovers. We don't press a lot, so that's 22 turnovers off of a half-court defense.
- We want our opponents to shoot 40% or less.
- We want to get 58% of all rebounds. This is important.
- We want to get 12 steals per game off of a half-court man defense.
- We want 30 plus deflections. Scoring is hard. But deflections are easy.

At the bottom of the page, we put WIN! Our players have these in their notebooks and after every game, we go down the stat sheets. I hate the stat sheets. They want to look at their individual totals. We really don't talk about stats too much except for team areas. I think a stat sheet will help you in your program because you can identify specific items.

We have two pennies that are different colors than anything else that we wear. One is black with a red heart and called the "heart award." The other is a gold penny called "chairman of the boards." After every game, the high rebounder gets to wear the gold penny. The other award is subjective. The coaching staff chooses someone; who tried the hardest, who had the best attitude? We really emphasize that. Occasionally, it will be the same person, and then you find out a little about your kids because they choose which penny they will wear. Once we gave the heart award to someone who only played two minutes. But she was up screaming on the bench the entire game. You can send a message to your players.

OFFENSE

A large part of our offense is the fast break. When you choose an offense, you are going to make some bad decisions. We all do. When you do, just tell your kids that you made a mistake and change it.

(Diagram 1) We like to work a lot out of the triangle. We want to teach players how to read the defense. 3 is the post; 2 is the guard.

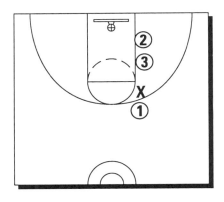

Diagram 1

(Diagram 2) 3 screens for 2 who pops out to the wing. Only use one side of the court. You then play 3-on-3. We tell the post what type of defense to play; high, front, or low. 1 passes to 2. Basketball is a game of triangles and two. Teach 2 to read the defense so the pass is made away from the defensive post.

Diagram 2

(Diagram 3) 2 may use the dribble to improve the angle of the pass. Stress spacing. Keep the triangle. If the post isn't open, 1 moves away and replaces herself. 1 goes to the circle for a straight-on pass from 1 to 3.

Diagram 3

(Diagram 4) The post defense plays on the other shoulder. 2 penetrates and passes to 3 or 1 and then to 3.

Diagram 4

(Diagram 5) Have players ready to go on the other side of the floor and just move your point guard to save time.

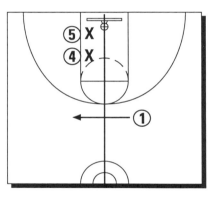

Diagram 5

(Diagram 6) Inside out. The defense is behind. 1 must be taught to take the defense to the box and then come back out to receive the ball.

Diagram 6

(Diagram 7) If the post is double-teamed, the guard must read the defense. If her defensive player moves to the top shoulder, the guard moves low.

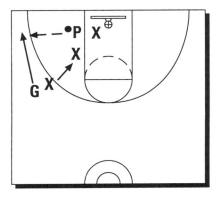

Diagram 7

(Diagram 8) If the defensive guard drops on the lowside, the guard moves high. You must know where the defense is. Most of our turnovers come from feeding the post. But you must get the ball inside.

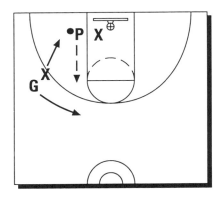

Diagram 8

(Diagram 9) Always be in a triangle. Even if 2 goes to the baseline, it is still a triangle. 3 pins the defensive player. Split the top leg of the defense. The post must get her top foot over the top of the defensive player's foot. Offensively, you want to establish contact.

Diagram 9

(Diagram 10) This is "constant 4-on-3." There are three teams of four players each; circles, triangles, and regular. 1, 2, 3, and 4 are the regular team, and they come down against 5, 6, and 7 of the circle team. The other circle player, 8 is at mid-court. Triangles 9, 10, and 11 are at the other end of the court. The regular team plays 4-on-3. After a score or a turnover, the circle team comes the other way, 3-vs-4. Player 8 joins in after the ball crosses half-court. 1, 2, 3, and 4 only play defense until half-court. The same thing happens at the other end of the court between the circles and the triangles. 12 waits until the triangles cross mid-court coming the other way. The game is played to 12 points. One point for a score; three deflections is a point; a charge is worth five.

If you don't have assistant coaches, bring in the post players fifteen minutes before the perimeter people, and then keep the perimeter people fifteen minutes after practice or vice versa. Spend fifteen minutes extra two or three times a week on individual positions.

(Diagram 11) We have two passers on the perimeter and the post players will go block to block. We teach three moves; the dropstep, the pivot and score, and the hook. We teach the dropstep from the block on the baseline side and also dropstep in the other direction. We discourage the use of the dribble on this move. The "pivot and score" is a little different. Instead of dropping the foot, you pivot on the foot. It's still a low-post move. You pivot on the lead leg, the same leg you would move for the dropstep. Then we do hooks. So, there are six shots, three to each side.

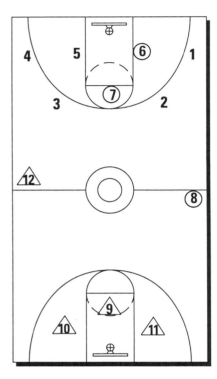

Diagram 10

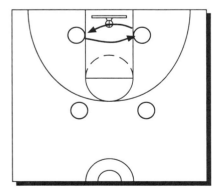

Diagram 11

(Diagram 12)   We never want to use a low-post move. We always want to post in the mid-post area. We don't want to post low or post off of the lane.

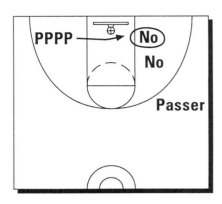

Diagram 12

(Diagram 13)   We also work at the high post, a turn and shoot, or turn, fake the shot and drive.

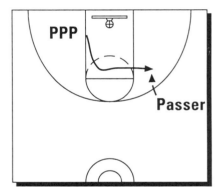

Diagram 13

(Diagram 14)   We have a back-screen in our offense. We will play 2-on-2 or add a passer. I practice without defense and shoot quickly with repetition. As the season progresses, I put more defense on the drills.

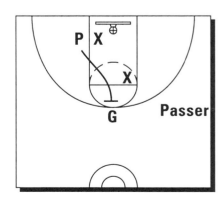

Diagram 14

(Diagram 15) Pop Outs for Guards. The guards pop out, pivot, take a shot, or else fake the shot and drive. Pete Newell convinced me that the guards should use the inside foot as the pivot foot. We do this without any shooting at first. If you don't pivot in this fashion, on one side of the floor you are changing a 14' shot into a 17' shot. We teach a rocking chair and a jab.

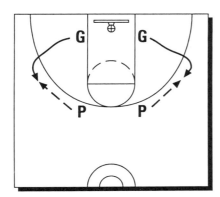

Diagram 15

(Diagram 16) They can do foul line extended jumpers, or they can break to the corner. They can also pop out and drive before taking the jumper.

Diagram 16

(Diagram 17) If the defense follows through the screen, the guard curls.

(Diagram 18) If the defense goes over the top, the guard flattens to the corner. Every time someone sets an off-the-ball screen, you are either going to curl or flatten.

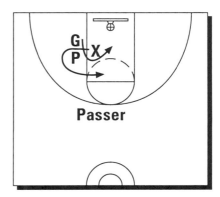

Diagram 17

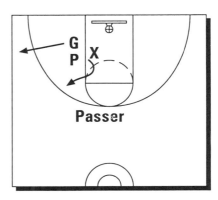

Diagram 18

We have covered some of the concepts. Now I'd like to show you some of our half-court offenses. We name them after states. Let's start with a man-to-man offense. Every drill I have shown you will fit into this offense.

(Diagram 19) Illinois. We start in a double stack. 1 passes to 2 and you have the triangle.

(Diagram 20) 4 posts for two seconds and then screens away. 5 comes across.

(Diagram 21) You have the triangle. 2 can pass to 5, or 2 to 1 and then the straight-on pass from 1 to 5. We also have the weakside flash.

Diagram 19

Diagram 20

Diagram 21

Diagram 22

Diagram 23

(Diagram 24)   Georgia. We start in the double stack again. 2 pops out and gets the pass from 1. 1 passes to 2 and then breaks to the corner. 5 screens for 4 who comes high and sets a screen for 2.

Diagram 24

(Diagram 22)   After 1 passes to 2, when 4 screens for 5, 1 screens for 3.

(Diagram 23)   A variation is for 4 to screen for 5 and then come to the high post for the jumper. We want to end up with two people on the blocks and three on the perimeter.

(Diagram 25)   1 is in the corner. 2 has the ball. 4 sets the screen. 5 is on the block, and 3 has spotted for the three-pointer. You can play 2-on-2. 2 comes off the screen hard for the pick-and-roll and goes to the basket. The players defending 3 and 5 must make some decisions. 5 can duck in.

Diagram 25

(Diagram 26)   2 can penetrate and take the jump shot. 2 can pass to 3.

Diagram 26

(Diagram 27)   2 passes to 3, but 3 doesn't have a shot. 2 goes to the corner. 5 moves across the lane. 4 is the screener and comes across and screens for 3. The guard who makes the pass, always goes to the corner. Once you are a screener, you are always the screener for that possession.

(Diagram 28)   We use options (colors). 4 comes out to screen the ball, but slips the screen and rolls to the basket. This works when the defense starts playing the post high. This is our "green" option.

Diagram 27

Diagram 28

(Diagram 29)   Tennessee is a quick-hitter. This is a box set. 2 is a guard, 5 the post. 1 dribbles to the side. When that happens, 2 sets the screen across the lane. 2 is your shooter. 5 posts.

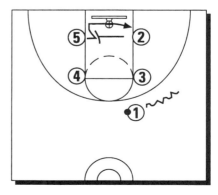

Diagram 29

Commodore Offense

I don't consider myself a system coach; I work with the talent I have in the gym. Maybe now, since we've had a little success, we can recruit the type of player that fits what we like to do. When I came to Vanderbilt, I had eight players on the roster over 6 foot tall and a 6'10" center, so I immediately had to make an adjustment on how we were going to play. As often as possible, we went to a 4 out, 1 in, set, or a 3 out, 2 in, set. Off the fast break, we are going to be on the side of the floor.

(Diagram 1)   2 and 3 are interchangeable. And 4 and 5 can be interchangeable. We initiate the offense with either a dribble or a pass. If 1 dribbles toward 2, we run a "zipper." This means back-screen. 2 sets a back-screen for 4, and we are in the 3 out, 2 in, set.

Diagram 1

(Diagram 2)   1 passes to 2; 4 screens across for 5. Very often 5 will be open for a pass from 1. 1 must get to the foul line extended; we don't feed the post above that line. We are a big penetrate and pitch team, but we have some rules when we penetrate on the dribble.

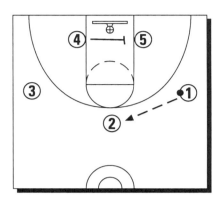

Diagram 2

(Diagram 3)   2 passes to 3. If 3 penetrates on the dribble, 4 fishhooks. 5 will dive into the lane. 1 will go to the baseline. One of the most effective passes we have in our offense is a pass across the baseline under the basket. No team teaches a defensive rotation that brings players under the basket. 3 can pass to 4, 5, or to 1. Our rule for dribble penetration is the fishhook on the ball side, the duck in from weakside and other wing goes to the corner.

Diagram 3

(Diagram 4)   2 reads when 3 dribbles, but usually when 1 gets the ball and doesn't shoot, 1 passes out to 2 who has the three-point shot.

(Diagram 5)   If 3 were to drive to the lane, 1 spots up, 4 steps off the block, 5 ducks in, and 2 reads the defense and steps down or up. We have good rebounding with 4 and 5 and 2 coming in from the wing.

Diagram 4

Diagram 5

Diagram 6

Diagram 7

Diagram 8

(Diagram 6)   From the same look we have the "chase" play. Instead of the back-screen by 2 on 4, 4 will down-screen for 2. This can be run on either side of the floor. We bring 1 down so that she can feed the post. We don't feed the low post from above, but we will feed the duck-in from higher than the foul line. Also, from this position, 1 has the proper angle to skip-pass to 3.

(Diagram 7)   Stepback. In effect, it is a high pick-and-roll. 1 passes to 2, steps in and steps back to get return pass from 2. This keys 4 to set a screen for the pick-and-roll. 5 ducks in; 3 spots up.

Diagram 8)   4 will either roll or step back for the 3.

(Diagram 9)   Stepback II. Same action except as 4 comes over, 1 comes off of 4 with the dribble and 2 screens for 4.

(Diagram 10)   4 can fade for the three-point shot, or can go to the basket off of the screen.

Diagram 9

Diagram 12

(Diagram 13)   4 passes to 1 and screens for 2. 3 screens for 5.

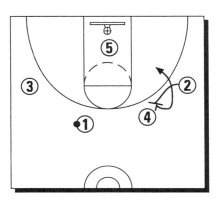

Diagram 10

(Diagram 11)   We end up with 4 out and our big center isolated inside.

Diagram 13

(Diagram 14)   "Dive Special." 1 passes to 2 and cuts through. 3 sets screen for 1, and 3 then goes to corner. 4 replaces and receives pass from 2. 4 dribbles at 1, and 4 and 1 have a dribble handoff.

Diagram 11

(Diagram 12)   "Dive." This is everybody's offense. 1 passes to 2 and goes through to the block. 4 replaces and gets pass from 2. 3 screens down for 1.

Diagram 14

(Diagram 15)   As 3 goes through, 5 and 2 set staggered-screens and 3 should be open for the three point shot. All of these plays can be run on either side of the floor. 5 and 4 must decide who is in what position, one on the strongside block, the other trailing.

Diagram 15

(Diagram 16)   We run this against big teams off of our transition. 4 and 5 set staggered-screens for 2. 3 comes across the top to make it more difficult to switch.

Diagram 16

(Diagram 17)   If the defense trails, 2 will curl and 4 will flare to the corner. 5 is isolated in the low post.

(Diagram 18)   If the ball is passed to 3 and 3 drives baseline, our rules are in place. The only option not in place is the fishhook because 4 isn't in place. But 5 will duck in the lane; 4 steps to the baseline looking for the pass from 3; 2 trails and 1 spots up on top.

Diagram 17

Diagram 18

(Diagram 19)   One other sequence that we use in our break is when 1 passes to our trailer, 4. 1 comes back at 4 for a dribble handoff. 3 screens down for 5, and 5 comes to block. After the hand-off, 4 screens down for 3.

(Diagram 20)   1 is now in position to feed the post; 5 is on the low post; 4 is weakside; 2 and 3 are on the perimeter. If 1 skip-passes to 2, 2 can dribble baseline and we have our fishhook, duck in, and pass across the baseline.

(Diagram 21)   One of the drills that we use has a coach at half-court with four players (letters). The coach will tell them what to do defensively against five players (numbers). Another coach is at the end of the floor. That coach has a ball, and an extra player (P) at mid-court. The defense may sit in a zone, may only have two players back and have two attack. The five will run the options in the break, recognize the defense and make decisions relative to getting shots. When we score, the coach with the ball throws the outlet pass to P, and the five players who scored must get back and must contest the ball. We are working on recognition as we go down the floor.

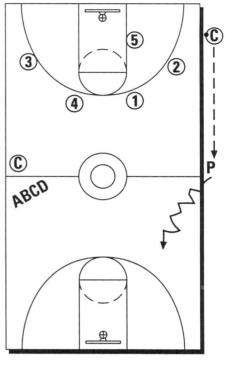

Diagram 21

Diagram 19

Diagram 20

(Diagram 22)   Sometimes A will challenge the ball. Sometimes we send two up. It's always against 4. Then we work on transition and getting back on defense. You must work on this for teams who change defenses. Don't expect your team to do it if you don't drill it.

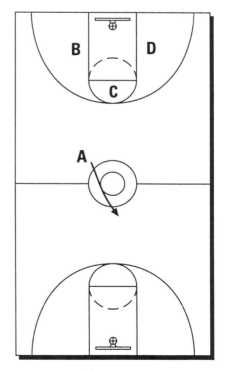

Diagram 22

(Diagram 23) Once we start this drill, the players can't cross half-court. It's continual 3-on-2, but the only shots that we can take are three-point shots and layups. We start with a jump ball. After the jump, A and 5 change ends and that's the last time anyone crosses mid-court. Having had that occur, A, B, and C will be attacking 1 and 4. 5, 2, and 3 will be attacking D and E at the other end.

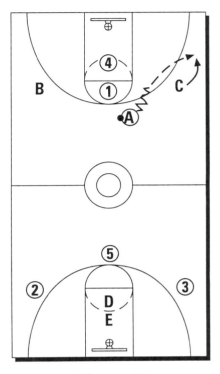

Diagram 24

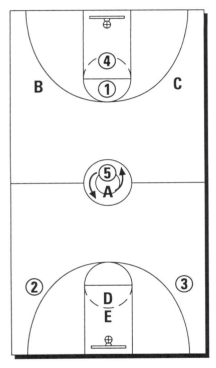

Diagram 23

(Diagram 24) Suppose that A, B, and C are attacking. You will get good shots if you make good decisions because you are going 3-on-2. We play for 10 minutes and we keep score; a 3 is 3 points, a 2 is 2 points. Suppose A, B, and C score.

(Diagram 25) Now 4 and 1 must bring the ball in. We put one player on the ball; one player faceguards 1, and one player plays behind 1. So it is 2-on-3. 4 must pass to 1 before the ball can cross half-court. 1 can either pass across half-court to 2, 5, or 3. D and E will try to intercept. Anytime the ball goes out of bounds, we don't inbound on the offensive end.

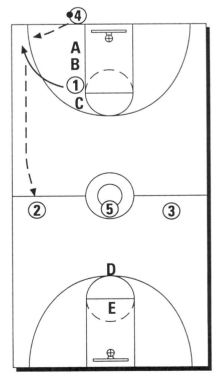

Diagram 25

(Diagram 26) We always inbound on the defensive end from the side. 1 must get open.

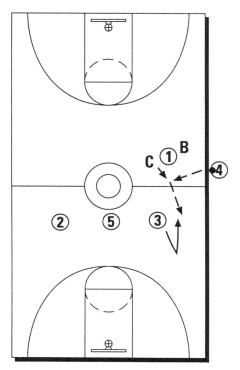

Diagram 26

(Diagram 27) Our rules still exist. If 3 is driving baseline, 2 must get to the corner and look for the pass coming across.

Diagram 27

(Diagram 28) If 3 drives here, 2 must spot up either up or down. 1 will fill for the three-point shot.

Here are plays for a good post player with a good jump shooter coming off the screen.

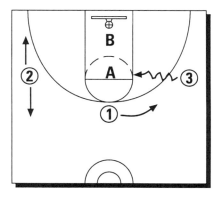

Diagram 28

(Diagram 29) "The Stack Play." 3 and 5 stack, with a 2 guard front. 4 is in the high post. 1 passes to 2. 3 pops out on the pass to 2, and 2 passes to 3. 1 goes away.

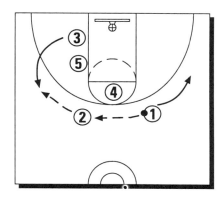

Diagram 29

As 2 passes to 3, (Diagram 30) 4 back-screens for 2. This is the first isolated look to 5. 3 can pass to 5.

(Diagram 31) If the pass isn't there, the ball goes to 4 and then 1 comes back for the pass from 4. If 5 is good at sealing, 4 will pass to 5 instead of passing to 1.

(Diagram 32) 1 has the ball. 2 screens for 5, and 1 looks to 5. 4 screens down for 2. You end up with your basic set and can go into the dribble series. If 1 dribbles baseline, you have the fishhook, the duck in, and the baseline pass.

Diagram 30

Diagram 31

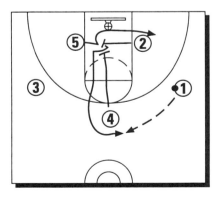

Diagram 32

(Diagram 33)   If 1 dribbles middle, 3 spots up, 4 ducks in, and 5 steps out.

Diagram 33

(Diagram 34)   This is a quick-hitting play. As 1 dribbles, 4 steps out and back-screens for 2. Occasionally, 2 will get the ball, but really you are keeping the defense honest. 2 goes to the corner. 3 is the shooter.

Diagram 34

(Diagram 35)   3 puts her head under the net. 4 gets pass from 1. 5 screens down for 3. 3 can curl, fade to the corner or come to the elbow.

(Diagram 36)   4 must read. If 3 curls, 5 can step out. 3 or 5 will be open. Here are a couple of dead ball sets.

(Diagram 37)   Box set, guards on blocks. 4 and 5 down-screen, and 2 screens for 3.

(Diagram 38)   You end up this way, and you are into the dribble series.

Diagram 35

Diagram 38

Diagram 36

Diagram 39

(Diagram 40)   This year we changed it so that 4 and 5 screen out for 2 and 3. This makes it easier to enter the offense.

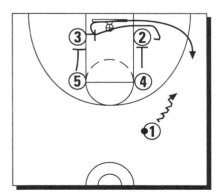

Diagram 37

Diagram 40

(Diagram 39)   Because teams like to switch and bump us off, we changed this a little. 5 and 4 down-screen. 3 goes to screen for 2. If the defense switches, 2 curls around 5. 3 then comes back off the same screen.

Motion Offense

We stress four areas in practice with the execution. The first is the purpose of the drill. Each drill has a purpose of what we want to get done for the day or the season. The second is teaching the "why." If you teach the "why," you will get better execution. The third is demand teaching good habits. Coach Knight says that the best coaches are the ones who are the least tolerant. It doesn't entail yelling at a player or berating a player. It is just the nonacceptance of a bad habit in practice. The fourth is to teach the players how to play.

We don't teach an offense at Indiana; we try to teach them how to play the game. We want them to recognize the various situations. We want them to anticipate situations. We want them to use their imagination in the offense. We have 13 players. Develop roles for your players and demand they play them. Motion offense is not an equal opportunity offense. It is an offense that tries to get your scorers, or your shooters, a shot. There is a difference between a scorer and a shooter, but our offense is set up for either one of those to get a shot. Our players must know who is a scorer, a shooter, a screener and a passer.

We build our motion offense around four concepts. The first is shot selection. Pete Newell says, "To beat a team, you must get more shots and better shots." We try to develop that thought for each individual player.

Next is ballhandling. Many players today need to improve handling the ball; passing, catching and dribbling. This is true at all levels.

The third concept is nothing more than movement; cutting, taking advantage where the defense is, reading the situation.

The fourth is a team concept. Help each other get open by screening and unselfish play.

Now, for the components of our offense. Usually, there will be a combination of three of these components at any one time. First is cutting. We run a V-cut, changing directions to set up the cut. You can act faster than the defensive player can react. The defensive player always must give you one or the other.

(Diagram 1) A is the defensive player guarding on top. A must choose whether he is going to play on the highside, the lowside, or head up. He tells us what we are going to do. Our eyes are on the defensive man. The offensive player does not move to find the ball. The ball finds the open man in our offense. If A is on the highside, we take him higher and cut to the basket.

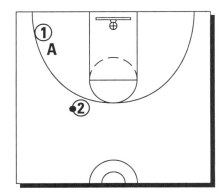

Diagram 1

(Diagram 2) If A plays low, take him lower and cut to the basket. Use what the defense gives you. We use a phrase in practice, "be hard to guard."

The second component of the offense is screening. The screener goes to the defensive man.

(Diagram 3) The screener, (2), does not wait for the cutter, (3), to cut to him. The screener goes and gets the defensive man. It is not up to the cutter to run the defensive man into the screener.

We have four screens. They are the down-screen, back-screen, cross-screen and flare-screen.

Diagram 2

Diagram 3

(Diagram 4) The down-screen is on the left side of the floor. The back-screen is shown on the right.

Diagram 4

(Diagram 5) The cross-screen. The ball-side post is the screener.

Diagram 5

(Diagram 6) The flare-screen. The flare-screen is an excellent screen for a guard who can score. The screener comes to the middle of the floor; the offensive man sets up to the middle and pops out to the side. The ball is brought to the action, and we have the entire side of the floor to exploit the drive or shoot the jump shot.

Diagram 6

The third component is passing. The ball goes to the action in our offense. This is a burden for the guards. Can they get the ball to the action?

(Diagram 7) 4 is the better screener, and 2 is the better scorer. Pass the ball to the same-colored shirt. Pass away from the defense. This depends on the angles you use in your passing. The passer reads the defense as well as the cutter.

Diagram 7

(Diagram 8) 1 has the ball. A is guarding on the highside of 2. 1 must know how A is playing so that he is ready when 2 makes the backcut.

Diagram 8

The fourth component is dribbling. We use the dribble for four reasons.

1) To improve the passing lane.

2) To initiate the offense, we use the dribble against the press.

3) We use the dribble to take the ball to the basket.

4) Attack the zone. More about that later.

GOES here ←

The fifth component is the shot fake, pass fake. In reviewing 30 tapes from last year, 30% of our scoring possessions came from the shot fake. A shot fake can move a person two feet. It keeps the defense at bay.

Any three of these five components are combined with any one play we use.

We also have rules for the offense. One of the great things about motion is the imagination your players can use. If they are going to take advantage of what the defense gives you, keep rules to a minimum.

(Diagram 9) By dribbling, 3 improves the passing angle to 5.

Diagram 9

(Diagram 10) The first rule is spacing. Spacing (15'-18') gives you floor balance. If you are moving and screening, you aren't always going to be that far apart. If 1 makes a basket cut and goes to the corner, 3 moves to the high-post area. The idea of spacing gives us purpose for the next movement.

Diagram 10

The second rule is hold the ball for a two-count. We hold it two seconds when we screen, catch the ball, post, everything. It gives us timing in our offense. Catch, face the basket, look in and see what you have.

(Diagram 11) The third rule is that the player closest to the middle of the floor is the screener. 3 is closer to the middle, therefore, 3 is the screener on a down-screen situation. The same is true for 4 and 5. 4 sets the back-screen for 5.

Diagram 11

(Diagram 12) There are exceptions. One is the flare-screen. Things change depending on your personnel. If 1 is your scorer, screen for the shooter.

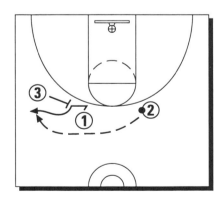

Diagram 12

(Diagram 13) Keep the ball off the baseline. The best defenders on the court are the baseline and the sideline. On defense, we force to the corner.

Offensively, we do the opposite. We have the ball in the high-post area. From the top of the key, we can go either side, drive, reverse the ball.

Diagram 13

(Diagram 14) We have a line on our practice floor. The only reason a player goes below this line is to post-up or make a cut. The team then has proper spacing. The ball does not go to the baseline unless you have a shot.

Diagram 14

(Diagram 15) Constantly fill the high-post area. If open, flash to it. Don't flash a player who is not a threat from the high post into the high post.

(Diagram 16) No two consecutive cuts in the same direction. If 1 goes into the high-post area, 2 will not follow. 2 will run the replace yourself cut.

We have a four-pass rule. We don't shoot unless we get a layup. Usually with four passes, we get two ball reversals.

Diagram 15

Diagram 16

(Diagram 17) We use four cuts off the top of our offense; cut and replace yourself, the basket cut, the inside cut to the corner, and pass and cut away.

Diagram 17

(Diagram 18) We use the inside cut for a guard off the down-screen.

Diagram 18

These rules, with our cutting and screening, etc. give us the motion offense.

Here are the drills we use. Everything we do in practice is the part/whole method of teaching. We break it down and then build it back up.

(Diagram 19) 2/1. Coach has the ball; A is defense on 2, the cutter. These drills are run in five-minute segments. We switch from drill to drill quickly. We will address the problems after practice. You correct a drill with the teaching of the players, but not the drill itself.

Diagram 19

The first drill is the down-screen. There is no defense on the screener; the emphasis is on the cutter reading the defense. The cutter's eyes are on the defense. We are looking for a good screen. The cutter has options. If the defense is playing high, take him higher and cut low.

(Diagram 20) The cutter must constantly read the defense. He may take A low, then pop out for the jump shot. On the right side of the court, 2 is running the tight cut. If the defense follows 2 over the top of the screen, 2 continues shoulder to shoulder with the screener and runs a curl.

Diagram 20

(Diagram 21) We run the back-screen for five minutes. If the defense is playing on the highside, we set him up and cut behind.

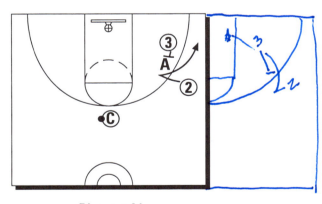

Diagram 21

(Diagram 22) If the defense is on the lowside, take him low and come over the top.

(Diagram 23) If the defense plays off, cut in, and pop back for the shot.

(Diagram 24) Flare-screen. The key is for the cutter to get one foot inside the top of the key. That buries the defensive man. There are options off of the flare cut. The cutter can cut into the middle and keep going on a basket cut.

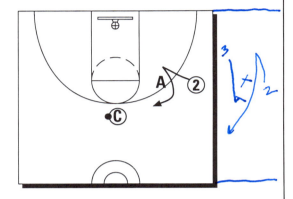

Diagram 22

Diagram 23

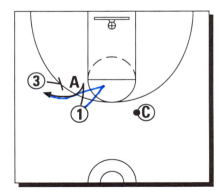

Diagram 24

Diagram 25) 2/2. We break down in small groups so we never have more than one player rotating in. On the left side, we work 2/2 with the down-screen. If it is a tight cut, the screener pops back. On the right side, 3 pops out with the screener making a basket cut. The screener, as well as the cutter, must read. We do this for the back-screen, down-screen and the flare-screen.

Diagram 25

(Diagram 26) The cross-screen with 2/2. The strongside post becomes the screener. He posts for a two-count, then screens. The cutter, must step off of the lane five feet. If he doesn't step off the lane, there is no room for the cut.

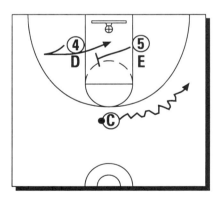

Diagram 26

(Diagram 27) If 4 cuts low, 5 cuts high after the screen. If 4 cuts high, the screener comes back low. The drill can be changed with the addition of two managers on the wings to be used to feed the cutter.

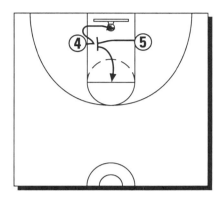

Diagram 27

(Diagram 28) 3/3. We go 10 minutes in group situations. Start at half-court. The coach is in the high-post area and is used as a release.

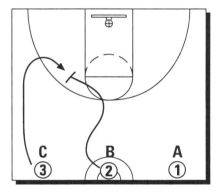

Diagram 28

(Diagram 29) 3/3 inside with two coaches on the perimeter.

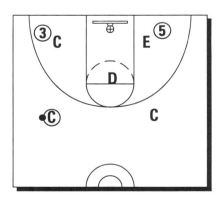

Diagram 29

(Diagram 30) 3/3 and a post. There is a new post and defensive post every three times. The ball goes to the post at least on every fourth pass. Work on relocation in this drill. When the ball is passed into the post, the perimeter player relocates. We don't cut much off of the post man. That takes away from our spacing.

Diagram 30

(Diagram 31) For example, 1 is relocating after a pass to 5 while 2, the man closest to the middle of the floor is setting a down-screen for 3.

Diagram 31

(Diagram 32) 4/4. This is our best drill. It gets all our players involved. With 4/4, you must maintain your spacing. Some teams put lines on the floor and want one player in each section except for the screen.

(Diagram 33) 5/5. We have a series of alignments. This is "regular." This is 5-man motion; all five are interchangeable, screening for each other.

Diagram 32

Diagram 33

(Diagram 34) "Post Exchange," which is 3 out and 2 in. The two inside players work together, and the three outside players work together.

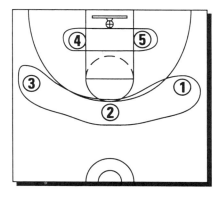

Diagram 34

(Diagram 35) "Triangle." This is 3 in, 2 out. If 1 takes ball to the right, 5 posts for a two-count and screens away. 4 comes across low. 3 screens down for 5, who comes high. 2 must come to the top to keep the 18' spacing.

Diagram 35

(Diagram 36) This is hard to guard. If 1 plays well inside, 3 can back-screen for 1 and make him part of the inside triangle.

Diagram 36

(Diagram 37) 4 out, 1 in. The four perimeter players work together, with one post player.

(Diagram 38) 1 out and 4 in. Use this when you have a good guard.

We use restrictions in practice to get our players to do what we want. We may count so many screens before we can shoot. We may use so much time before a shot can be taken other than a layup. We may only allow one certain player to shoot. These help in getting your players to execute the basics of cutting and screening. We may give points for a good screen, an open shot, an offensive rebound, a

Diagram 37

Diagram 38

defensive rebound and a point if the offense doesn't score.

(Diagram 39) 2/2 drill against a switching defense. The coach has the ball. There is a spot when the defense switches that there is a crease directly to the basket between the two defensive players. The screener sets a screen, then cuts down the crease to the basket. This is a slip-screen. Sometimes 2 will not go all the way to set the screen. 2 may recognize the crease and use it immediately.

Diagram 39 **Diagram 40**

(Diagram 40) This same thing can occur on the back-screen.

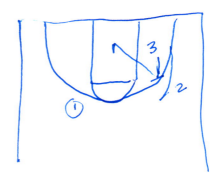

DEBBIE HOLLEY

How to Blow off Steam without Burning Your Team

Let's talk about the following survey.

- Identifying basic emotions

- Understanding your own emotional makeup

    - Emotions I handle easily

    - Emotions I avoid

- Expressing appropriate emotion

    - The emotion I avoid

    - Inappropriate emotion

- Expressing emotions appropriately (e.g., Anger)

    - Definition

    - Kinds

    - Expressing anger...confrontation

- Creating an emotional advantage

Look at #2. Using the four feelings, mad, sad, glad, and scared, under "emotions I handle easily," I want you to take any or all of the four emotions you feel you don't have a problem feeling. For example, "Mad." You are comfortable speaking your mind when you need to. "Sad." If you go to a funeral, you are comfortable crying. You aren't uncomfortable sitting with a grieving friend. If so, you can handle sad. "Glad." You can be a cheerleader. It is not hard to take a positive view of something. "Scared." If it doesn't cause you to freak out, you may like watching a scary movie.

Now look at the next part. What are the emotions, the feelings that you avoid? I personally don't like funerals. I feel sad of other people's pain. My husband cannot handle being scared. He does not go to scary movies. List the feeling that you hate. This effects your coaching. There is no right or wrong here; one is not better than another. This is just differences. Here is the hardest question. When you feel the emotion you have coming on, what do you do? What do you feel instead? Most of us run to another feeling, one that we are comfortable with.

For example, I'm glad, so when something sad happens, I'll tell you why it was really a good thing. I don't want you to be sad. My son hates to be scared. It took me awhile to realize what he does when he is scared. He goes to glad, and starts laughing. He was once called into the principal's office and couldn't stop laughing. That's his reaction to fear. It happened several times when I had disciplined him. Picture disciplining one of your players and they respond with a smirk or a giggle. This kid is probably not arrogant, but scared. If you understand this, you will be better able to understand that kid. When my husband gets scared, he gets mad. This is a real pitfall in coaching.

Anytime you are in a close game, what is the appropriate emotion you are feeling? Scared. But if you don't like being scared and move into mad, what's going to happen? You are going to blow! The coach isn't really mad; he's scared and is responding by going crazy and blowing up at his team. His team is obviously scared and confused because they don't know why he is mad. This occurs because the coach isn't really in touch with what he is really feeling. Sometime take your top two or three returning players and do this with them. It will make you a much better coach, and you will know what that kid is really feeling. A couple other things. Let's take a feeling that you don't like to feel. Let's say that it's mad. But I've got news for you. You are going to get mad. If you aren't able to express that feeling, and feel that feeling, your kids will feel that anger and they will not know why you are mad. Maybe you can't handle the feeling of glad and your kids will feel that they aren't measuring up. Nothing they do pleases you. It's never right; it's never good enough Why? Because you can't say 'UNBELIEVABLE, AWESOME."

We are back to my basic premise. To be an effective coach, you must be able to feel and handle all four feelings. You are going to need all four during the season. Let's talk about using these emotions to motivate your team. Many coaches make the mistake of trying to motivate their teams using one emotion. Probably it is the emotion that comes easiest to you. That's the one that you will probably go to and use as your primary motivator. You may disagree with me, but I think that you are making a mistake when you use one of those emotions almost exclusively for your team. Let me show you why. Let's use anger. Let's say that you are really convinced that, to motivate your team, you must be on their case, be mad all the time to keep them going. If that's true, here's what I see wrong with that. If you use just one emotion to motivate your team, it will lose its effectiveness because your kids tend to tune you out no matter what emotion it is.

My husband and I were at a Division I basketball game, sitting right on the floor. One of the coaches is a coach who stays in mad all the time, from start to finish. He never lets up, never sits down, goes on and on. He was on the other side of the court. There was some kind of break in the play, and one of the players was standing next to my husband and my husband said "how do you put up with that?" The kid looked at my husband and said, "We don't pay any attention to him." Why? Because they are tired of it. The kids blow it off, no positive response whatsoever. If you only use one emotion, you must keep turning up the intensity of that emotion. If you run a practice with mad, and you really want to get their attention, you must go into a rage to even get their attention. Whatever emotion that you use with your team is the emotion that you have to live in. Do you really want to be mad all the time? Do you really want to be scared all the time? You'll have to be if that's your primary motivational tool.

Finally, if you just use one emotion, it's contagious. It will infiltrate your team. If you are angry with your team all the time, you will have a team that gets on each other, that treats each other as you treat them. You will have a team who is resentful toward you and one another. You can actually sabotage your own team. The same is for scared. If you are scared all the time, your team will play that way, and teams don't play well when they are uptight. My opinion is that of the four emotions, glad should be your primary emotional tool. That's psychology 101. Kids flourish in an environment where there is positive motivation, encouragement, where there is someone telling them that they can do it, where things are upbeat. That's in every scientific study that has ever been done. There must be times in every feeling where you will need to put fear into your team. You see your team approaching an easy game with lethargy. You must get them scared. There will be a time when you use sad because of their behavior or something. And there are times when you must get angry when them. That's part of coaching.

Look at #4. It is important to express an emotion appropriately. Here's where we are going to get into dealing with anger. Before I tell you how I think anger should be handled, I want you to see how you think anger should be handled. So, look at the three question survey.

ANGER SURVEY

- Do you ever feel angry?

    - Not very often. I'm basically an easy-going person and little things don't bother me.

    - Yes, some things really get to me even though I know they shouldn't.

    - Yes, in fact I feel angry a lot. Sometimes everything seems to bug me.

- Yes, I can take a lot, but now and then I need to blow off steam and clear the air.

- Other..................

• How do you feel about expressing anger?

- I don't think it's good to express anger.

- When I get angry it seems to make things worse.

- I feel much better after I've blown my top and cleared the air.

- I can do it if I know I'm right.

- I have to be pinned in a corner before I'll admit I'm angry.

- Other...............

• How do you express anger?

- I don't because I really don't ever get that angry.

- I usually keep it to myself.

- I don't ever come right out and say I'm angry, but if I am, people seem to know it.

- I usually just tell people how I feel and why.

- I get really mad. Sometimes I lose my temper.

- Other....

Can you find yourself in this list? Let's spend some time in a general discussion of anger. I learned about anger 15 years ago when my husband left home and we were on the verge of divorce. My husband made one visit to the pastor who had married us for a one-time counseling session. When he came back, I asked, "How did it go? What did you learn?" He said, "He didn't understand; he said we must be really angry with each other." Neither of us felt that we were angry with each other. Oh no! We were just getting divorced. We weren't angry, not mad at all. We actually thought we weren't angry with each other. I've always been taught it was never OK to be angry. Anger wasn't a good thing. You should always be in control of your emotions. I would never admit that I was angry. Now, what is anger? Anger is a feeling. It is an emotional tool that signifies that something is bothering you. That's all it is. It's an emotional tool. It's not right; it's not wrong. It's not good; it's not bad. It's a feeling that comes over you that says that something isn't right. Let's start there. What we choose to do with that feeling can make our anger constructive or destructive. We always have a choice.

Let's talk about the different types of anger. We have already touched on appropriate and inappropriate anger. Let's start with inappropriate anger. When you are really feeling another feeling like scared or sad, but it vents itself in anger, that's the first kind of inappropriate anger. Another kind is when you don't have all the facts, but you think you do. But when you find out all the facts, you are confused. The feelings are real, but the anger itself was inappropriate. Is that uncomfortable feeling that I'm feeling really angry. My husband and I would not admit to that when we were separating. Were we angry with each other? Yes. Is it appropriate? You must answer that yourself. Do you have all the facts? Do you know why you are angry? Half the time you will only start questioning yourself, and you won't be angry anymore. You will realize that you are just having a bad day, or you just don't have all the facts.

There are two more kinds of anger; repressed or expressed. Repressed anger is common to the passive personality. These people like to deny that they are angry. They like to pretend it is not there. The problem with that is anger accumulates and it doesn't just go away. It is not a function of time. It's like pushing an air-filled ball under water. No matter how deep you push it or how long you hold it under, it will eventually surface. Then, look out! Our goal in coaching is to make sure the anger is appropriate and to express it. Make sure that we do not repress it. How and when are other questions.

Controlled or uncontrolled anger. Uncontrolled anger is usually a result of a more aggressive personality. You tend to fly off the handle. It is usually a result of acting too quickly. Folks who have a temper need to use time. They need to cool down. They need to think. You let your feelings rule your behavior. You don't think about the consequences or how the other person is going to feel. If someone hurts us, we will hurt them back. Uncontrollable anger can become irrational and can be destructive. And listen to this carefully; it never solves the problem. If you only hear one thing out of this seminar, I want you to hear this. UNCONTROLLED ANGER NEVER SOLVES THE PROBLEM! But it always creates another one.

Sometimes when you use this with a team you justify it by saying that they had it coming. My message today is that they didn't have it coming. They had something coming, but they didn't deserve uncontrollable, destructive, hurtful, abusive anger. They needed to be dealt with, but not in that manner. Uncontrollable anger always shuts down all effective communication, especially with girls. With boys you must relate to their ego; with girls you must relate to their feelings. If you treat girls in an uncontrollable way, you have lost them. Every woman in here is shaking her head. Husbands take this home. You absolutely lose women when you verbally abuse them or are too angry or emotional with them. We're lost. We can't hear a word that you are saying. Anger also needs to be well-directed, not misdirected. How often are we angry at one person and take it out on another? See how difficult it is to handle anger? You must go through these mental gymnastics to find out why you are angry, if you should be angry, who you are angry with, how you should handle it, and how you are going to express it. By this time, you are not angry anymore.

Expressing anger in a confrontation. This is the hard part. Once you decide that you have reason to be angry, you know the facts, and the feeling you have is anger, and you've decided to express in a controlled way (that's always the goal as coaches) and the goal of communicating is to be heard. But that's another seminar. You want this player to hear why you are angry with her or with him. How can you accomplish this? Let me give you a couple of quick ideas for handling confrontation.

Number one, get all the facts. Suppose that you have a player who is always late, and today he is late again. Do you have a right to be angry with him? No, you don't have all the facts. The first thing you need to do is to get the facts. He may have a very good excuse for the first time. So protect yourself by getting all the facts. Number two, pick the right time and the right place, especially with kids. They are so susceptible to peer pressure. If you're confronting a kid in front of his friends, all he can think of is how embarrassed he is. He's not hearing you. He is being humiliated, even if you are doing it in a straight forward, good way. At that moment he hates you.

Whenever you can, call that kid aside and do it in private. You have a chance of being heard in private. That's not a guarantee, but you have no chance of being heard in public. Avoid things like "always." The minute you make that statement, the kid is thinking of the one time that he didn't. Avoid generalities and stick to what he did today that made you mad. Try not to make demands on the kid, but try to stick to phrases like "I would like it if you would..." You are requesting. You have a right to demand it if you are the coach, but your goal is to be heard. You must be careful of name calling. "You are so lazy." And finally, be careful of comparing him with someone else. You build resentment between teammates.

DEBBIE HOLLEY

The last thing we are going to do is to build an emotional advantage. It took all this time to get to here. Why? Once you develop the ability to feel those four feelings, and you learn that it won't kill you, you can handle them. Once you have learned the appropriate feeling to feel in certain situations, once you have learned to express feelings in a way that other people can hear, then you are free to take those four feelings, they are all at your disposal now, and use them to create an emotional advantage for your team. In most cases, coaches are powerless over creating advantages. You can't create a height advantage for example. It's just there. But here is an area where you have power. You can do things that will create an emotional advantage over the other team.

Let me give you a couple of ideas. Save those moments for the time when you are really going to need them. Know that some time next year your team is going to need a bucket of cold emotional water thrown on them at some point in a game or in practice. You need to get their attention. So save that controlled, uncontrollable fit that you can throw. To your players, it looks like you are having an uncontrollable fit, but you have chosen every word; you have thought it through; you have practiced it at home. You don't use personal words; you don't hurt anybody, but you are just having a temper tantrum. Know who's really good at that? Hubie Brown. Hubie Brown used to coach the Kentucky Colonels when I worked for the Spirits in St. Louis in the ABA. We played the same teams so I saw them many times. Several times we would be behind their huddle during a time-out. And Hubie would go crazy, uncontrollable, veins popping out, face was red and language that I don't suggest you use. He would go nuts. I thought that he was out of control. As the players turned to go back out on the floor, Hubie was kneeling, looking at the people, and this one time he looked up and said, "Ladies, I'm really sorry about that. But sometimes you just have to do those things." I thought, "he wasn't even mad, he just threw a fit because his team needed him to throw a fit." Sometime next year your team is going to need you to throw a fit. Save it. All of you glad people....that one moment where you are so disappointed...you can only do that once or twice and then they turn you off.

Now, how did you create an emotional advantage? In spite of what you were feeling, scared, angry...look at your team and ask what your team needs. Assess the situation. What does your team need? You may or may not be feeling those things, but this is where you get your advantage. It doesn't matter what you are feeling. You don't respond to your feelings, you are going to respond to the players and react to the situation. See the differences. You don't sit on the bench and roll with your feelings. You are choosing your feelings, thinking, choosing your spots to have your controlled, uncontrollable fit, your moment of utter disappointment, to be the cheerleader cheering for them. You must talk to yourself and ask yourself what is best for your team.

Full-Court Pressure

We press because it allows us to take advantage of our superior conditioning in the last five minutes of the game. I now have one area where I have the advantage and that is conditioning. When you press, because it takes a high amount of energy, you have the tendency to play more players. Over the course of the season you develop more depth. You now have the opportunity to truly control the tempo of the game. Some people have the impression that tempo means slow. If you don't play with a high level of intensity when you press, you get destroyed.

From a coaching standpoint, all good pressing teams have one thing in common. That is, commitment from the coach. So, you go into the season ready to press and you have one of those games where you get blown out, and there is the tendency to go, "ooooh boy, I don't know about this pressing stuff. Maybe we should soften it up." My point is this. One of the main characteristics of a good pressing team is commitment. You must see the thing through.

Let's review some of our fundamentals. First is our stance. We press from an open stance. In other words, all five players face the ball. We do not close down and deny. We do not faceguard. Our inside foot, the foot toward the middle of the floor, is slightly ahead of the outside foot. Our hands are facing the ball with our thumbs above our shoulders pointing inward. We always want to play the ball and see our man. If our man is behind us, we will back up in an open stance and see our man and play the ball. We are denying the ball inbounds, but we are denying by seeing the ball. The steal we want is not the steal you get from closing down where you see the ball at the last second. We want the steal where we shoot the gap on the inside ear.

We Basically Have Two Alignments.

(Diagram 1) One is the 1-2-1-1 press where X4 is on the ball, X3 is always left, X2 is always right, X1 is the back of the diamond and always ball side, and X5 is back. This is our White Press. Why X3 on the left, and X2 on the right? Because we want them there when we fall back into a 2-3 zone. X3 is back on the left; X2 is up on the right. X2 and X3 are usually your better athletes.

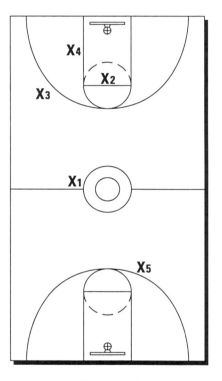

Diagram 1

(Diagram 2) The 2-2-1 is our Black Press. I am going to use the Black Press to explain the fundamentals of our press with the understanding that these two presses are the exact same when the ball comes inbounds. Note that when the ball is out-of-bounds, this press is a zone press. We cover certain areas and there are certain areas we will not approach. For example, if X1 is guarding a player and he comes forward, X1 would take him to this dotted line and then there would be a switch. I don't want to cover switching yet. But, I want to make the point that when the ball is out-of-bounds, we are in zone areas. When the ball comes inbounds, the press is man-to-man or match-up. Match-up is probably the better term. We have basic rotation rules.

middle, we are in a diamond. Our players will match-up because it is a match-up press once the ball is inbounds.

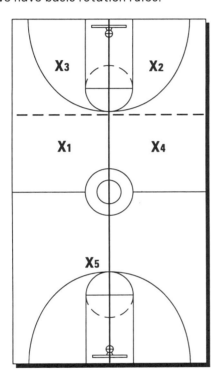

Diagram 2

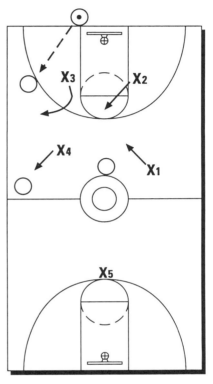

Diagram 3

(Diagram 3) The first rule is that once the ball is inbounds and the ball is on the sideline, your press should be in a box. If we are in a box, X3 plays the ball, X4 covers the sideline, X1 is inside the middle man, and X2 drops back in the middle. Sometimes that box will be slightly distorted as this one is.

(Diagram 4) If the ball is now passed to the middle, our press is now a diamond. X2 has the ball; X1 fans out; X4 is back and X3 comes to the middle.

(Diagram 5) If the ball is dribbled to the middle, X3 stays with the ball. X2 drops to the wing; X4 comes up, and X1 is at the back of the diamond. When the ball is on the sideline, we are in a box and they will play the ball and see the man. If the ball is in the

(Diagram 6) When do we trap? We only trap the ballhandler who is out of control. X3 is guarding the ball. We would not trap the ball in its present state. We tell X3 to play even with the ball in your open stance. We want our defender to get into the offensive player, to encourage him to dribble. We want him to go down the sideline. X3 puts extreme pressure on the ball.

Remember, if anyone can just put the ball on the floor and blow by our player, we have no press anyway. You have no defense, even at half-court if this happens. If X3 is doing his job, the ballhandler must change direction for one or two dribbles. We talk in terms of turning the man with the ball. We must guard his first move and his second move. When we are doing our job, we want the dribbler to dribble in an uncontrolled state. We only trap ballhandlers in an uncontrolled state. Why do we only trap on the speed dribble? Because the dribbler cannot see as his head is down.

When you are in a controlled state, good players will beat you, they will pick you apart with the pass. The theory here is that he is the easiest to trap. We trap with X3 and X1 on the sideline. We don't have any certain area, except sideline. We teach our players that when they trap, they form a T with their feet. (Note — toe of one man's foot perpendicular to the instep of the other man's foot.) We want to trap in our plane and look to deflect in our plane. Don't reach. Get the hands up, and pantomime the ball. The trap must move and follow the ball.

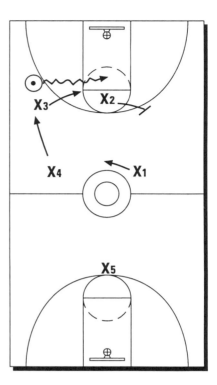

Diagram 5

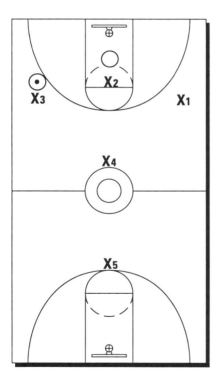

Diagram 4

(Diagram 7) If X3 doesn't do the job and the ball is dribbled toward the middle, we backtip. If we get beat middle, we want to "level off" and backtip. X4 comes to the dribbler and level off the dribbler. We want to make him change direction, other than a straight line path with the ball.

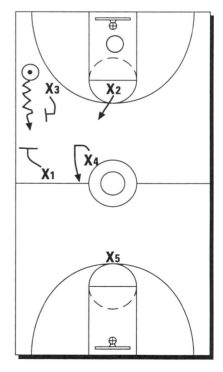

Diagram 6

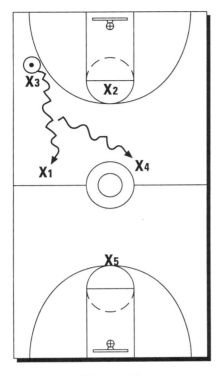

Diagram 7

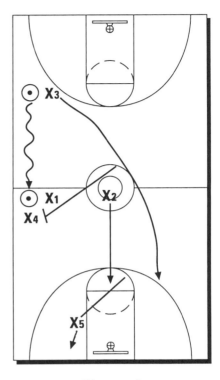

Diagram 8

Remember, he has just screwed up, and we are now giving him the opportunity to make a good play. X3 runs through the ball and backtips. We have backtipping drills. We don't lunge at the ball in an effort to backtip. Sprint to the level of the ball and tip the ball through. Don't lunge. X3 must run hard.

(Diagram 8) Let's get X5 involved. X3 has made the uncontrolled ballhandler go down the sideline. As X1 comes to set the trap, the ball is advanced by the pass. When the ball is thrown out of the trap, the player over whom the pass has been made turns and retraps. In this case, X1. The ball is still above the old hashmark, so we are going to retrap using X1 and X4. Our rotation is going to be X2 to the high post, X5 to the low post on the ball side. X3 sprints out of the trap to the opposite side.

(Diagram 9) When the ball crosses half-court, we must, at all times, have three areas filled; the low post by X5, the high post by X2, and finally, the furthest point opposite by X3. All the players not involved in the trap must be lower than the level of the ball. You must run as hard as you can. We don't get a lot of turnovers out of the trap. We get turnovers from our back pursuit.

(Diagram 10) Let's say that X3 and X1 are trapping and the ball is advanced with the long pass below the hashmark. Our rotation is slightly different. That is X5's signal that he must come out and trap. X1 must still retrap as the ball was thrown over his head. Now we have the trap by X1 and X5, and we must still cover our three areas. X4 covers ball-side block. X2 covers weakside; X3 comes hard through the middle. X2 and X3 may exchange assignments. But you must cover ball-side block, weakside block, and the middle.

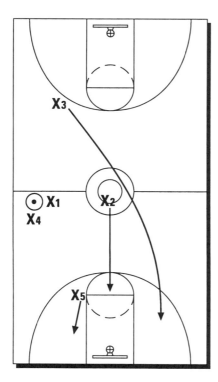

Diagram 9

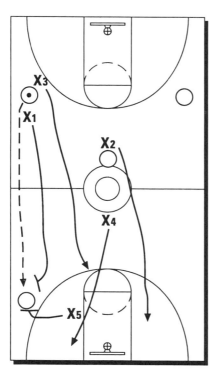

Diagram 10

(Diagram 11) When the ball is passed to the middle, most players want to run to the ball. If you are going to be a good pressing team, you cannot do that. You must teach your players to fan out. X2 is split between two offensive players. The most dangerous pass against the press is the pass to the middle and the return pass.

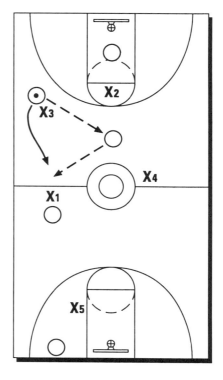

Diagram 11

(Diagram 12) X3 is not in a trap, so when the ball is passed to the middle, he does not turn and follow the ball. He looks middle, but he must stay with his man and shoot the gap for the steal. X4 can't run to the ball. X4 must take a step up, and fan out to cover the back man who is now going long. X2 stops the ball. We don't backtip on this. We only do that on the dribble. This is a pass to the middle of the floor. We want our players inside the passing lanes, not behind the ball. X4 may have stunted at the ball, but he knows he has fan-out responsibility.

(Diagram 13) This is a zone press when the ball is out-of-bounds.

Now let's deal with the concept of switching. In some press offenses, you get this action, a screen and bringing someone else into the area. We will verbal switch in this case.

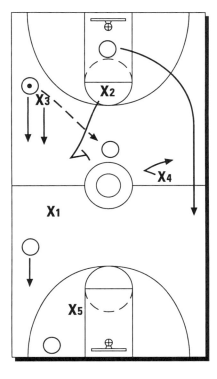

Diagram 12

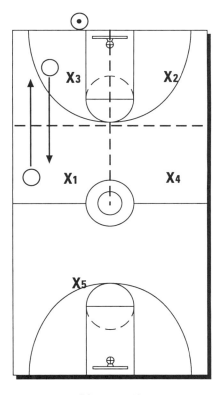

Diagram 13

(Diagram 14) If we have a screen from one side of the floor to the other, we will verbal switch.

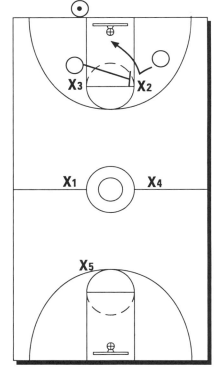

Diagram 14

Skill Development

In our program, we pay a high degree of attention to individual offensive skill. I want to talk about that this session. We do this in a formal manner. The NCAA allows us 20 hours a week. We only use 16 to 17 hours per week for our team practice. We set aside the other three to four hours to just spend individual time with our players working on individual offensive skill development. As the season starts to wear on, particularly as we get into league play, the great majority of us have a tendency to spend time on team oriented things; zone offense, zone defense, man defense, man offense, press offense, special situations, scouting reports and whatever. We get caught in this rut of doing team things and don't allow enough time for individual skill development. We set this time aside for the individual players. They come in between classes, in the morning, before practice, etc.

We have a maximum of three players with a coach and all they do is work on individual offensive skills. That is a big reason why we were able to take a group of players who, everyone said, didn't have much talent, and mold them into competitive Big Ten players. Each session takes one hour, and the focus is to put as much into the hour as we can. We not only try to develop skills, but since we are a pressing team, we use it for conditioning. They also come back that day for team practice. It helps our level of conditioning. We call it "Pro Time."

(Diagram 1) Full-court dribbling and shooting. Start on the end line, with the left (off) hand. Speed dribble the length of the floor with the ball in the left hand. We want them to pound the ball to develop control. Spread the fingers. At the old hash mark, we angle dribble to the basket and take a straight layup. Our layups are always taken above the block. If you are below the block, you expose more of your body to the defender and allow the shot blocker into the game. Go both ways. Take a straight layup at both ends. Do it again, but take a jump shot off the glass. We want to load our shot as quickly as possible. How? When we come into the shot, the last dribble is going to be our hardest pound.

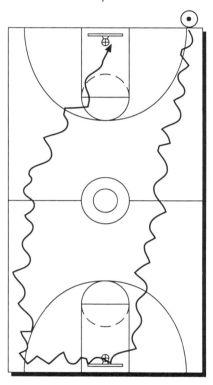

Diagram 1

(Diagram 2) The third time down, we circle to the corner for the jump shot. The fourth time down, crossover at the hashmark and take an elbow jump shot. We want to crossover tight and below the knee to make us ball quick.

(Diagram 3) The fifth time down, crossover at the hashmark, and crossover again at the elbow and take a layup off the glass.

STU JACKSON

Diagram 2

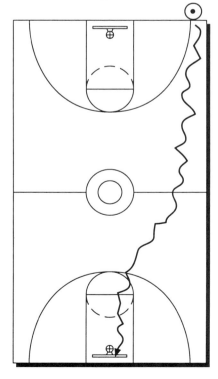

Diagram 3

(Diagram 4) Half-court ballhandling and shooting. Start on right side at half-court, speed dribble to hashmark and speed dribble in for straight layup.

Get the ball out of net, take the ball out-of-bounds and outside the lane. Now they will speed dribble by an imaginary man at the second marker. At half-court, they will crossover, tight and below the knees, right hand to left hand and repeat this from the left side with the ball in the left hand. Layups only.

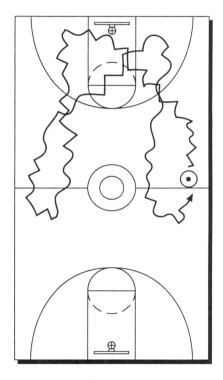

Diagram 4

(Diagram 5) Second move, change of pace at a chair. The body stays down; ball stays down. Layups only. Come back the other way, left hand on left side. Third move, inside and out. We push the ball in and then out. Take the same route and go inside and out at the imaginary man. The fourth move is the stutter. Stutter in one spot. Drive the defensive man back on his heels and then explode out of the stutter. The fifth move is the crossover. We will repeat these five moves with jump shots. The third segment is technique shooting.

STU JACKSON

Diagram 5

(Diagram 6) There is a rebounder, a passer and a shooter at these nine spots. Take five shots per spot. We want rapid fire jump shooting. We teach our players to two-step into the ball. From grade school to junior high to high and above, time is of the essence. You have less time to shoot.

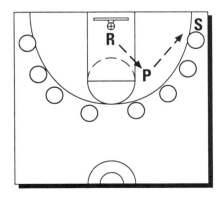

Diagram 6

What about the big people? Same thing, but obviously they will be shooting within their range. The rebounder, passer and shooter rotate positions after every five shots. In the corner you shoot ten shots.

We chart every shot a player takes without defense. If a man comes in and says that he can shoot three-pointers, show him the proof. Don't let a player take a bad shot which is taking away a shot from a good shooter.

We then repeat the technique shooting drill using the ball fake. Ball fake is a big cornerstone for us because we spread the floor. We don't teach the jab fake. The ball fake is simply that the body stays down and the ball comes up.

(Diagram 7) We like to take shots off of a downscreen. You may want them off of a player screen, a curl. We will shoot from the spots where we get shots in our offense. Then, we will do it with the ball fake. We take the post players to the low post. We want to teach players how to finish the shot. We give pro names to the low post moves. We always have our big people post up on the first marker. They move their man. They seal and move the defender up the lane. Or, we have them move the defender down the lane. Receive bounce pass, jump hook. Then, we teach the "up and under." Post up at first marker. Ball fake up, bring the ball in, through and under, step through and finish. Then, do same thing to the middle of the floor.

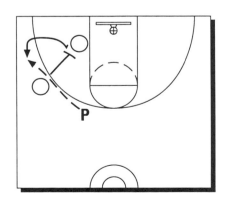

Diagram 7

STU JACKSON

There is the "Bernard King" move. Ball fake violently at the defensive man in one direction, keep the ball up, turn, jump shot. Do it in both directions. Post up wide, and fake into the defender's face.

Then the "Sikma" move. When you have a defender bodying up to you, we want to create space. Don't turn away from the man. Make an inside pivot and move away from the defender. Put the pressure on the defender. The defender has gone from someone who was bodying up, to someone who must make a decision. Do I play him at 8', or do I stay off? If the defender closes, ball fake and go by him. If not, straight jump shot.

Last, we do a "Ron Seikely." Similar to the Sikma move, but take the ball to the defender's feet. Inside pivot, take the ball through very low, and go. Attack the rim. Go either direction. Make these moves quickly.

Philosophy and Secondary Offense

OFFENSIVELY:

- Take advantage of the strength's of your players
- Be flexible
- Should allow for a certain amount of creativity
- Produce the best percentage shot
- Have good rebounding position
- Execute the best half court - offensively

Fast Break Off Of A Made Basket
- 4, 5 run left seam off the floor or opposite the ball
- 3 takes it out on the right side
- 1 and 2 get open, then run their lanes

If 1, 2 go down left side of the floor, 3, 4, 5 go to the right side which keeps the ballside open. Preferably, 1 pushes the ball, but 2 can help release the pressure. The break can be run to either side. If 1 or 2 is being pressured, 3 can come back and set a screen on the ball.

Secondary Break
(Diagram 1) 1 passes to 4 who cuts off of the upscreen by 5. Options: 1 dribbles toward basket and passes to 2 who passes to 4 cutting to the basket after 1 clears.

Diagram 1

(Diagram 2) 4 takes post - then upscreens for 5 who receives a pass from 1 or 2.

Diagram 2

Starting Offense (Entry)
(Diagram 3) 3 takes the ball out of bounds and passes to 1. 2 moves to his position in front court. 3, 4, 5 move to their positions.

(Diagram 4) 1 passes to 2 and cuts to the basket. 2 passes to 1 if open. If not, 5 screens for 1 who comes off of the screen headed back to the top of the circle. 4 moves down to screen 1. 2 passes to 1 near the free throw line for the shot.

MIKE JARVIS

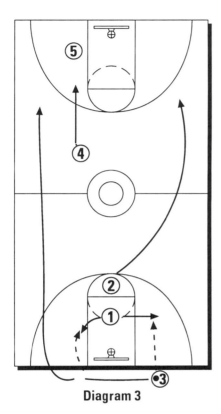

Diagram 3

Diagram 4

(Diagram 5) 1 dribbles toward 2 who clears toward the basket and screens for 5. 1 passes to 5 if open. 2 moves toward the top of the circle and receives a screen from 4. 2 passes to 1 near the free-throw line.

(Diagram 6) 1 dribbles toward 2; passes to 2 and screens for 5. 5 breaks off of the screen to the corner and receives the pass if open. 2 then comes up the lane and cuts off of the screen set by 4. 2 looks for 1 open at the free-throw line.

Diagram 5

Diagram 6

(Diagram 7) 1 dribbles toward 3 and rubs off of screen by 4, then passes to 3. 1 cuts to the basket looking for a pass and cuts off of a screen set by 5. If 1 didn't get the pass before the screen, 1 is rescreened by 4. 3 passes to 1.

(Diagram 8) 5 goes baseline after the screen in order to avoid confusion with 4 coming down to screen.

MIKE JARVIS

Diagram 7

Diagram 8

(Diagram 9) 1 passes to 2; 2 passes to 3. 4 is high and 5 is low.

Diagram 9

(Diagram 10) 1 and 2 exchange positions. 4 slides down on the strongside, and 5 comes high on the weakside.

(Diagram 11) 4 screens up across the lane for 5 who goes low strongside looking for a pass from 3. 4 breaks to strongside high post.

Diagram 10

Diagram 11

(Diagram 12) 4 slides down on the strongside. 5 slides across the baseline, then moves up and across to the strongside.

Diagram 12

(Diagram 13) 1 passes to 3 on the wing. 4 breaks to the corner to get open. 5 slides down the lane. 2 comes to the point while 1 cuts down the middle looking for a pass.

Diagram 13

Diagram 14

(Diagram 14) 4 has the ball in the corner. 3 breaks for the basket and curls to set a screen for 4. 4 drives the baseline.

(Diagram 15) 1 dribbles toward 2. 2 clears across the lane. 4 moves high and 3 comes to the point. 5 stays low. 1 tries to drive for the basket.

Diagram 15

TANYA JOHNSON

Summer Program: Make Use of What You Have

One of the things we are noted for at Marillac High School is making the most of what we have. Ten years ago, in my first year, we won the conference championship and I really didn't appreciate it. Nine years later, we got the second one and we are still celebrating. Our conference is very strong with several state champions in it. Many teams are highly ranked. In making the most of what we have, summer camp is a very big key. So, I thought I would talk about what we do summer camp wise. I know we are all restricted in one way or another in what we can do. The varsity players are really encouraged to do the following. We can't demand that they go to camp, but over a period of time, they just know that it is expected. They want to be part of a successful program. If they are to continue in the program, these things are expected.

VARSITY:

- They attend a four-week high school summer basketball camp. Within this time, we will spend three days a week in a two-hour strength training session.
- They play in two summer high school leagues between June and July. They probably play three or four times a week during a six-week period.
- They attend a shooting camp, at least one time, preferably before the sophomore year. This is a big thing for me. I don't have one varsity player who hasn't been to a shooting camp. I have worked at a particular camp for seven or eight years now. I believe in the method that he has, and we run those same drills. That is a real key for us. We may not be the most athletic, but our shooting percentage has gone up.
- They attend a position camp per discussion with varsity coach. Currently, I have several tall players. I have had discussions with those players about the route they should take. For example, this summer I have four players going to go to post camp and have others attending guard camp.
- Strength training. They work on strength training three times a week throughout the summer. I'd like this to continue throughout the preseason.
- I'd like them to attend a team camp. This isn't the most important thing on this list. But, I like the team bonding that results. Usually I don't go. It gives them an opportunity to know one another. We say that just because you are called a team, doesn't mean that you are one. Last year, we went to a team camp out of the area where we didn't know any of the other teams. It was a great experience. I wanted them to see different teams.
- I want them to participate in one tournament during an evaluation period.

The reason we do this is because we want to be competitive. Other people in our area are doing the same thing. If we don't do it, we can't keep the competitiveness.

SOPHOMORES:

- They must attend a two-week high school camp. This group needs a lot of attention.
- They also play in one designated summer league between June and July.
- We really encourage all of our kids to get to a shooting camp between the freshman and sophomore year.
- We direct our players to position camps. I'm not telling them that they must go. I don't bring that up. It's when they come to me or the parents come to me.
- They are also involved in strength training three times a week.

TANYA JOHNSON

FRESHMEN (INCOMING):

- They attend a two-week high school summer basketball camp. The camp runs two hours a day. Many of these players go on to other camps like volleyball. This is an age where you get a lot of phone calls from parents. They ask what camps do we recommend? The shooting camp is the one that I emphasize. I direct them to the shooting camp that I go to.
- They play in one designated summer league between June and July.
- They attend the shooting camp if possible. I think you get more out of a camp if you work the camp or if you attend. They are evaluated four times during this camp, and I'm there for the evaluation. So, we get the maximum benefit.
- They get strength training education three times a week throughout the camp session. Many of them have never had any instruction in weight training before.

When you make your camp brochure, it doesn't have to be elaborate. I think that communication with other coaches is essential. As assistant athletic director, I am in charge of the summer programs and so the volleyball camp, the soccer camp, the tennis camp, and the cross country camp are also listed.

SUMMER CAMP CHECK LIST

When considering whether or not to have a camp, you need to consider the five W's and an H: who, what, when, where, why, and how. To do this takes a lot of time and work. It's not something that you want to devote the entire summer doing.

Who is the camp for? Is it for your own high school program, for kids grades nine through twelve? Do you want it just for the varsity? If you are an assistant coach? Are you working with the head coach? Are you targeting one age group? We have to provide grammar school camps.

What are your camps going to offer? Be specific. I know what I am going to offer to the varsity, to the sophomores, to the freshmen. We know exactly what is going to be taught in that time period. On day one, you would see the very same thing being taught at all camps. The only difference is that the varsity girls are moving faster, but the same drills are being taught. You must ask yourself what is it that you want those kids to learn? For us, it is a four-week time frame. At the end of those four weeks, we have reviewed and broken down our defense, and gone over offensive drills from the ground level. This is a time to experiment. We had become predictable. We changed our thinking during that time. With the sophomores, we worked a lot on defense. Defense is a constant for us. It's review of defense, and the zone offense. We spend time reading defenses for the motion offense. For the freshmen, that's where we really use our staff. Patience is really a requirement when working with them. Many of them were "superstars" at the grade school level, and they must find out that many of them aren't as good as they thought they were. We really work on defense at the freshman level.

When will the camps be offered? You better ask your players because they are the ones you want to come to the camp. The families may have scheduled vacations. We schedule our camp to go the four weeks immediately after school is out. We have everything finished by July 4th. We tell our freshmen if you want to continue in the program, go to the camp. People will be asking you in January; I get calls from parents. Communicate with your players. Some players may be going to summer school. My response to parents is that they must make a choice. They can't do everything. What are the times of the camps? The varsity players like to go early. The length of time for your camp is a personal thing for each coach. I am thinking of going to three weeks if all of the returning players are accomplished. You must resolve conflicts with other coaches concerning times and dates. Communicate with other coaches well in advance to set up camp dates that allow students the opportunity to participate in as many camps as possible.

Where do you run your camps? Do you run it at the high school, or through the park district? Is the camp in the name of the school or does it have your name on it? If you have your own camp, you are responsible for the insurance. If you run it through the school, you are covered by the school's insurance. From the PR standpoint, I want parents to know that when they sent their daughter to Marillac High School, they got something positive. You will be known. People will send their daughter to your school just because you've been there for awhile. You must think about how many baskets you have and how many players you can handle at each basket.

Why are we doing this? Sure, to make some money, but I want to help the program. If you do something and you don't do it well, it will come back as a negative for the program. It is also possible that some of the kids will attend your high school because they had a positive experience at your camp.

How do you decide whether or not to start a summer program? I have good administrative support. They are supportive of the basketball program and supportive of me. An option would be to hold it through the park district. Or, maybe you would have a connection at another school. If I were going to take a position at another school, one of the first things that I would ask about is whether or not I would be able to run a summer program. If the answer was not, I would not be interested in that position. You must also look at the community.

Who else is offering camps? Where we are, I think that there is a need for the parents to get the kids out of the house for a couple of hours a day. If you are in a small area, you must ask yourself what is the smallest amount of campers you must have to run a camp. I will run a camp with eight or nine kids. You must also ask yourself if your current program is in place. Are the students from your school willing to attend summer camp? Maybe basketball isn't a primary sport in your school. My attitude would be that I'm coaching basketball and I want to see it grow. You must develop that attitude. You must develop the program. Get freshmen who want to play and then you can make some inroads. If I were to take a new position, one of the first things I would do is to meet with the current team and tell them what I planned to do. It might be hard, but you can get it done. There are good kids out there who want to play. It isn't going to happen overnight.

Fees—How much do you charge? Who is going to work this camp? What kinds of awards are you going to give? Does everybody get a tee shirt? Maybe you can get them donated. Do you have to pay for the postage of mailing the brochures and printing the brochures? Do you have to pay for the custodial help? Do you have to give a percentage to the school? How much will you actually make for your work?

As I look back, I know that camps have been a big part of our success. You must evaluate your talent. You must decide where each player will fit. Then you must make the adjustment. Do you have a small team? Do you have a post player? You must be able to adjust to that. And you must communicate. You must make sure that your team understands what you want.

QUESTION: HOW MANY CAMPERS DO YOU HAVE AT EACH BASKET?

Answer: From six to eight. We have a coach at each basket, either myself, assistant adult coaches or varsity players. It is great for the varsity players. They get frustrated trying to teach the younger players. The younger campers really look up to the varsity players.

We are in an area where the parents are very supportive. They know that in order to continue on the path, the kids must go to camp. So the parents arrange their activities around the camp. I really think the players must understand that if they are not in our summer weight program, they won't be playing basketball. It's to the benefit of the kids who are really serious about it. I don't recruit. I don't have parent problems because I have never promised anything, but the camps help because when the kids attend grammar school camps, that is the time the parents see the staff and also some of the varsity players. Our enrollment is increasing. That must mean we know what we are doing. Know what you want to teach and be confident that you are teaching them the right thing.

LON KRUGER

Expectations for Players/Coaches

Sometimes at clinics we concern ourselves too much with the X's and O's as opposed to the "whys" behind them. Successful programs do what they do very well. Let's start by listing some goals that are common to all of us in the coaching profession. Often times at the start of the season, we are asked what our goals are. We want to do things as well as possible. We want a high number of possessions, the highest percentage of the time during each game. If we do that, and have that as a long range goal, winning will take care of itself.

HERE ARE FOUR SHORT-TERM GOALS:

- Create an atmosphere that is enjoyable. If they enjoy what they are doing, they are more apt to "buy in."

- We want our players to play extremely hard every day in practice and play with a tremendous amount of awareness on both ends of the floor. They must prepare every day to go to practice to compete.

- As coaches, it is our responsibility to put people in positions where they can be successful. It only makes sense that if players feel comfortable with what you want them to do, they are going to do it with more confidence.

- Do things in a game that we do every day in practice, and we want to prevent our opponents from doing what they do in practice. We go into a game attempting to take away one or two things from each of the opposing players.

Remember the long-term goal—To play as well as we possibly can each possession of every game. Here are four things to go with that.

- It all starts with our expectations as a coach. We must expect a lot from our players. The more we expect, the better the results.

- Communicate those expectations to our players. Do it in a very positive way. Be specific, talk to them individually, talk to them as a team. Be very fair; be very consistent, and always be very positive.

- Through practice, develop habits so you can transfer those expectations from the meetings to the practice floor. Get everyone on the same page. If it is a late game situation, then everyone must have the understanding of what you want.

- Take it from practice to the game situation. We must deliver the right messages.

Regardless of size, speed, quickness, etc., we need a check list for our team. I am going to go through several possessions and tell you what we expect of our players. Assume that we just scored, or the opponent just got the rebound and gained possession. The first thing we talk about is transition to the defensive end. We must have an immediate reaction. First, we want to meet the ball early. We do that with any of our perimeter players. We also talk about protecting the basket. Our guard has the basket until the first big player gets there to relieve him. As you go back, be in good position relative to the ball and the man. Get off the man toward the ball. It is very important not to give up easy baskets. Never allow the ball to be dribbled by you.

After we stop the transition look, we get into our half-court defense. You must be ready for the fight, down low, ready to compete. We must be in a good starting position. By that I mean two things. One, the defensive stance. Two, be in good position relative to man and ball. Be off the man toward the ball so you can see both. If you are in good starting position, you have a good chance to have a good possession. Especially our post people. We want one 5/5

LON KRUGER

defense, not five 1/1's. It's not a matter of "my guy scored" or "your guy scored." It's a matter that we either stopped them or they scored.

When the opposing team takes a shot, the first thing that we want to do is to communicate that the shot has been taken. When "shot" is called, this is the cue to go into the block-out mode and contest all shots. We chart how effective we are contesting shots. Then, think about getting to a rebounding zone. The zone varies as to where the shot is taken. Normally, it is about 5' to 8' around the goal. We even tape it out in practice. We want our players to get to that position on every shot, make contact there, and go after the ball aggressively. I don't understand how you can play in a game and not block-out. There is nothing else to be thinking about when the shot is taken. The average number of times that people will block-out during the course of a game is between 20% and 30%.

Now, it is our ball. We want an immediate reaction. We want to run out. Too many times there are two or three steps before a player gets to full speed. Minimize the number of easy baskets we give up, but gain as many opportunities as we can on our end. We run, attack the glass when we have an advantage in numbers and we are trying to score. If we don't, then with our secondary look, we want to push the ball into the defense. We want to stretch the defense. Look inside. If the opportunity is not there, swing it, and look inside again. You might get the same shot after you reversed the ball as before, but the defense is not going to be as steady.

In the half-court offense, you are always looking for good spacing, good ball movement, good movement of people without the ball, good balance, and inside scoring opportunity. When the shot goes up, we want three players on the offensive board. People only block out 25% of the time.

You must talk to your players individually in meetings. When you go on the floor to practice, you have the regular communication during practice, but there are no opportunities to have long discussions. You want to talk to them about what you expect from them and their role on the team. If you allow a player to shoot the three-point shot in practice and you don't let him shoot that shot in a game, you are going to have a problem. If you don't think a shot is going in, then you must consider it a bad shot. You must bring that to the player's attention.

After a loss, we have the players' attention in practice and we make progress. We must get that same type of attention after a win. Why not? That's why there are upsets. We challenge our players to come to practice every day to get better. During the course of the season, the length of practices vary, but the intensity never does. We always go hard. The players must develop that habit. We never talk in terms of winning. We talk in terms of playing as well as we possibly can. It's important to make that distinction. Often we will be as disappointed after a win as we are after a loss.

As a coach, it is important to teach what we know, and to teach what we are comfortable with. If you are going to try something new, you must spend some time with it. Visit some other coach and learn as much as you can about it. You must be able to sell your players on the fact that this is going to work. Talk about slippage. For example, take a rebounding drill. Everytime, the defensive man will block-out the offensive man. Then go 2/2 or 3/3, and there will be some slippage. There will be more slippage in a 5/5 situation. Go to the game, then there is more slippage about 25% of the time. There is slippage of intensity. There is slippage in every part of the game. Our objective is to minimize the slippage.

Always build confidence, reinforce the players. You must have confidence to play this game well. A lot of this is done in individual meetings. Very seldom do we get after a player in front of his teammates. It is very important to be very positive in everything we do. It is very important to treat each player individually. We tell our players early on that if you are concerned with spending three hours in a study hall and someone else only spends one hour, then you are going to be frustrated all season. We have our expectations for each player individually; what they need to be a good person and player.

When we practice teamwise, we go three possessions. If we are on offense, we change to defense and then back to offense again. We talk in terms of winning each of the three possessions. Their attitude is so important regarding winning each possession. We want to get every player to play as if the game is tied and there is one possession left; then we will be very good.

Out-Of-Bounds Underneath

You cannot just take what we do and copy it. You must gear it to your personnel's ability, what they do and don't do well. It allows us to move people around, to run the same action for any number of different players. Our point guard is 1; 2 and 3 are swing men; 4 is the power forward and 5 is the post. We have several "options" for out-of-bounds underneath. We always inbound the ball with the point guard. These are all against a man-to-man defense.

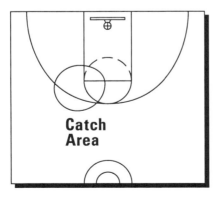

Diagram 1

(Diagram 1) Strong Action. We inbound the ball to the "catch area." We may have to pass to the wing first, but we want the ball to go to this area.

(Diagram 2) We inbound to the catch area. We are then going to make a guard-to-guard pass. On the pass from 4 to 3, 5 shuffle cuts off the screen of 1. 4 then down-screens for 1 and then posts.

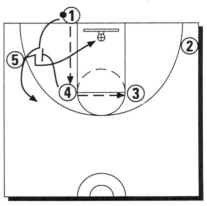

Diagram 2

(Diagram 3) 3 then passes to 1. 1 looks to 4 or 5. You have three looks; the shuffle cutter, the point guard, and the pass inside. We can put any player in any of those spots.

Diagram 3

(Diagram 4) If we want to shufflecut the post man, we call "43 strong." That means 4 receives the pass. The big man, not in the call (5), will be in the corner on the ball side. The perimeter man not in the call will be corner opposite (2). 4 and 3 will influence to the baseline. 4 moves to the elbow to receive the pass. 3 breaks to the other elbow to get the pass from 4. When 4 passes to 3, 5 shufflecuts off of 1's pick.

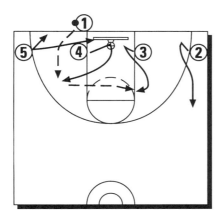

Diagram 4

(Diagram 5) 4 down-screens for 1 for the jumper.

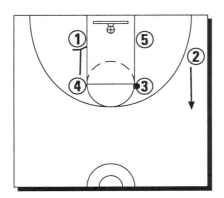

Diagram 5

(Diagram 6) "35 strong." If 3 is a good post-up man, run this. 3 gets the pass in the catch area, and makes the guard-to-guard pass to 5. 3 then down-screens for 1 after 4 makes his shufflecut. 3 posts-up.

Diagram 6

(Diagram 7) How can this be stopped? If you start with four men on the baseline, the other team must get on the top of four. But, you have the basket there to keep people honest. If that occurs, we call "50" which is the automatic lob. 4 takes one step back into the defense and knifes to the goal. 4 can also start up the lane and turn and loop back to the basket.

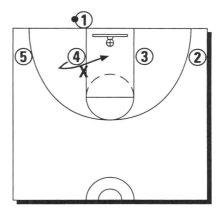

Diagram 7

(Diagram 8) Put 1's defensive man on top. This is an automatic. This keys 4 to seal X1, and 1 passes to 5 who makes the return pass to 1 for the shot.

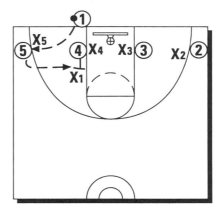

Diagram 8

(Diagram 9) Some teams try to take away the guard-to-guard pass. 3 comes high and then goes backdoor to receive the pass from 4. 2 must move to keep the defensive player away from the ball.

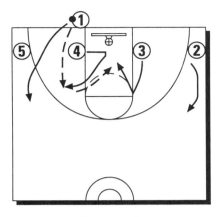

Diagram 9

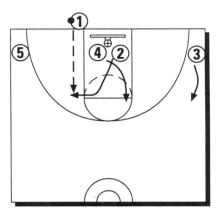

Diagram 11

(Diagram 10) "43 counter." We use this against a team that overplays. On the "counter" call, 2 steps hard and high. 3 must backcut. The ball goes from 1-4-3, or from 1-4-2-3. 2 feeds 3 as 3 posts.

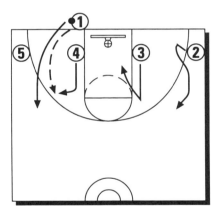

Diagram 10

Diagram 12

(Diagram 13) 5's defensive man usually steps out to help on 2. We then "slip the flare pick," and 5 cuts to the basket for the pass from 4.

(Diagram 11) "24 weak." We use this for a good perimeter shooter. We start with 2 and 4 stacked in the lane. 2 can use 4 to get into the catch area. 4 then goes to the opposite elbow.

(Diagram 12) Now instead of shufflecutting, 5 sets a flarepick for 2. 2 flares for the skip-pass from 4. 1 goes higher than the free-throw line extended. He must take his defensive man away from the basket. 2 and 5 have the entire side of the floor. 5 rolls to the post area. 5 can also pick for 4, who can come to the top of the key.

Diagram 13

(Diagram 14) "42 weak slip." 5 picks for 4. The others must keep their people out of the way. They must play act and influence their men out of the area. We can run this play for any of our players. We can call 35 weak, 52 weak, 24 weak. You can run that jumper for anyone. When your opponents walk through some of your plays, you can give it a completely different look by changing the positions of your men.

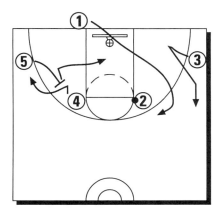

Diagram 14

(Diagram 15) "Weak 42 opposite" is a variation. This is a jump shot for 2. 4 uses 2 and goes to the catch area. On the "opposite" call, the big man not in the call goes to the corner opposite. 5 flare-screens for 2. 1 goes to the ball side of the floor keeping his man away from the action. The ball goes from 1-4-2.

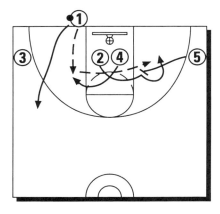

Diagram 15

(Diagram 16) "42 opposite slip." 5 can slip that for a pass from 4.

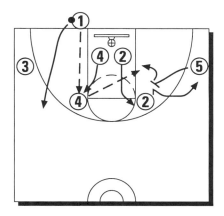

Diagram 16

(Diagram 17) "24 post." With a strong point guard, post him. Whoever you want feeding the post, have him catch the ball. It looks like "strong action." 1 passes to 2 who fakes the pass to 4. 5 makes the shufflecut; 2 passes to 1 who has posted up. 5 cuts to get a part of the defensive man of 1.

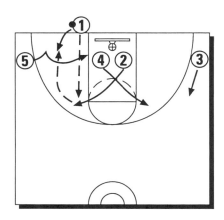

Diagram 17

(Diagram 18) The entire side of the floor is open for 2 after the pass to 1. Anytime you feed the pass, you must move. Occupy the defense.

(Diagram 19) "42 post." We set it up so that 2 always feeds the post. 5 will always be on the side of 2. The ball goes from 1-4-2.

LON KRUGER

Diagram 18

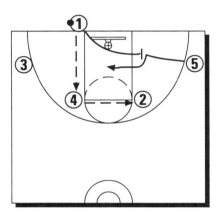

Diagram 19

(Diagram 20) Sometimes 2 must dribble to improve the angle to feed the post as shown on this "24 post."

Diagram 20

(Diagram 21) "25 gut." 5 sets pick for 2 who gets the ball in the catch area. 2 then looks low for 5 who steps to the ball. The big man not in the call goes to the corner ball side. 1 sprints out to get his defensive man out of the way. Everything is spread along the baseline and 5 is isolated.

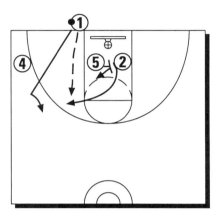

Diagram 21

(Diagram 22) "50." This is a lob in front of the goal. 5 can V-cut back to the goal or make a loop. We want 5 going toward the goal when he catches the ball. Whoever is on the opposite block, must dive hard to the baseline to clear the area.

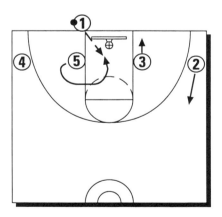

Diagram 22

(Diagram 23) "50 seal." 5 steps into the open area. 2 sets a backpick for the same type of action as a "50." Sometimes 2 is open for the shot.

LON KRUGER

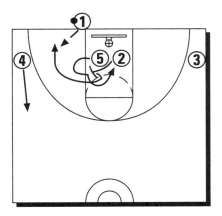

Diagram 23

(Diagram 24) If 2 gets the pass but doesn't have a shot, 5 steps back to the ball.

Diagram 24

(Diagram 25) "53 strong." We can line up this way also. 2 breaks opposite; 4 goes to the corner; 3 goes to opposite elbow and 5 to the catch area.

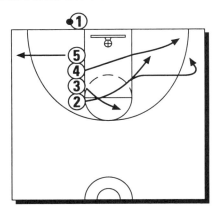

Diagram 25

(Diagram 26) After the shufflecut, for a variation, 1 can backpick for 4 who breaks down and posts-up. The ball can go from 2-4-2-1 or 2-4-2-1-4.

Diagram 26

(Diagram 27) Against a zone we can run "24 weak." It is a little different. Usually against a zone we must inbound the ball through 5, who then passes to 2 in the catch area. 2 passes to 4, and 5 screens the top man in the zone. 2 steps wide.

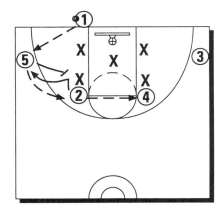

Diagram 27

(Diagram 28) The baseline man in the zone now has both 1 and 2 to guard. 4 passes to 2 who can pass to 1.

(Diagram 29) We can run "42 opposite" against a zone. 5 is in opposite corner. 1 inbounds to 4. 5 seals the top man in the zone. 1 goes to opposite corner as 2 comes off the pick of 5. 4 passes to 2 who can pass to 1.

Diagram 28

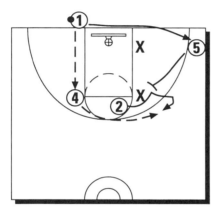
Diagram 29

(Diagram 30) "42 strong" against a zone means that we lob. The ball goes from 1-4-2. 5 shufflecuts high to influence the middle man of the zone. 1 seals the back man in the zone, and 4 goes to the basket for the lob. After the pick by 1, 1 steps out wide.

Diagram 30

(Diagram 31) Sometimes on the "24 weak" against a zone after the pass from 1 to 2 to 4, 5 sets the screen on the top man of the zone and then breaks into the middle of the lane for the jumper.

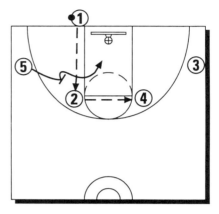
Diagram 31

(Diagram 32) We can run a "42 strong" from the sideline out-of-bounds. We inbound the ball with the man who is not in the call. 1 gets the pass coming off of the double pick. 1 dribbles to the wing.

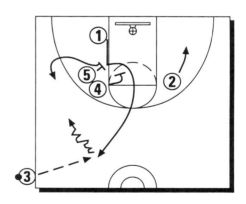
Diagram 32

(Diagram 33) 4 receives the pass from 1 in the catch area. 2 goes opposite. 1 goes to the post; 5 shufflecuts out of the corner, and 3 is wide opposite. So, we run exactly the same thing from the side. You can run any of those actions from the sideline inbounds.

Diagram 33

THE LEGENDS

A Panel Discussion

Moderator:

Bob Murrey

Panel:

Bighouse Gaines, Winston-Salem (Retired)

Ernie Hobbie, Shot Doctor

Billie Moore, UCLA (Retired)

Ralph Sampson, James Madison

Jerry Tarkanian, UNLV (Retired)

Morgan Wootten, DeMatha Catholic High School

Bob Murrey: This is a time when you have a chance to ask questions about the game of basketball. We usually don't have as many people available.

Question: What is your opinion of the physical play of teams like the Knicks? It seems to be filtering down to college and high school.

Morgan Wootten: I think the game we see in the pros is not the high school game. This is not the game that we, as high school coaches, coach. It is a physical game; there is contact, but there is good physical play. But with the pros, that's a different world.

Jerry Tarkanian: I agree with Morgan. You like to see physical play and people be aggressive, but some of the play in the NBA, their plan is to knock you down if you try to drive. That goes too far. My biggest complaint about the college game is that every time you have a really big game, the officials take over and start calling every little thing, and all the good players have three and four fouls early. That part bothers me more than anything else. If the game is called right, the college game is about as physical as it needs to be.

Billie Moore: At one time basketball was considered non-contact, but it has gotten away from that. I agree with Jerry that the hardest part is knowing how to adapt to the officiating. It's more of an attitude of how the game is officiated. The hardest part is what's allowed from game to game.

Ernie Hobbie: I agree with Tark, but I think we can take it a step beyond. Just recently, a kid got fined, but he wasn't fined as much as someone else because the punch he threw didn't land. I have difficulty with that. To me, it doesn't matter. He swung to hurt somebody.

Bob Murrey: This question might have a specific direction toward Bighouse because you had some problems in your conference didn't you?

Bighouse Gaines: There is a tremendous influence. I think there are several things that have hurt basketball. One has been the dunk. I don't see any specific skill needed to do that. The other thing that bothers me about that is the kids see it and decide that "you aren't going to dunk on me, not in my face." That has a tremendous effect. I just retired from the rules committee. They are describing the rough fouls. Fouling from behind when someone is going to the basket has had a tremendous negative impact on college ball.

Bob Murrey: Let's hear from a player who has played for 10 years.

Ralph Sampson: I think that these coaches made

THE LEGENDS

the correct comments. The NBA has the high visibility among the public and every time there is an outburst of fighting or whatever, it often gets blown out of proportion. There is no room for fighting or the throwing of elbows in the game of basketball, but players do get excited. I think it effects the young kids a tremendous amount. Kids try to emulate Jordan or Ewing instead of learning the fundamentals of the game.

Question: This is for Coach Tarkanian. You preach getting the all out intensity, what do you do to counteract the players from going a step too far?

Jerry Tarkanian: I think you want aggressive play. I don't think you can win big in the college game unless you are aggressive. I don't think anyone can win without toughness. But, I believe there is a difference between being tough and trying to hurt someone, or fighting. I want to see our players be aggressive, beat someone to a spot, front the post, etc. But it's different when a player is going for a basket and your job is to make sure that you knock him down. I hate to see games won on intimidation.

Question: The rule has been changed to 35 seconds. It looks like we are going more and more to what the pros are doing. Is this so?

Jerry Tarkanian: I like the 35-second shot. Any team who wants to get a shot off, can in 35 seconds. It will help late in the game where you see the intentional foul. With 35 seconds, there should be less intentional fouling. I agree that the college game is more popular, but I think the reason it is more popular is because they play fewer games and it is more exciting. The players are fresher and are able to play at a higher level.

Bob Murrey: Coach Moore, do you have any comments on that from the women's tandpoint?

Billie Moore: The women have a 30-second clock. We have had this for 25 years and we still see zones. As you watch the men's game in the last two or three minutes and you watch a women's game, you will see much more intentional fouling in the men's game. I think the clock will get the game a little more up-tempo. The less time that you have on the shot clock, the more the team with the better athletes will win.

Question: Not counting the pros, if you had to make one change in the rules, what would it be?

Bighouse Gaines: I would just adopt the international rules. I am in favor of the 30-second clock. I can't remember losing the game because of the clock. As far as the lane is concerned, we should adopt one lane for all of basketball. For the last minute, the clock should be stopped on every made field goal. The biggest problem the rules committee has is how to play the last two or three minutes so that it won't take a half hour. So, we have the 45 down to 35, and it will eventually go to 30. I think the lane will be changed; I don't know if it will be NBA or international size. The South American groups changed the concept of basketball, Oscar and the three-pointer. We went to South America and got beat by the three-pointer.

Bob Murrey: And you think that stopping the clock near the end of the game will be a big help?

Bighouse Gaines: Everyone seems to think so.

Question: What will the women's game look like in the future?

Billie Moore: In the next 10 years you are going to see more of what has happened in the last ten; bigger and better athletes playing the game at a much higher level of intensity. The three-point shot for the women, there's really not that same

THE LEGENDS

impact on the women's game. We may only have one or two players on the team who can shoot the three. That may be the biggest change coming, that teams will have three or four, maybe all five players shooting threes.

Question: What's the possibility of another women's pro league?

Billie Moore: There was a rumor a couple of weeks ago about the NBA getting involved in such a league. Obviously, those of us involved in women's basketball would like to see that happen. Right now we have about 75 to 100 of our athletes playing in Europe. Japan used to be a big market, but they closed that because of finances. I would like to see such a league. I would want the game to be played as it is.

Jerry Tarkanian: I have a suggestion for a rule change. Nothing bothers me more than the five foul disqualification. You can go on the road, or even at home, and the officials can take that game away from you. Two or three questionable calls can go against your big man or your number one player and it destroys everything that you have worked for all year. That bothers me. I would like to see two intentional fouls and a player is out of the game. But, the incidental fouls, I don't think there should be a limit.

Question: For Coach Wootten. You've sent a lot of kids to college to play ball; what is your feeling about the requirements regarding the test scores, and the Prop 42 and Prop 48?

Morgan Wootten: Basically, I think the NCAA has the right thought when they encourage a kid to be a student athlete. I disagree with the SAT being used as one of the yardsticks to judge. The SAT exams have nothing to do in terms of predicting success in college. That's been proven. The SAT was never intended by the people who made it to serve that purpose. We have the world's number one expert at DeMatha, someone who tutors this course. We have presidents of some of the biggest corporations in America flying their children in for him to tutor, and he can raise their scores 300 points. It means that it isn't a valid test to be used like that. But the idea is good. We want good student athletes. The newest rule they are proposing for sophomores now is ludicrous. It actually awards the underachiever. The lower your grade average in school, then you need a higher SAT. So, if you don't work up to your potential, nail the SAT, you won't be a Prop 48. If they are going to stay with the SATs, then when the kid goes in, he should get four years of playing time. It doesn't make sense, a kid goes in as a Prop 48, he's a marginal student anyhow, and they say he has four years to graduate and he can't play the first year. I think he should have that extra year. So, I don't like the SAT as a yardstick. The idea is right, to be the best student athlete they can be.

Bob Murrey: Let me ask Ralph (Sampson) a question. As a young man at age 22 and moving into the pros, what kind of advice would you offer young kids who have the opportunity to go into the pros?

Ralph Sampson: First thing, I would tell those who go hardship to stay in school because of the mere fact that you don't know how long you will play in the league. But, you will never get the opportunity to go back and be a college student again. That's one of the greatest experiences in life you will ever have. The biggest transition point, from college life to the NBA is the travel, the time on the road, the living out of suitcases, the wear and tear on the body and the mind, from one hotel to the next.

Bob Murrey: Jerry, on the transition from a successful college coaching career, moving into the NBA, what do you think was your biggest adjustment?

THE LEGENDS

Jerry Tarkanian: First of all, it's a different game. It will take 30-35 ballgames to really get a good feel for it. I also think that it is an adjustment for an NBA coach going into the college ranks. It bothers me when you hear all these NBA people talking about how a college coach can't coach in the NBA. It will take a little time to adjust either way. The biggest problem from my standpoint was that we just didn't have any practice time. We had six days of camp and started our exhibition season and played a game about every other day. You know what you want to do with your team; you know about the weaknesses, and I'd get excited about practicing. A player would remind me that we played the next night. The toughest thing is knowing when to rest them. It is one of the keys to being an NBA coach because I know you want to keep the legs fresh, but you want to drill them properly and do what needs to be done, and you must understand that you have only one day. Really, what can you do in practice? The other thing is that you must guard people away from the ball. That changes the game totally. If you have a poor post man, you can send him as far from the basket as you can and you've got to go guard him. Offensively, the NBA game is basically a one- and two-man game. Get your great player and you post him up. Create a double-team and attack a double-team. Whereas in college, you are working on help defense and a lot of different things.

Question: What weaknesses do you see in the high school players coming out of grade school?

Morgan Wootten: Basically, it is fundamentals. They don't know how to get in a defensive stance; they don't know the basic steps, the retreat step, the swing step, the advance step. A lot of them have poor shooting habits because they start very young and have two hands on the ball. They use their body to shoot outside their range, so their shooting fundamentals are very poor and need a lot of work. A big weakness I see in high school all the way through the pros is a lack of individual offensive moves. There are so many players who catch the ball and have no idea what to do with it. If they are open, they can shoot it, but in terms of being able to create their own shot in a one-on-one situation, they just don't have them. Ninety-nine percent of the post players don't have a move, so they put the ball on the floor and try to get open.

Ernie Hobbie: I've spent 40 years in education and have taught kindergarten through high school. When I hear a question like this, it bothers me. We are supposed to be educators; we are supposed to be teaching young people. One of my concerns is that everyone wants to emulate someone else. Here is one thing I learned from Hubie Brown when I went to some Knick practices. He said, "Hey, they know who I am. I'm Hubie Brown. I'm the same every day. My players know what to expect." This is very important. If you are coaching kids don't be somebody else. Learn to communicate with your kids so that they have some trust and confidence in you. When you send a kid out to perform and he misses a shot, don't crucify him. As a coach, your job is to teach every kid how to handle the ball, how to shoot the ball, how to defend. Try this one day. Make all your big kids guards, make all your little kids front liners just so they have the perspective of how difficult the other position is.

Question: What is the value of scouting services for kids in high school?

Jerry Tarkanian: Most of the major colleges subscribe to them. The scouting services make recruiting more national. Now there really aren't any great players that you don't know about. There are about seven or eight scouting services and you can double and triple check. For the college coach, it's good. From the high school kid's perspective, it has to be good if he is interested in going to college. It would open a lot of doors for him. It saves colleges a lot of money.

THE LEGENDS

For $150 or $200, you can subscribe to these services instead of sending out a coach to check out the player.

Question: Ralph, why did you choose the University of Virginia after all the recruiting was over?

Ralph Sampson: My high school coach and I set up guidelines to stop all the illegal recruiting that was going on. I narrowed the list to four schools; Virginia, North Carolina, Kentucky, and Virginia Tech. I chose Virginia because it was one hour from my home town and my mother could see me play, it was in a good conference, it had a good coach and I could get a good education. Basketballwise, they were one player away from being a very good nationally ranked team. They had a lot of good players but they didn't have a center. I wanted to go and play.

Question: Coach Wootten, as a high school coach, what is your biggest challenge every year?

Morgan Wootten: I think that you have new players, a new type of team coming up. It is your ability to adjust, to make sure that your system bends to get the most out of your players. One year we might have some decent size, and the next year we won't, so you must make changes offensively and defensively to bring out the best in your personnel. I think the coach must stay fresh and have the ability to adjust to coach different types of kids.

Question: With the lessening of scholarships and the raising of requirements, many people will have to go to junior colleges. Is this going to have a major effect on balancing the talent across the board?

Jerry Tarkanian: I really think that raising the standards is good. A lot of kids who go to junior college should go to junior college. The biggest problem you have academically is when you get a kid in college and he is surrounded by kids who scored 1100 and 1200 on the Boards, and he scored 700. How can you expect him to compete? I think that a kid who doesn't measure up to the normal standards of your admission policy should go to a junior college for a year or two. If the junior college upgraded their standards so that every course you had to take was a college level course, you would be doing the kid a favor. We recruited a lot of junior college kids, and I'm amazed at how many high school coaches around the country think it's a sin to send a kid to junior college. I went to junior college myself. Junior college can be a great service, especially for a kid who is struggling academically. He's much better off going into junior college for two years, having some success academically, building some self-esteem, maturing, and being more serious about his education.

Over the 19 years at UNLV, I'd say that 50% of our players came from junior college. It's another misconception that the media has that if you recruit from junior college, you have thugs and bad guys, and if you recruit freshmen, you've got good guys. I want to guarantee you that some of the nicest guys I ever had came from junior college, and some of the worst kids came from the freshman class. That can go either way. It bothers me when people take the negative approach to junior college.

Question: Coach Wootten, how many people will this effect? What percentage of these top 100 players will these new requirements effect?

Morgan Wootten: One school of thought is that if you raise the requirements, the kids realize this, and they will reach higher, extend further and will meet the requirements. I don't think as great a number will qualify. There may be a 10% drop-off. Maybe in a few years they will catch up again. But I do like the emphasis being put on the student athlete. Right now we have good parity

THE LEGENDS

in college ball as it is. There are a lot of good teams out there. Maybe the quality of play isn't as good.

Question: What about the NCAA policy of reducing the number of coaches on the staff? What does the future hold for young coaches?

Bighouse Gaines: It doesn't make sense. North Carolina, for example, grosses two and a half million dollars and a $16,000 limited earnings coach is cut. You can make people lie, steal, and cheat. I know someone who has a wife and two kids, and he is making $16,000 coaching. Someone is supplementing him someplace. If a coach can make a half million, let him make it. There shouldn't be any limit, but they should also be able to pay their assistants.

Ernie Hobbie: I know people who are struggling. One is a grad assistant with $60,000 in loans. He is trying to make ends meet. He can't get married. That problem concerns me. Basketball revenue makes 80% to 82% of the budget of the NCAA. Yet, how much do the basketball coaches have to say about their own rules? If a coach is driving to practice and one of his players gets hurt, he can't stop the car and take him to the hospital. If he puts him in his car, it is a violation. If there is a tremendous storm and he gives the player a ride, it is a violation. There are so many rules. I'm all for rules, but some of these rules are ridiculous. No one can go in and help a college player during the season. You can't even volunteer. It's a violation. I'm all about helping young people, and sometimes the rules we have aren't helping anyone.

Bob Murrey: We haven't had six such people where we could sit and ask questions for many years because of tight schedules. It's great to be able to listen to over 150 years of experience (from these six people). They have given a lot of time to the game. It's crazy. Kids go through basketball even at the collegiate level and they don't know the history of the game. It's sad. We old-timers do. Do you? Do you teach your kids the history of the game? It will only be through the efforts of you, the coaches. That's why we do this. We call it "The Legends." It's a great chance to learn about basketball.

Teaching Man-to-Man Defense

In teaching defense, you must develop a great pride in stopping the other team. This must start from the very first day of practice. The basic keys to defense as we see it at St. John's are:

- Pressure on the ball. We pick people up at the "door." This means we pick people up three feet outside the NBA three-point line.

- Make the next pass difficult. Force a player high and wide to get the pass.

- Helpside defense. When away from the ball, get in the lane to give help. Players must learn to contain the dribble. We don't want the ball in the middle third of the court. We funnel everything to the sideline. Once the ball goes below the foul line extended, we force the ball to the baseline. We don't want to give up easy baskets, especially on transition defense. We want to hold the opponent to one shot. We emphasize our guards should rebound as well as the big men.

DRILLS WE USE TO TEACH DEFENSE ARE:

(Diagram 1) 1-on-1 full-court defense. The defense passes to the offense to start the drill and then sprints to half-court. He then turns and picks up the offensive player, forcing him away from the basket.

(Diagram 2) 3-on-3 full-court defense. The coach throws the ball to the offense who is lined up on the baseline. The defense sprints to half-court and then turns and picks up the ball. The two defenders whose men don't have the ball must sprint back below the line of the ball and stop any penetration. We call this "building a wall."

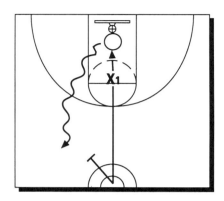

Diagram 1

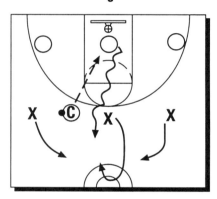

Diagram 2

(Diagram 3) 4-on-4 full-court defense. This is the same as the 3-on-3 drill with another offensive and defensive player added. The responsibilities are the same for the defenders. To make this drill more difficult, you can change who the defense is guarding so they can't just sprint back and pick up a man. They might have to change sides of the court to pick their man up.

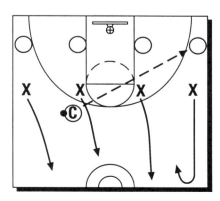

Diagram 3

(Diagram 4) Contest the shot. This is a drill of three defensive players versus four offensive players. We allow no dribbling, just passing by the offense. We allow only jump shots at first, and then we allow baseline offensive drives. The defense stays on defense until they get the rebound.

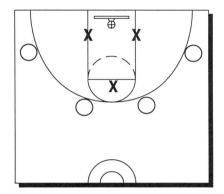

Diagram 4

We run a shell drill to work on several things:

- Defend the Pass and Cut. (Diagram 5) We tell our defenders to jump to the ball and front the cutter. The offense rotates on the pass and cut.

Diagram 5

- Defend the Down-screen. (Diagram 6) The man on the ball must pressure the ball. The man being screened has the right of way to get through and get to the ball. We encourage his teammates to pull him through the screen.

Diagram 6

- Help and Recover. (Diagram 7) The offense now looks to drive when they get the ball. Emphasis is on the defense stopping the penetrating dribble.

Diagram 7

(Diagram 8) "Diamond" Drill. Every third pass must go to the post. We are emphasizing the defender on the outside "digging down" on the pass to the post and then getting back out to the pick-up man. The offense can pass, cut, screen, etc. We encourage a skip—pass and drive to force the defense to have to recover and stop the drive.

(Diagram 9) "Spit Out" Drill. This is a four-on-five drill in which we have an open post. The post, however, can only catch the ball on the block. Every third pass must go to the post. The offense can make any cut they want. We run all these drills four to five minutes everyday. If a drill isn't going well, we'll go on to the next drill and then come back to it later.

Diagram 8

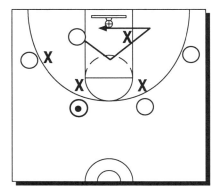

Diagram 9

1-4 Press Offense

turn and look up court. He should be a good ballhandler and free-throw shooter. He should also be a good "finisher." If you have a player who can't do anything, you could put him here. Just have him go "down and out" and get out of the way. He should line up by putting his butt toward the sideline. 2 is your small forward. He should be a good ballhandler and "finisher." He should be confident, mobile, and able to move. 3-point guard and best ballhandler. He must want the ball and not run away from pressure. He will get the ball 90% of the time. He should be a good decision maker on the break. 4-center and good ballhandler and passer. He will fill the middle vs. the press. He lines up opposite 1 with his butt facing the sideline opposite 1.

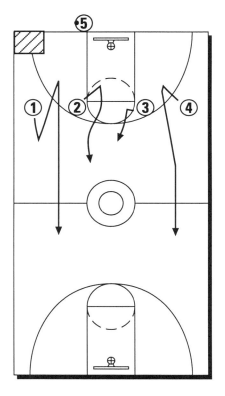

Diagram 1

We use this offense because it is simplistic, and good against man and zone pressure. We find that teams don't press us anymore, but if they do, it isn't for very long. We also can score off this offense, not just cross mid-court. We assign specific positions to this offense.

(Diagram 1) 5 always takes the ball out-of-bounds. He must be a good decision-maker and a good ballhandler. He must be a good free-throw shooter and be able to make the baseball pass. 1 is your power forward, usually the second tallest player on the team. He must stay out of the corner when breaking for the ball. He must be able to get free for the inbound's pass and upon catching the ball, must

(Diagram 2) First option. 1 breaks to the ball, getting open but staying away from the corner. 2 breaks to the 28' marker; 3 cuts to the middle of the floor, and 4 cuts wide filling the outside lane.

Diagram 2

Diagram 4

(Diagram 3) Option two. 1 and 4 cut wide and fill the outside lanes; 2 breaks to the ball, and 3 breaks to the middle to get open. If 1 can't pass to 2, he looks to 3 cutting in the "pocket." If 2 or 3 aren't open, 1 looks to throw the diagonal pass to 4.

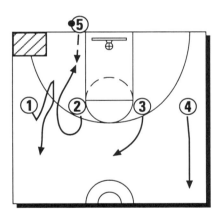

Diagram 3

Diagram 5

(Diagram 4) If 2, 3, or 4 aren't open, 1 looks to pass back to 5.

(Diagram 5) Another option we use to inbound the ball is called "weakside." 5 inbounds to 4 who has faked a cut down court and comes back for the ball. 4 now has three looks: a. pass to 3 on the sideline. b. pass to 2 in the "pocket." c. diagonal pass to 1.

(Diagram 6) Against man-to-man pressure, we run what we refer to as "Double."

3 and 4 change positions with 3 starting off on the outside, and 4 lines up in the inside. 1 goes long; 2 moves across the lane to set a double-screen with 4. 3 cuts off the double-screen looking for the inbound's pass. 3 can cut low or high off of the screen.

(Diagram 7) "Fade" cut. Third option.

(Diagram 8) 5 should not throw the ball to 3 until he has cleared the lane. If 3 cannot get open off the double-screen, 2 spins to the ball and 4 curls into the middle. 5 passes to 2 and then moves inbounds to back-screen 3, then open for the return pass.

Diagram 6

Diagram 7

Diagram 8

(Diagram 9) As a special wrinkle that we run off "double," has 2 coming across setting a backscreen for 3 and then cutting long for the homerun pass.

The 1-4 press offense can be run against a 2-2-1, 1-2-1-1, 1-3-1, 1-2-2, or 4-1 zone press. When facing a zone press, look to see what zone press you are facing as they cut to their assigned spots.

Diagram 9

(Diagram 10) Against a 2-2-1, we line up as normal and 1 cuts to the ball. 5 passes to 1 and steps inbounds, staying behind the ball. When 1 gets the ball, we tell him to get the ball to 3 in the "pocket" or to 4 on the diagonal pass. We don't want to pass the ball to 2 because this pass actually helps the defense set up the trap.

Diagram 10

(Diagram 11) If 1 can't pass to 2, 3, or 4 for the break, he passes back to 5. 5 dribbles toward the opposite sideline; 3 moves back behind the ball to be the safety valve; 4 breaks to the middle; 2 cuts down court to the opposite sideline, and 1 fills the lane on his side.

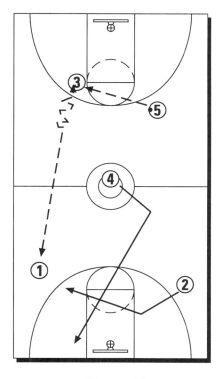

Diagram 12

(Diagram 13) If, as 3 dribbles the ball up court, 1's man moves up to trap 3, 1 runs a curl move and 3 looks to get the ball to 1 who turns and takes the ball to the basket.

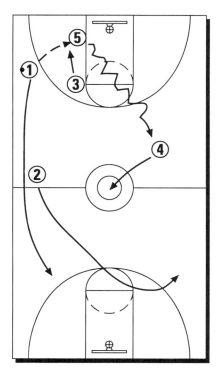

Diagram 11

(Diagram 12) If 5 reverses the ball to 3, 3 dribbles once or twice up the sideline and looks to pass 1. 4 runs a cut to the basket, and 2 cuts across the lane.

Diagram 13

Offensive Drills

The first thing I am going to do is give you the drills in a practice situation. This will give you a good idea of practice organization as well as what drills we run and when in practice we run them.

(Diagram 1) One of the first drills we do is UCLA. There are four lines on the baseline. We go full-court working on fundamentals. We talk about the positioning of the body. We start with a jump stop. We have a coach for each line on the free-throw line. The first person will run to the coach and jump stop. We want to hear the sound as they make a two-foot stop. We want the knees bent. We want them on the balls of their feet, but not on the toes. They do it again at half-court and again at the other free-throw line.

Next, we talk about pivoting. We do it the same way, except we add the pivot. We jump stop, then pivot on the left foot. We do it again with the right foot. It's amazing how many kids want to move their pivot foot while doing a pivot. We only let them put their foot down twice in pivoting a full circle. Then we add the position of the ball. With the forwards, we talk about "elbow to nose." We want the forwards to have the ball high, so when they pivot, their elbow is at nose level of the defense. For the guards, we have them bring the ball through below the knee. They bring it through with the elbow first.

(Diagram 2) Three lines, with the post players in the middle line. Use two balls. This drill works on catching the ball while you are moving; it works on getting the ball from the dribble to the pass quickly; it works on your reaction in finding the ball and catching it quickly. It also works on the ballhandling, and you must look before you pass. The people in the outside lanes must dribble with the outside hands. As 1 passes to 2, 3 is passing to 2. The timing should be that 1 passes and immediately turns and catches. We run the floor; there is no sliding. We don't shoot. We don't switch lines. We try to get a two-dribble maximum. The ball always goes to 1.

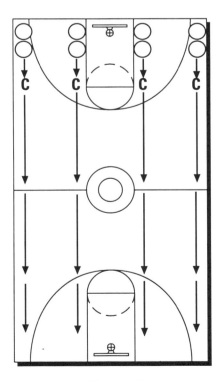

Diagram 1

Diagram 2

(Diagram 3) Triangle Box Out, 3/2 and 2/1. You can start this drill 3/3 with two coaches, one coach shoots the ball. The defenders must box out. This is especially crucial for the weakside person. The offense crashes the boards. When the defense gets the ball, then run the floor and play 3-on-2 at the other end. 1, 2, and 3 attack two tandem defenders at the other end. One takes the ball and the other takes the first pass. The person who scores or shoots the ball now plays defense going the other way against the two people who were the tandem defensive players. If a shot is taken and a teammate gets an offensive rebound, she then shoots. Therefore, she is the one playing defense. The last person to touch the ball, either 1, 2, or 3, plays defense going the other way.

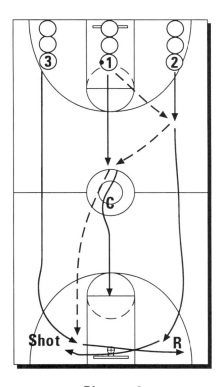

Diagram 4

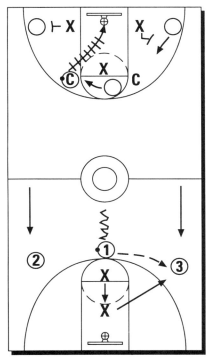

Diagram 3

(Diagram 4) "100% Effort." 3 lines. 3 just sprints the floor. 1 passes to 2 and back to 1 and then a long lead pass to 3. Sometimes we put a coach at mid-court. 3 should not have to wait for the ball. She should not have to break stride; she just sprints. 3 shoots; 2 rebounds.

(Diagram 5) 2 rebounds, passes back to 1, who outlets to 3. (2 and 3 have crossed underneath.) 2 sprints the other way and the same thing happens.

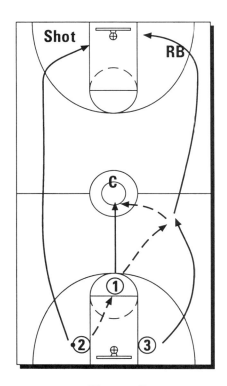

Diagram 5

(Diagram 6) "Weave with a trailer." You all know the weave, pass and go behind. The weave is a good drill for footwork and passing, but we have added something to it. The goal is that you must make eight in a row. Each shooter must make two in a row, but we will have more than one group running. All the trailer does is sprint the floor and get a layup. So, the three players who are doing the weave must be looking up the floor to be able to pass to the trailer when she is in position. The trailer must help by calling for the ball. The ball cannot hit the floor. When she takes the layup, the three people in the weave must sprint the floor and take the ball out of the net.

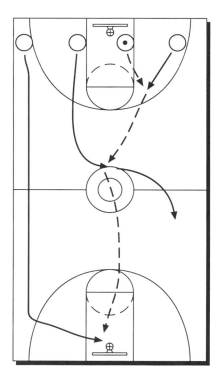

Diagram 6

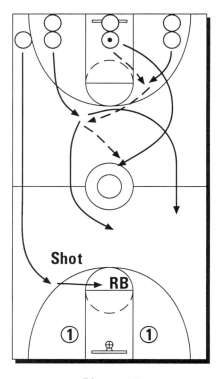

Diagram 7

(Diagram 7) This is the same drill except that the trailer shoots the three-point shot. This now becomes a great offensive rebounding drill. When the shot is taken, the other three players must rebound these three positions. The shooter rebounds long in the middle. We want an offensive putback. We want the ball kept high and shot quickly. Then we go the other way.

(Diagram 8) "Weave and 2 Shooters." We have a player with a ball in each of the four corners in addition to the ball being used by the weave. On the weave, whoever has the ball when you get to half-court, takes the ball to the basket. The other two players fill the outside lanes and call for the ball from the player in the corner.

(Diagram 9) The person who dribbled in to take a layup now goes in the other direction with the two players who were in the corners with the balls. The two outside players rebound their own shots and stand in the corners. We try to get a weave on the return, but it usually is more spread out. This is a continuous drill. We usually make 55 shots in three minutes. Every drill you do should have a goal.

(Diagram 10) "The Eleven Man Break." 1, 2, and 3 attack 4 and 5. On the turnover or score, let's say that 5 gets the ball. 5 then outlets to 6 and 5; 6 and 7 then go against 8 and 9. 10 and 11 are ready to go back in the other direction. This is a continuous drill.

MUFFET McGRAW

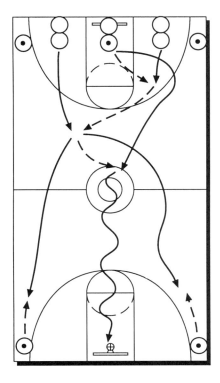

Diagram 8

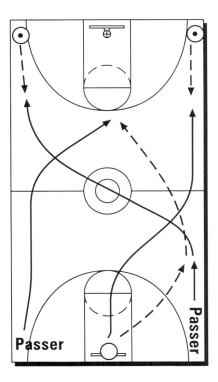

Diagram 9

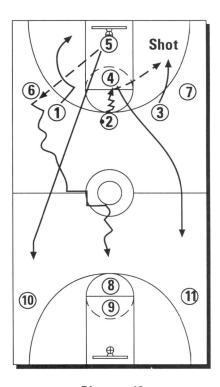

Diagram 10

(Diagram 11) "Trash Drill." This is for your big people. Put a ball on each block and have a rebounder for each block. 5 is the shooter. All she does is bend down, pick up the ball on the block, and power it up. She does not get her own rebound. She immediately turns to the other block and does the same thing. She must shoot with the left hand on the left side, right hand on the right. Remember to put a number on it. She must make a certain amount. She just goes from side to side.

(Diagram 12) This is a shooting drill for post people. Post breaks to the mid-post area and gets a pass from the coach. We found that we had trouble scoring when the defense played directly behind us. The coach varies the passes; the players can vary their position.

MUFFET McGRAW

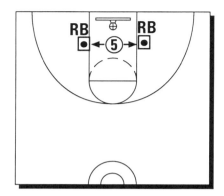

Diagram 11

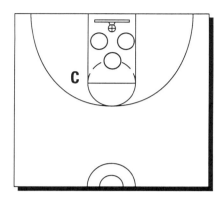

Diagram 13

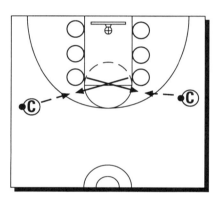

Diagram 12

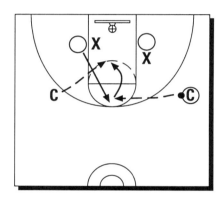

Diagram 14

Diagram 15

(Diagram 13) This is a rebounding drill. The coach shoots. Don't call anything and it is the player with the ball against the other two. The player with the ball can use the coach as a passer if the player with the ball gets in trouble. We want a player to shoot even if she has little chance of scoring because many times she will draw the foul.

(Diagram 14) We play a lot of 2-on-2. We use two coaches for passers. We want the post players to work on playing together.

(Diagram 15) We use this with the perimeter people, three players, two balls. We are shooting threes. You can shoot anywhere you want. One player shoots, follows her own shot and passes to the player who doesn't have a ball. The open player must call for the ball. The passer then runs out into position to get the next pass.

Diagram 16) Work 3-on-3 with no dribbling allowed. This teaches them to move without the ball. They can screen away, they can back-screen, give and go, etc. We want the guards to stay low because they create space and keep the defense away. When they stand up, the defense can get in their face.

MUFFET McGRAW

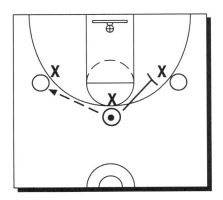

Diagram 16

IRISH OFFENSE

We run a lot of different things. We run the flex and the power game. We always work 5 on 0, at least five minutes every day. Count the passes, run every option of every play. When you do your offense half-court, make it a game. If the offense doesn't score on three out of five possessions, the defense wins.

One of the best things we did this year was to have a controlled scrimmage. I would go to the offense and say what I wanted them to run each time down the floor. I'd give them instructions for about three possessions, and now the defense doesn't know what the offense is running. It's more like a game situation.

We do a lot of special situations in practice. One of the things that is good is to say to one of your players "you have four fouls." Hopefully, the offense will attack that person so you are working on two things. Put seven seconds on the clock and make it a game-like situation. We will scrimmage as if it is the last five minutes of the game, with a specific foul situation and score. I tell my players, I don't want you to shoot it when you feel it, I want you to shoot it when I feel it. That's the rule. We will also do situations where I want a certain person to shoot the ball. We will then have a five-minute game scrimmage and a five-minute press scrimmage. We have a score on the clock, we are up ten, down ten, etc.

THE FLEX

This is the first year we ran it. The reason was because I have an assistant coach who is very, very, good and he ran it a lot in his program. I like the motion offense, but I think my team wasn't real good at it and it is important to match your offense to your team. Two years ago I decided I was going to the passing game. I studied it and I knew it. First game, 41 turnovers. Second game, cut it to 35. We had big people outside with the ball who didn't know what to do with it; guards were inside, it was a mess. So, this year we tried the flex. If you know where someone is supposed to be, it's easier to concentrate on it. You don't have to first find them, and this is a big thing with us.

The flex is an equal opportunity offense. Last year we had a player who was very good; she led the team in every single category. I knew she was the best player on the team. I assumed that our team knew she was the best player on the team. Wrong. She would go through a game and sometimes only get five shots. I would be constantly yelling to get her the ball. That was a big mistake. I found that out in the end of the year conferences. They asked, "Why don't you think I'm good?" I'd say, "I think you are good. I never said you weren't any good." They said, "you never said it, but you wanted the other player to shoot." With the flex offense, you need a post player who can come away from the basket. If you have someone who can't shoot, don't let the post shoot from a position where she won't be successful. You can alter this offense to suit your personnel. A negative thing is that you need good passers. I think passing is a lost art. Too many parents are telling their kid to shoot the three. Against the flex, teams will switch.

(Diagram 1) We worked on that daily.

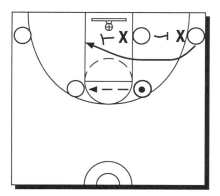

Diagram 1

(Diagram 2) When the guard moves out and screens for the post in the corner and the defense switches, they have a guard defending a post on the block. We had to set this up against a team that switched. We hand-picked our players for the various spots. That's why the guard is starting on the baseline and the post in the corner.

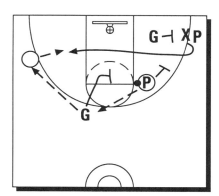

Diagram 2

(Diagram 3) Then the guard could come off of a staggered-screen for the three-point shot. If the defense stays high, the guard cuts right to the basket, but you must read the defense. I'd like to talk about a couple of entries we have.

(Diagram 4) 3 is our best player. Our guard, 2, screens down for 5. 2 then flares to the corner. 1 passes to 5.

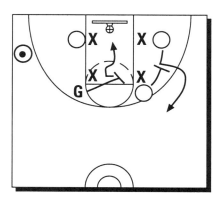

Diagram 3

Diagram 4

(Diagram 5) 4 screens for 3, and she has a lot of options.

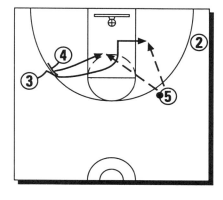

Diagram 5

MUFFET McGRAW

(Diagram 6) If she wasn't open, she went through to the block. 5 dribbles toward the middle and initiates the offense with a pass to 1. 3 back-screens for 2, and we are into the flex.

(Diagram 7) If you have a three-point shooter, she can play with the screen. 2 can go to the screen and then fade to the corner for the 3.

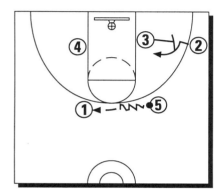

Diagram 6

Diagram 8

(Diagram 9) "1-4." 1 dribbles toward 3 who goes to the block. If 3 doesn't get the ball on the block, she back-screens for 4. 5 then back-screens for 3 who comes off for the three-point shot. We screen the screener.

Diagram 9

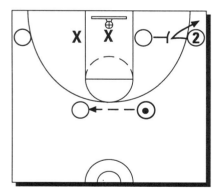

Diagram 7

(Diagram 8) "Push." This is the play we use when we want to stay inside. This works best when the defense is switching. 2 literally pushes the player on the block to the other side of the lane. The post then comes down and screens for 2. 2 is open for the three-point shot. The thing I like about the flex is that when you run a quick-hitting play and it doesn't work, we run right into the flex.

(Diagram 10) 4 is now on the block; 1 on the wing. When 1 passes to 3 and 3 doesn't have the shot, 5 pops out to get the pass from 3. 3 then screens down and we are into the flex.

(Diagram 11) We drilled this 3-on-3 with one extra offensive player.

(Diagram 12) If there was a switch, the person on the down-screen would go find the defensive post. Many times this screen will be in the lane.

MUFFET McGRAW

Diagram 10

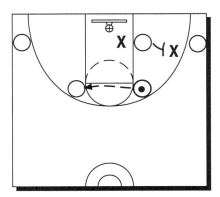

Diagram 13

Diagram 11

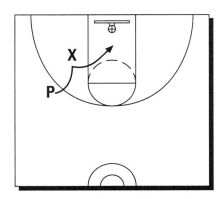

Diagram 14

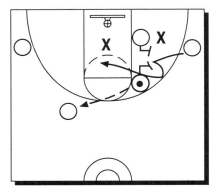

Diagram 12

(Diagram 13) We tell our post players, when the ball is at the elbow, look for it. Once the pass is made, don't post up.

(Diagram 14) If this is the post, the defensive player will be way off of her. Go down, bump her, and go around her.

(Diagram 15) My theory on the block is that you are either open on the first or second pass. You can't take them both away. If you have a good post player, she is going to get open. If you pass to the wing, how are you going to guard her? If you guard her topside, we pass to the elbow and then inside. If you are going to front, we will go high-low.

(Diagram 16) When they switch on the down-screen, the person coming off of the screen always stays. That's the rule. Don't go out. After the down-screen, she replaced herself if she was a guard. If she was a post, she would stay on the block.

(Diagram 17) We also encouraged the slip. She came down as if to screen; she would slip into the lane for the ball. A team either switches or they don't.

Diagram 15

(Diagram 18) We set up in a 1-2-2, usually with the posts out. The posts screen down. The key to this whole thing is that the point guard must give 2 and 3 room to read the screen. They can't just pop out to the wing every time. The defense will just wait for you to go out and you have nothing. If the defense plays high, 3 fakes high and flattens out.

(Diagram 19) If the defense plays behind, we want her to curl. Tell your point guard to choose a side of the floor just off the elbow and allow her to get open.

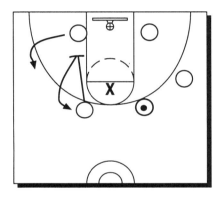

Diagram 16

Diagram 18

Diagram 17

Diagram 19

(Diagram 20) Now you have 4 and 5 on the block. We want to go to the side of the best post player and away from a good passer. We want 4 to be able to handle the ball at the high post. 1 passes to 3 and screens down for 4. 4 comes to the high post.

Diagram 20

Blizzard Defense

We started playing this defense at George Washington because we really weren't very good. We had our real strong concepts of man-to-man defense and great pressure, but we were being blown out so we needed another way to play to stay on the court with these people. So, we came up with a match-up zone that we call "Blizzard." Since we have used this defense, our program has just skyrocketed. We have gone from a program that was (9-19) when I came in to three 20-win seasons playing national competition. This defense kept us in games against the better teams and gave us an opportunity to be competitive on the national level. I think this works best in the women's game. We play with a 30-second clock which is not a lot of time. We control the tempo of the game and have a chance to hide a player who isn't very good. We can also take certain players out of the game. You may not want this as your main defense, but you can use it as one that you go to every now and then if you are strong in something else.

Basically, the Blizzard is a 1-1-3 match-up. This is the hardest defense we have ever had to teach because it won't work unless you have tremendous ball pressure. We play it from a half-court set and we nearly tackle ballhandlers. It's impossible to run your offense against this when we play it properly. The problem is when one person breaks down, it is easy for the others to break down.

(Diagram 1) We put our two guards in line with each other (1 and 2). Sometimes we will change and put a 6' person at the top to create pressure and cut down on the passing lanes. 1 attacks the ball as it comes across half-court. Everything in this has man-to-man principles. 1 wants to force the ball out of the middle of the floor and this gives everyone else a chance to match up with someone. The wing on the ball side denies. The wings are interchangeable and the guards are interchangeable. We call 5 our "hoop" person, or middle person. 5 fronts anything low post ball side. 5 even tries to front the mid-post as much as possible. 4 drops off for weakside help. 2 is our floater and tries to steal the next pass or match-up with anyone in the high-post area.

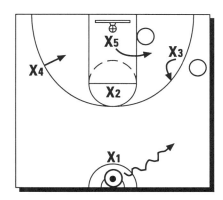

Diagram 1

(Diagram 2) If the ball is on the wing, X2 gets in line and X1 gets weakside, X5 is still fronting and X4 gives weakside help. This is a hard defense to play against because when the ball is on the wing, most try to run some type of screening offense away from the ball. We try to match up with people as they come off the screens and switch automatically. There's no fighting through screens. But this is not a passive defense, we are attacking the ball, and we don't mind getting beat on the dribble because we have help from inside or the baseline. When the ball is on the wing, we're trying to force the ball toward the middle. And the defense almost looks like a 3-2 when the ball is on the wing.

(Diagram 3) When the ball goes to the corner from the wing, we will do this three different ways, depending on who our center (X5) is. If she is immobile, we keep her in. If she is quick and agile, we will send her out to the corner and bring our weakside person (X4) around and run the long slide through with our wing. So the ball-side wing becomes the person on the weakside block. This is a difficult slide, but it is also very confusing for the offense because as soon as the pass is made, the person guarding her sprints away from her. Most people try to force the ball from the corner into the low post, and X4 (tiptoeing the baseline) tries to step in the passing lane and steal. Remember we have ball pressure by X5 in the corner, and we try to force everything baseline.

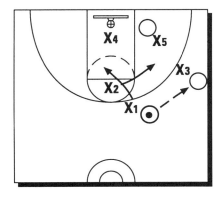

Diagram 2

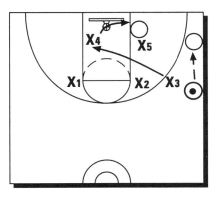

Diagram 3

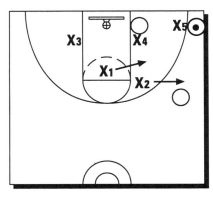

Diagram 4

(Diagram 4) X4 is fronting on the low post; X5 is on the ball; X3 is weakside help, and X2 is denying the return pass to the wing. X1 is responsible for the middle-post/high-post area. Anytime we get the ball in the corner, we want to keep it there and shut the offense down. What kills us is when the ball is reversed. The things that really hurt this defense are skip-passes and ball reversals. When the ball is in the corner, we try to take away the next pass. We try to disguise this by making it look like a man-to-man defense, but it really is a point zone with one person on the ball and the other people adjusting to that person. It's really not that complicated.

(Diagram 5) All match-up zones have gray areas. When the ball is in one of these areas, you must have a lot of communication. Suppose X1 is guarding the ball, and the ball is passed across to the other gray area. X4 must fly at the potential shooter.

Gray Areas

Diagram 5

(Diagram 6) However, we try to cover the ball in this area with our guards if possible.

(Diagram 7) When the ball goes into the high post, X5 sprints and attacks the high post. Both guards turn and help defend when the ball is in the high post. It is actually a triple team. Most teams don't pass well out of a triple team and the person who flashes to the high post usually isn't a good passer. We are trying to deflect the ball. We try to make the low post look like it is open when it is not. As X5 leaves the low-post area, it looks open but it is being covered by the wing (X3).

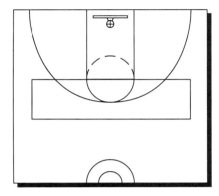
Diagram 6

Diagram 7

(Diagram 8) This is a breakdown drill that we do every day. Anytime the ball is in the high post, we drop both wings down and it really becomes a 2-1-2. We have a 7:00 a.m. running session for all players who miss the slides and the deflections.

Diagram 8

(Diagram 9) Another breakdown drill is for the two guards. It is 3-on-2 with one guard stepping in front of the high post for the deflection. We try to emphasize what will hurt us in a game and we can't let it happen.

Diagram 9

(Diagram 10) The short corner can really hurt you because of the pass out for the three-point shot. When I see someone open at the three-point line, I panic because in the college women's game, the shooting is so good.

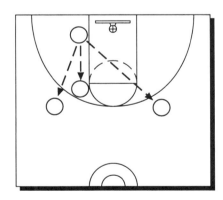
Diagram 10

(Diagram 11) So anytime the ball goes to the short corner, the wing and X5 will trap. We try to take away some of their options. This is an automatic.

Diagram 11

Diagram 13

(Diagram 12) When the ball is on the wing, we are forcing the ball to the middle. Anytime the ball is above the foul line extended, we force it to the middle. We will then trap with the X2 guard.

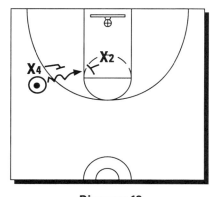

Diagram 12

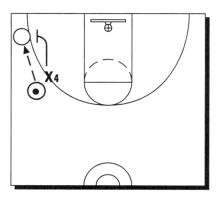

Diagram 14

(Diagram 13) Anything below the foul line we funnel to the baseline and trap. We run this defense several ways; we call them Blizzard 1, 2, and 3. For example, in #2, instead of attacking, she almost plays in between because on the pass, she must cover the corner.

(Diagram 15) Normally, we are trying to force the ball back to the middle. We are really trying to take away passing lanes and angles. We pick up at mid-court for the pressure and to keep them from doing what they want. We want to get the ball on one side of the floor and keep it there. We try to get the offensive guard to kill her dribble, and then we gamble a lot. We have something called "blue," and this means that we trap. We trap in strange spots, but that allows us to dictate what we want to do defensively rather than what they want do offensively.

We trap the better teams. The better teams are so well coached that they want to make the next basketball play, the fundamental play. The good teams will throw the ball away before they will take a bad shot. Why? We take away the normal, smart play and make the offense make something out of nothing. The bad teams, it doesn't seem to bother them. Honest, we had a kid bank the ball off the shot clock this year and beat us. The good teams are so smart that they out-think themselves, and that's why it works.

Diagram 15

(Diagram 16) We trap with our wing and our guard when the pass is made from the top. We find that this is one of the best areas in which to trap. We are trying to deflect the pass. We don't even deny the pass to the corner. But we try to get a piece of it.

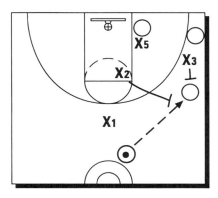

Diagram 16

(Diagram 17) We call this Blue Three and Blue Four. If the offense has a great player on the wing we use this to get the ball out of her hands. Sometimes we only trap one person.

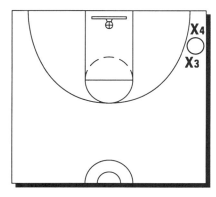

Diagram 17

(Diagram 18) If we are trapping and the ball comes back out, we don't want the ball reversed so X1 loops out to guard and tries to force the ball back to the same side. We don't want the ball reversed to the three-point shooter on the other side. Teams prepare for us in very strange ways. Before the ball gets to half-court, we run a 2-2-1 full-court containment press.

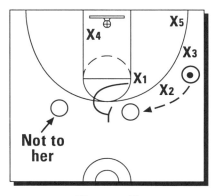

Diagram 18

(Diagram 19) We like to trap in the dead corner with X3 and X5. X4 tiptoes on the baseline and fronts. X1 will try to deny the pass back to the wing; X2 stays in and looks for the steal off the pass. If the ball does get into the low post, X2 drops down and takes the charge from the low post as she double-teams with X4. This is an all-out kamikaze-type defense the entire time that you are in it.

(Diagram 20) There is a series of breakdown drills at the end of this presentation, but I want to cover the main drill we use when we put everyone together. This is an 8-on-5 drill. Sometimes we play it for 30 seconds, for 60 seconds, or keep score with deflections being two points each, an offensive rebound will be a minus two, etc. This gives the defense the opportunity to make their slides. We only have one person on the ball and that person must call "ball" so that we don't have more than one person on the ball at a time. Work on stance and footwork, but must importantly, the slides.

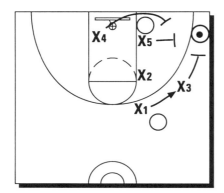

Diagram 19

Diagram 20

We don't have big kids. We had no post players when I got to George Washington. I want to share some ideas on how we develop our post players. The first thing is that you must work on their confidence. You must tell them that they are going to be a great player. That's the number one thing. As a coach, it is so easy to be negative. You must remain positive. I think that's the number one reason our post players got better. You must be realistic, too, and give them something to shoot for. Give them positive feedback. The drillwork we do is geared toward making it hard, yet enjoyable. We have a name for every drill we do. First we have the offensive drills.

(Diagram 21) When the ball is on the wing, the guards must "get in line" with the ball, which means that they must drop to the line of the ball.

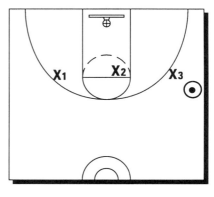

Diagram 21

JOE McKEOWN

Developing Post Players

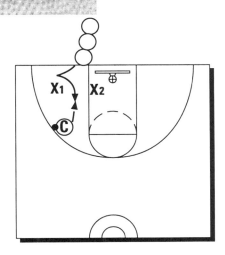

Diagram 1

(Diagram 1) Christmas Tree. We have a coach with the ball, two defensive players and a line of offensive players. I found out long ago that women's college basketball players do not like contact. They don't just play enough basketball. They aren't in the school yard with pickup games. We needed to help them overcome this fear of the physical. The offensive player steps between the two defensive players and gets the bounce pass from the coach. The two defensive players are facing each other, arms up and they lock each other's hands. After catching the ball, she pivots, and breaks through the hands and makes a layup. Go up strong, create contact. It's a confidence builder, make 5 in a row. Do it on both sides of the floor. We have gotten more three-point plays the old-fashioned way because of this drill. They aren't worried about getting bumped.

(Diagram 2) Road Runner. Two post players facing the basket with their hands up. It is a conditioning drill as well as a fundamental drill. A player has the ball facing the coach. We time this for a 30-second period. Pass the ball to the coach, and come off the screen for the return pass. They reverse pivot and dribble into the defensive player with a jump stop. Go up strong and make the layup. Catch the ball out of the basket, pass to the other coach, and go to the other side. You are doing two different footwork drills.

We teach what we call the permanent pivot foot. If you are right-handed, your left foot is your pivot foot. If you get the ball on the left side of the basket, you pivot and crossover. If you are on the right side, you bring the right foot back and explode to the basket. We use the permanent pivot foot to alleviate traveling calls. We try to get them to make 10 layups in 30 seconds. The defense starts out passive, but it gets tougher as the year goes on. Normally, we don't have our guards do this drill.

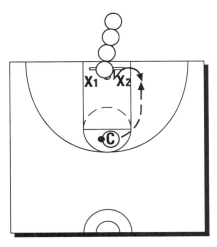

Diagram 2

(Diagram 3) The Visa Drill. Our post players aren't physical enough to work 1-on-1 inside. We let them front us. In this drill we have a double low post with defense. 4 flashes and gets pass from a coach. When this pass is made, 5 seals off her defensive person with her hips and we lob from 4 to 5. We try to step the defensive player up the lane. This helps our passing and our timing. A lot of post players defensively do not like to be held off with the hip of the offensive player. We do this from both sides. It helps the post players to play together on this drill.

Diagram 3

(Diagram 4) Hell Hole. For the first 30 seconds we limit this to perimeter passing. The defensive player works for defensive position against the post. This is a tough drill. It is a very physical drill. We spend the last 30 seconds trying to get the ball inside.

Diagram 4

(Diagram 5) Whenever a player crosses the lane, you must deny the cut with contact. We try to step her off with our hip.

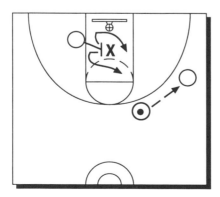

Diagram 5

(Diagram 6) We have several rules. Anything half way up the lane or above, the defensive player goes behind.

(Diagram 7) If the offense is low, then we go over the top.

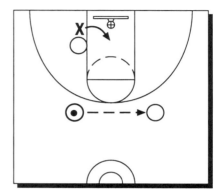

Diagram 6

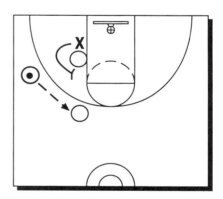

Diagram 7

(Diagram 8) During the second 30 seconds of this drill, try to get the ball inside. We feed the post with bounce passes. Sometimes players will work very hard to keep the post from getting the ball and when the post gets the ball, they stop playing defense. They must continue to play defense. Move your feet. When the post kills the dribble, get both hands up. Before that, have only one hand up. When they shoot, reverse pivot on the block out. You must block out on this drill or you go another minute. If you rebound the missed shot, you must outlet the ball.

Diagram 8

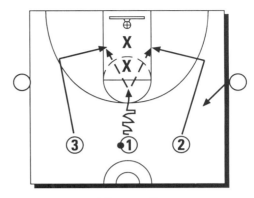
Diagram 9

(Diagram 9) The Terminator. Put our two biggest players on defense, one at each end. We run a 3-on-1 fast-break drill. This is a continuous drill. We outlet pass and fill the lanes. The offensive player cannot pull up and shoot, she must attack the basket. She must take a layup. Our post player starts half way up the lane. Her job is to read the offense, stop the dribbler and react to the pass. Only one pass from the center to the wing. The person must attack the basket. Then she tries to block the shot. The person who shoots the ball rebounds, makes the outlet pass and fills the lane going to the other end.

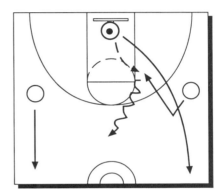
Diagram 10

(Diagram 10) We found this to be very good for our defensive player. We teach blocked shots. How do you teach blocked shots? You must use your outside hand. If you are on the left side of the basket, block the shot with the right hand across your body. Use your left hand on the right side of the basket. This means that the shot blocker is more or less facing the basket. We encourage blocked shots. This makes us aggressive. Go up strong, work on the timing.

(Diagram 11) Two-on-Two for Post Defense. The defense must adjust to the ball. The offensive players try to pin. Shot goes up, reverse pivot and block out.

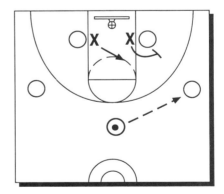
Diagram 11

(Diagram 12) When we switch, we switch and deny. 1 posts up for a second and then screens away. X2 turns her back to the ball and sits on the screen. X2 faces 2. This makes it easier to take the impact of the screen. Now, stop the cutter physically with an arm bar while maintaining contact with the screener.

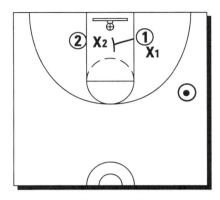

Diagram 12

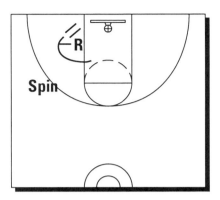

Diagram 14

(Diagram 13) We also have a drill for offensive rebounding. The coach shoots and the offensive player uses one of three moves to get inside position.

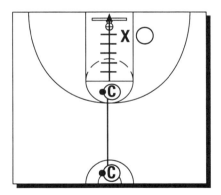

Diagram 13

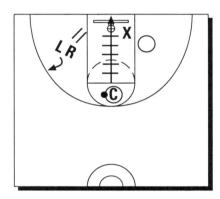

Diagram 15

(Diagram 14) To go around the defensive player on the left side of the floor, the offensive player puts her right leg between the legs of the defensive player and spins around the defense. Many times a defensive player thinks after they make the contact that they have you and they stop playing defense.

(Diagram 15) We also "walk" away which means we drop off after the original contact is made. The defensive player doesn't know where you are. In the women's game with the small ball, most of your rebounds are farther from the basket. Very few rebounds are directly under the basket.

(Diagram 16) We also "go swim." Step with the left foot across the back of the defensive player. We don't shove with the arms. It is the feet that do it. Then you can pin with the hip. So, "go swimming, walk away, or spin."

Diagram 16

(Diagram 17) The Four Game. Our power forward is not the back-to-the-basket type so we run 4 on the perimeter. This is against a good defensive team. If we pass the ball to 4 coming off the screen, that alleviates the weakside help on the post.

(Diagram 18) The ball went from 1 to 4 to 5. 4 lobs the ball to 5. 5 pins the defense and gets her shoulders to the baseline. Obviously, there is more to this with the perimeter people, but we are concentrating on post play now.

Diagram 17

Diagram 18

(Diagram 19) If 5 is defended on the lowside, the ball is reversed back to 4 who lobs on the other side away from the defense who is pinned by 5.

(Diagram 20) 1 passes to 2 as 5 sets a back-screen for 4. 1 moves away as 2 dribbles towards X1. 3 fills behind. If 4 can shoot the three-point shot, make a skip-pass to 4.

Diagram 19

Diagram 20

(Diagram 21) Sometimes we stack and either exchange the wings or pop them out. 1 passes to 3.

(Diagram 22) 4 flashes to the high post, and she can dump the ball inside to 5. You can get a lot of layups just on lobs.

If your best player is not a post, that doesn't mean that she can't post up. Make the defense make a decision. Put your point guard at the low post. We have done that and lobbed to her. If you teach it and you believe in it, your players will believe in it and it will work. If they don't believe it, they will be the first ones to tell you, and no matter what you say, it won't work because they don't believe in it. You've got to convince your guards, or they won't throw the ball inside to one of your smaller players. If you have a 5'10" vs. a 6'3" and she thinks she can get it and she works to seal etc., it will be successful. One thing we do not do. We do not spend time teaching our kids to shoot the ball left-handed. Maybe she will get it once a game. We would rather teach a drop-step, jump stop, face the basket and go up strong. We don't have many players who are gym rats. We just don't have the time to teach all of these things.

Diagram 21

Diagram 22

BILLIE MOORE

Teaching Fundamentals

It is difficult when you come to clinics and hear the various coaches saying that you must spend so much time on this and so much time on that. You say to yourself that you don't practice that long. How can you fit everything in? That's the first thing that you must make a decision on as a coach. Regardless of the level of your personnel, you must make a decision on what you want this team to represent. And that starts with fundamentals. You must make a decision on what three or four things you are going to do well. You must understand that you must put your emphasis on three or four things and be willing to not be as good at something else.

I always look at the game of basketball from three areas. We look at it from an offensive standpoint, a defensive standpoint and the fundamentals involved with each, plus we look at it from the transition game. Years ago, transition wasn't a big part. But now you must consider transition as much as you consider defense and offense.

Let's start with defense. What kinds of fundamentals do we have to teach? Your first decision is what kind of defensive team do you want to be? Will you emphasize player-to-player defense? Are you going to be a zone team? If so, what type of zone are you going to play? I think it is very difficult to be a very good man-to-man defensive team and also be a very good zone defensive team. It is very difficult to play two or three different types of zones. You must take a hard look and say just what you want to do. I really believe in fundamentals, regardless if you are a zone team; match-up zone, odd front, even front, it makes no difference, you must start first of all with the principles of man-to-man. You must make decisions and it starts with the ball. What type of ball pressure do you want? You must make a decision on guarding the ball. One of the most difficult things is the difference between putting pressure on the ball, being able to contain the dribbler, and being able to defend for the pressure. Those are three things that you must work on regardless whether you play man-to-man or zone.

Ball pressure. When we pick up the ball, ball pressure, we are going to dictate. Don't give the offensive player choices. Are you going to force everything to the left? Are you going to channel everything to the baseline? When we put pressure on the ball, we are talking about taking away the shot, taking away the look, and forcing the drive. That's the fundamental on defense, regardless of the type of defense we play. What do we mean by taking away the shot? We consider anyone within the three-point line a shooting threat. So, we pick up the dribbler. The second thing we do is to take away the look. That means we don't let the player make the easy pass inside to feed the post or reverse the ball. Now, by how you dictate, you teach your players to play the drive. And you must only play the drive in one direction. So many times players play defense and react to what the offensive player does. They wait and see what the offensive player is going to do. It doesn't make any difference what type of defense you are in. The point of attack of your defense starts with ball pressure. We start out by saying "guard as close as you can without fouling."

Early in the season, don't worry as much about direct penetration. What you are ideally trying to do is to drive the dribbler wide. How do I teach this player to defend? All coaches do it differently. Some coaches prefer the inside foot to be the lead foot. Some will say, shade the player on the ball side. Some will overplay the dominant hand and/or force the player to go left. It depends on what your philosophy is. But the fundamentals are still the same. You must take away the shot, take away the look, and think drive to the baseline.

(Diagram 1) This is penetration. I believe that the hardest fundamental to teach is guarding the dribbler. That causes more breakdown on defense, learning how to contain the ball.

Then, you must decide what are you doing on ball-side help? What position are you going to teach for ball-side defense? Are you going to contest one pass away? Are you going to teach only contest on passes towards the basket? And how are you going to defend the block? Are you going to front, play high on the hip, or play behind? The more I coached, the more my philosophy became to play dead front or dead behind. I don't like the hip because it is very easy to get sealed. We play dead front because we want to give quick help and early recovery. In your zones, how are you going to play the ball? So fundamentals on defense doesn't just mean teaching the basic zig-zag drills. You must also make decisions on helpside. What is your helpside philosophy on defense, both man and zone? Many zones dictate where you belong helpside because of the placement of the ball. So, teach how to guard the dribbler, with the good lead foot in a toe-heel relationship.

We use the theory of broomsticks. We make the players think they have a broomstick between the feet so we get short choppy steps. When you are guarding the ball, you must have short choppy steps. Once you get into the attacking area, you must have short choppy steps. We have our hands up, head high, and push with the power foot. If I am sliding to the right, the left foot is the power foot. If you believe in putting pressure on the ball, one of the more important skills you must teach is the close-cut. This is an extremely important skill, and it is not a skill that players automatically have. We teach the players to sprint the first 3/4 of the way and shuffle the last 1/4. When we shuffle, we have hands up, head up, weight back. We do many drills on this right on the sideline We have them close-out on the sideline. Take away the shot, take away the look, and then think drive. I am protecting myself on the drive.

(Diagram 2) We use areas of the court. We have our feet like this on these spots of the court. The position of my feet says that I must think drive, but I only need to think drive in one direction. I shade the player so that she goes in one direction.

Diagram 1

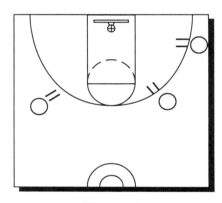

Diagram 2

(Diagram 3) You have many other decisions to make. Even in the zone, if the ball is in this corner, how do I play this pass? Do I play it so the ball cannot be reversed out of the corner?

Regardless of what system I am playing, there are certain fundamentals I must work on. If contesting or denial is an important part of your defensive package, then you must teach that as a fundamental before you try to put it into your defense.

When you contest, do you contest on the line up the line? Do you contest getting into the offensive player with the arm bar? You decide what is best for you. If you do contest, how are you going to open up? We always open up because we like to see the ball. Many teams deny turning the other way. But you must decide. What do you do against screens? You can't ignore screens even if you are playing a zone

BILLIE MOORE

because teams now attack zones with screens. These are all fundamentals of defense. Are you going to force the ball to use the screen? Will you switch; are you going to switch and recover? It becomes a time restraint. How much time can you devote to this? Take your fundamentals of defense and say that this is what you want to do. If you use more than two defenses, do you like what you see when you run your third or fourth defense? I think you must say to yourself, "Where do I want to be good?" If I want to really be good in man-to-man, then there is only one way to do it. Play it. You must play it. It is much easier to play man-to-man and then go into a zone than to play zone and change to man-to-man. There are a lot of technical things when you get into building a team defense. Then you get into things like the ball line, help line, etc.

Offense is the same way. There are some fundamentals offensively that you must decide on regardless of your offense. Take the fundamentals of shooting, something everyone thinks about. It starts with the feet and you must spend time on footwork; stops and pivots. Two minutes on footwork. You will see a big improvement in your offensive skills. Once you get past the fundamentals, the mechanics of shooting, we have a basic rule. We do game shots, game spots, game speed. We spend very little time on just shooting drills. We do it position wise. The guards would be at one basket, the forwards at another, the posts at another. Game shots, game spots, and the hardest thing, game speed. Why is it hard to get game speed? You do the shooting drills too long. Try to get your players to shoot shots at game speed. They break down about five or six shots, 15 or 20 seconds. The game speed is a lot more important to us to get the game speed. If I am shooting for the repetition of mechanics, that's something else. With our perimeter players, we are ball in the air, feet in the air when we shoot. Some people teach to step in. We want ball in the air, feet in the air. If we want to incorporate passing, we will work on what we call a split-court drill.

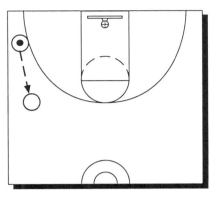

Diagram 3

(Diagram 4) Take a point, wing, and post. Put a defender on the wing and post. Let the point work on ballhanding and the entry pass. Then the wing will work on feeding the post or reversing the ball. We do 3/0, 3/1, 312, 3/3. That's the progression. When you look at the fundamentals offensively, look at shooting, ballhandling, pass, and movement without the ball. Then, start putting in the offense. So many times offenses breakdown because of passing skills. Work on the V-cut to get open. Some players don't understand how important it is. They think that the only time they use a V-cut is in transition and when they put their head in the basket and pop out. That's a fundamental skill.

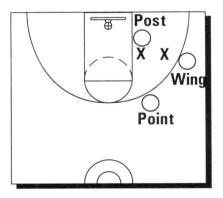

Diagram 4

Now, transition. What are the fundamentals of transition? We must talk about filling the lanes. I have a pet peeve. You must coach for game slippage. If you don't, you are going to be disappointed.

(Diagram 5) If you ask your players to run wide in the lane and you allow them to run here, what does game slippage do? You get this. So you must teach for game slippage. What is another fundamental of transition defense? Finding the ball. Assign a player if you want to slow down the ball. It is a misnomer when you say to stop the ball by half-court. What do they think they have to do? They shirk they have to pick up the ball. What you want them to do is to make the dribbler turn, change direction. We are slowing down the ball. We can't stop it. What do players do? They run at the ball and the offensive player goes right by. We want them to play an up-and-back tag game with the ballhandler to make her change direction, crossover, or a reverse. Many players think transition defense is running to the paint and then finding their player. Our rule is that our #1 guard is back under the basket, and the #2 guard has the responsibility of slowing down the ball. Our #3 and #4 will pick up the wings coming down on their side. Don't run from side to side to pick up a player. #5 matches up with the other center. Fit in your philosophy on what meets your personnel.

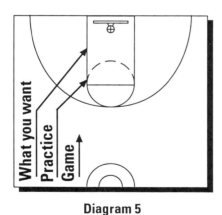

Diagram 5

Special Situations, Time, and Score

How much time do you spend on all the situations that come up in a game? If you are going to have play for the last 5 seconds, the last 10 seconds, for coming out of the locker room at halftime, etc., my approach to this, what I evolved into in my last few years of coaching, is trying to take something like a set that you might run in your half-court offense and run it for all situations. I have a zone attack that I run against all zones. I don't believe in having a zone attack that you run against an odd front and a different attack for an even front. Hopefully, you have an attack that will allow you to play against a match-up, an odd front, or an even front. It's the same thing I talked about earlier. The more you ask them to learn, the more watered down they become. If you can take one or two things and teach it, you are better off. Today, how to attack the match-up is the problem. When you get to what you are going to do against a zone, you must also include what you are going to do out-of-bounds, on the end line or the sideline. Do I have things that are just out-of-bounds against a zone, or do I have things that work against both the zone and a man defense?

Same thing when you talk about your man package. Maybe your transition is your primary attack. What are you going to do when you must set up in a half-court set? The most difficult pass to make in this set is the entry pass. I must have something that gives me more than one option. We got to the point where our number one offense was our transition game. We looked to run off a make, a miss, a turnover, anything.

We found that our secondary break became our primary offense. It just meant that it started from the endline instead of coming down and setting up in a half-court offense. I liked it because we were coming down the floor and going right into the

BILLIE MOORE

attack. When you get into time/score, you must decide what you are going to do in a comeback situation. When do I start it? How many points down and how much time is left? I must know my personnel, and their ability.

On the other hand, there is a time/score situation when I am milking the clock. I must decide on the last-second play. Do I have something in my plan for a last-second shot? I'm telling you that you can call time-out and draw the neatest play, but they are not going to go out and do it. Two will remember it; two won't, and the other one doesn't have any idea what is going on. So, it's a lot easier if you can just say to them what they are going to run. How many of you find time to work on end of the game situations daily in practice? Not many hands are up. This becomes a time problem.

One of the things I started to do the last few years of coaching is that I played three-minute games. Put any score on the clock you want, and then give them a three-minute situation. That will allow you to work on these situations. If you suddenly get a game and you start yelling "green, green" because they need to foul and you haven't had to do it in your first 10 games, they won't have any idea what it means. But if you have practiced it during some three-minute games and set up that situation, they will do it.

How about free throws? What do you do with the other team on the line and five seconds on the clock? What do you do made or miss? Do your players know? What if you are down by one? What do you want to do? Do your players know what you want to do? Do you call time-out? You must make that decision. But you should make it on the practice floor in a three-minute game. Your players have the ability to run what you want because you have worked on it.

(Diagram 1) We come down in our transition, our secondary break. The point guard comes to the side. We have choices what we can do with the pass to the wing, the pass to the lag (#4), or a dribble out to the wing. So, we have more than one choice.

Diagram 1

(Diagram 2) Let's say we run our curl option or our look option. 1 dribbles toward 2; 2 comes off the screen of 5, and 4 and runs the loop. We now have the possibility of a 1 and 5 two-man play. If 2 is a good shooter, 1 passes back for the shot.

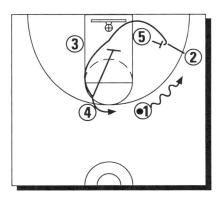

Diagram 2

(Diagram 3) We never let 1 get below the forty-five degree angle unless she is taking it to the basket or is feeding the post. Don't let your wings set up in the corners; it is difficult to reverse the ball from the corners. When we run our shooting drills, we run some for the point guard attacking the glass.

(Diagram 4) 1 can reverse to 2; we run a side post. 4 screens; 2 dribbles off the screen. 3 can stay, and 2 and 3 run a two-man game, or 3 can go to the corner. We run this same set from out of bounds on the sideline, from a time-out.

Diagram 3

Diagram 5

Diagram 4

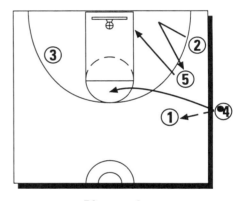

Diagram 6

(Diagram 5) We take this skill with 4 and 2 and work on reading the screen. Do they switch? Probably not because you have big/small. There is a philosophy on screening. If you screen big/big or small/small, you will get switching. Make your screens small/big, or big/small. Then you force the defense to do something other than switch. If they trail, 2 will penetrate. If they shoot the gap, we automatically read that and set a quarter screen.

(Diagram 6) We run a variation of this from out-of-bounds. 4 inbounds to 1. We can run a curl. Or, 1 dribbles toward the middle. 2 pops out and 5 is on the post.

(Diagram 7) 4 comes over and we run the same thing.

(Diagram 8) Out of the same philosophy, keep 5 low.

Diagram 7

BILLIE MOORE

Diagram 8

(Diagram 9) Now we can reverse the ball. 1 passes to 4, reverse it and post up 5. 2 backpicks for 4 for the lob pass. If the lob isn't there, 4 comes back out. Now, we run the counter.

(Diagram 10) 1 to 4 to 3. 4 and 1 set a double-screen for 2. 5 comes to the ball. Transition.

I prefer not to call time-out in the last few seconds. We will run one of these options. And we have the same philosophy from out-of-bounds. We don't try to just get the ball in from out-of-bounds. We will run our offense from there. We try to score. In 25 years of coaching, making the entry pass hasn't gotten any easier, so you need more than one option. We run the same attack against a zone. The hardest thing in coaching is to get your players to play basketball and not play plays. The more plays you give them, the more you make them play plays. Give them the structure and let them play. Remember, run those three-minute games. Recognize the defense, man or zone, and run it. But you practice it. And you don't have too many things to practice because you haven't given them a play for every situation.

Diagram 9

Diagram 10

The Nebraska Offense

We organize our plays by "colors." If we run a set play and we don't get the shot, we go right into motion.

(Diagram 1) Blue. This is a box set, the posts on the elbows, the wings on the blocks. The point dribbles to either side. When he gets to the foul line extended, the posts set a double-screen for the wing on the opposite block. This can be a staggered-double.

Diagram 1

(Diagram 2) 1 passes to 2.

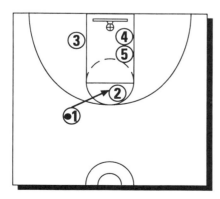

Diagram 2

(Diagram 3) If 2 doesn't have a shot, he passes to 3 coming off of the double-screen. If 3 shoots, 4 has the weakside rebound position.

Diagram 3

(Diagram 4) 2 can also pass to 1 who is going backdoor.

Diagram 4

(Diagram 5) Black. This is a diagonal screen. 1 dribbles to the side away from the post who is going to the block. 2 screens for 5 who will either go high or low. 4 steps high to be in position to go screen.

(Diagram 6) 1 passes to 5.

Diagram 5

Diagram 6

(Diagram 7) If 1 doesn't pass to 5, 1 passes to 3 coming off of the staggered-pick set by 2 and 4.

Diagram 7

(Diagram 8) Silver. Same philosophy. Everything looks the same except now there is no diagonal screen and 3 back-screens for 4 on the side of the ball. 4 posts up big on the block. This screen is very hard to defend.

Diagram 8

(Diagram 9) 1 passes to 4.

Diagram 9

(Diagram 10) If 1 can't pass to 4, 3 steps out and gets a pass from 1. When 3 gets the ball, 5 screens down for 2. 2 must set up the screen with a V-cut. 5 posts up. 3 can pass to 5 or to 2. This is a quick-hitter.

(Diagram 11) Gold. Same look. 1 dribbles to the wing. Notice we have one post low (5) and one post high (4). Until now we have had both 4 and 5 at the elbow. 2 steps across the defensive man and then steps out for the pass from 1.

DANNY NEE

Diagram 10

Diagram 11

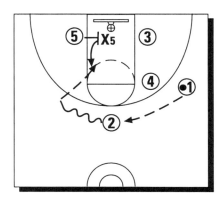

Diagram 12

Diagram 13

(Diagram 12) 1 passes to 2. 5 steps across the face of X5 and seals 5. 2 makes several dribbles for position and passes in to 5. You must teach 5 to make the moves to get the shot. What I am doing is helping you to put your people in position to score to win. Don't worry about the three-second count on 5 in the lane. There is too much happening, especially late in the game. They won't call it.

(Diagram 13) If 2 doesn't pass to 5, 2 will pass to 3, who is coming off of a staggered-pick by 4 and 1. This takes care of the helpside defense. X3 cannot get through both of these picks. Anytime you come out of a time-out or at the start of a quarter, you should be running a special play. Watch the NBA. They are always looking for a way to isolate their best shooter. And the kids just love it.

(Diagram 14) Green. I really like this. I like double stacks because it gets everyone away from the point guard and you can see what the defense is. 1 passes to 4 coming off of the double-screen. Don't get locked into the numbers on these drawings. Anybody can come off that pick. You can invert this set with 2 and 3 on top.

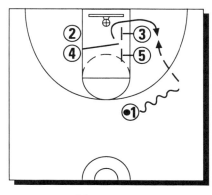

Diagram 14

(Diagram 15) If 1 can pass to 4, good. But that's not the priority. After 4 comes off the double, 1 passes to 2 coming up the lane and you have a 1-on-1 opportunity.

Diagram 15

(Diagram 16) 2 can go backdoor. Those pro sets help you get shots for players in situations throughout the season. It's not an offense. These are complementary plays. If that's all you use, they won't work. Why? Predictability. We don't run all the plays every game. We change.

Diagram 16

(Diagram 17) Offense #1. This you can use as an offense. PW stands for priority wing. PW is the wild card and can be anywhere. PW loves this offense. W is the opposite wing. 4 and 5 are on the boxes. 1 is the point guard.

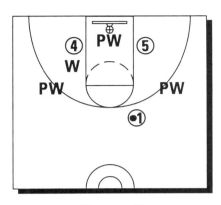

Diagram 17

(Diagram 18) There are endless options. The PW can come off 5, run a curl, or go backdoor. PW can come off the double and run a curl, or pop to the corner. PW can go anywhere.

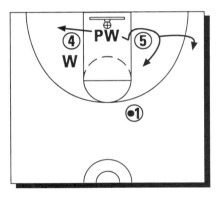

Diagram 18

(Diagram 19) PW starts on the outside behind 5. PW can come back on the same side, can pop to the corner, can go around the double and go backdoor.

(Diagram 20) PW starts outside the double-screen. PW can run along the lane and come out the other side, can V-cut back out, can curl around either side.

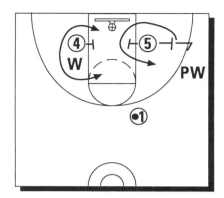

Diagram 19

Diagram 20

(Diagram 21) 1 passes to PW and the opposite wing pops out, and we are ready to start, 3 out, 2 in.

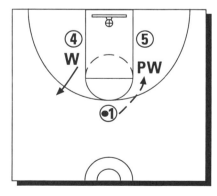

Diagram 21

(Diagram 22) This is an offense so once the PW gets the ball, everybody must do certain things; there must be predictability. First option, 4 sets a backpick for 1, big man setting pick for little man. PW can pass to 1 if he is open. We really want PW and 5 to play a little 2-on-2.

Diagram 22

(Diagram 23) If this doesn't happen, PW passes to 4 who has stepped out.

Diagram 23

(Diagram 24) 4 has the ball in the middle of the floor. I like stepping 4 out. Seldom do players deny that pass. I want the ball in the middle of the floor. This is the way we get ball reversal in our league. PW gets on baseline side of 5 and sets a double. W goes headhunting for 1. 1 comes out looking for ball from 4.

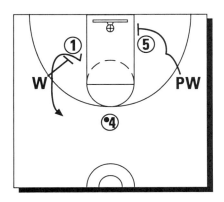

Diagram 24

(Diagram 25) But what we really want is for W to come off the double-screen.

(Diagram 26) If W doesn't get the ball, PW and 5 cross, 5 flashes hard into the lane, he steps across the face of the defensive man. PW comes off of 5 and breaks into the lane. The diagram doesn't do this justice. He's open.

Diagram 25

Diagram 26

(Diagram 27) 4 can pass to any of the four. We have a 1-4 set where there is no helpside defense. Attack! Shoot it! Go to the glass! If not, we have 3 out, 2 in motion. You can't use this exclusively because of its predictability. You use it, then put it away for awhile. This isn't our whole offense.

Diagram 27

(Diagram 28) Everyone in the country is looking for a way to get a three-point shot. This is what I am comfortable with. I start with the box offense again. This is called "Three." Everyone is interchangeable. The wings are on the elbows now. 1 dribbles toward the wing. 2 sets screen for 1. 1 looks for the three-point shot. 3 blasts to the corner; 5 sets the screen.

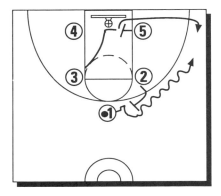

Diagram 28

DANNY NEE

(Diagram 29) This is set up by the movement in Diagram 28. After 2 has set the screen for 1 and 1 has dribbled off the screen, 4 comes up and screens for 2. Notice the angle of 4. His back is not to the basket; it is to the sideline. 1 makes a skip-pass to 2.

We score on our out-of-bounds plays. We run a series. We put one in; we put another in a week later; then another week later, we put in another one. We run our plays in sets; a box, a straight line, or a circle. We signal our out-of-bounds play by the inbounder's feet. The feet are either together, apart, or staggered. We want to score on our out-of-bounds plays.

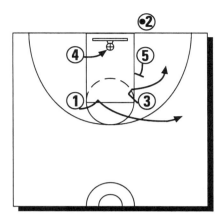

Diagram 30

Diagram 29

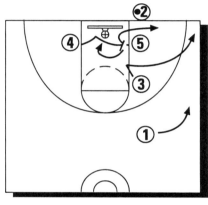

Diagram 31

(Diagram 30) Box, feet together. The play starts when 5 moves to screen 3. 5 comes up the lane and gets on an angle to the corner and screens for 3. 3 steps toward the basket, and then comes off the screen of 5. 1 cuts to ball-side wing. 4 steps toward 2. Sometimes 4 gets the ball from 2.

(Diagram 31) 4 steps toward 2 and then goes diagonally up the lane and screens for 5. 5 goes to the basket; 4 rolls toward 2. 2 looks for 5, then 4, then 3, and then 1.

(Diagram 32) Box, feet apart. Everything is the same, but this time 4 blasts to the corner. 5 comes up on the inside of 3 and back-screens. 3 comes off the screen; 5 rolls to the basket. 1 goes to the wing ball side.

(Diagram 33) Box, feet staggered. Same set, looks the same. 4 screens diagonally for 3. 3 comes off. 5 sets screen for 4 and rolls back to basket. 4 gets 5's screen and breaks out to the corner. When you put these three box plays together, they complement each other. If I were a head coach, I'd give an assistant coach the responsibility for the inbound plays. These plays work against both zone and man-to-man.

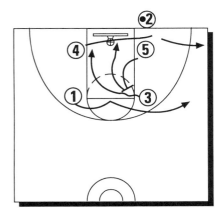

Diagram 32

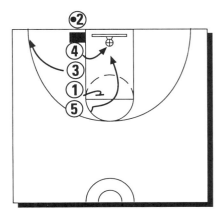

Diagram 34

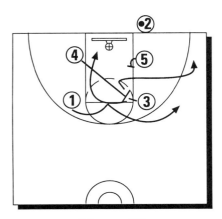

Diagram 33

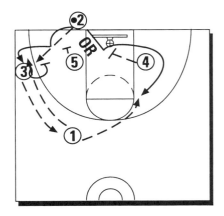

Diagram 35

Diagram (34) Line, feet together. The players in the line face the lane. 4 is above the block. The play starts when 4 cuts to the basket. 4 tries to step across the defender. 4 wants the ball. 3 busts out to the corner. 1 steps up the lane and screens for 5. 5 cuts down the lane.

(Diagram 35) If the ball is passed out to 1, 3 sets a double-screen with 5. 2 steps in behind the double-screen for the pass from 1.

(Diagram 36) If 2 passes short to 3 in the corner, 3 will pass to 1, and 2 will come off a screen set by 4 for the return pass from 1. So, if we throw it long to 1, we set a double-screen with 5 and 3. If we inbound short to 3, we reverse the ball, and 2 comes off the single screen by 4.

(Diagram 37) Line, feet apart. 4 breaks to corner. 1 blasts out to far corner. We have both corners filled. 3 screens up the lane for 5. 5 blasts down lane.

Diagram 36

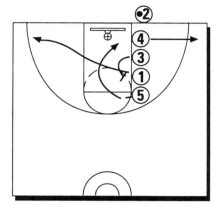
Diagram 37

TOM PENDERS

Guard Play

I've always felt that great guards are made; they are not born. The guards work the hardest. When's the last time that you saw a big kid work on his own on the playground? They never work on the skills they should be working on. Forwards and centers seem to need supervision to work on their game. No matter what level, you can develop people to be guards. Point guards should be an extension of the coach, and it's unusual if that isn't the case. It's smart to have your guards learn both guard positions. If we are playing a team that has a great point guard defender, we would change assignments to throw off the other team.

This is my philosophy of what a guard must be.

- They must be leaders, players who are respected by their teammates both on and off the court.

- They must have great attitudes, which comes from being a leader.

- The guard should understand what the coach wants, both offensively and defensively. This is the most important thing.

You must communicate with your guards more than with the other players. Defense starts with the guards. Pressure the ball.

Evaluate the skills of your guards, and then let them show you what they can do. I try to figure out what each guard can do and then let them do it. You can't yank a kid out of a game if he misses some three-point shots when he hits in practice. Encourage him to do what he does well in practice, and downplay what he doesn't do well. We never accept unforced turnovers. We never accept traveling violations. That is the most ridiculous thing that can happen. We teach them what passes to make. A great guard knows where the other nine people are on the floor. You never see a great guard get stripped from behind.

Guards must know where everybody is on every play. This is one of the drawbacks of the motion offense. Each player should catch, turn and read the defense. That's great if you have five players who are that smart. Some teams who run motion make a lot of turnovers because all five people must make guard-type decisions. You can teach a guard to become a better shooter. Much of shooting three-pointers has to do with the footwork.

We teach our right-handed players to pivot on the left foot. This almost totally eliminates the travel situations. Why? Everytime, your left foot is the pivot foot and your right foot is the jabbing, faking or take-off foot. How about when you go left? The only thing we teach is the crossover; swing the ball down low, step with the right foot, push the ball out and go.

When we stop, we always come to a stop with the jump stop. The jump stop allows you to be square to the basket totally balanced. We want to catch the ball in the air, and square up immediately. If you catch the ball on the wrong foot, it is a difficult push-off situation. You are shooting against your body and you are going to drift. Keep the same foot as a pivot foot and you eliminate the travel.

The only exception to that is in the post. We teach three basic moves; the jump hook, the drop-step, and the Sikma turn (a front turn). Three good moves is enough at the high school or college level. Experiment with your three-point shooters. Have them shoot some threes off of the wrong foot 50 times. Then have them step in and have them shoot correctly 50 times, stepping into the shot. It won't be close. We average 94 points a game, but we don't turn the ball over much. One game we had 20 turnovers, and that was early in the season. Great guards are going to make turnovers, but they are going to be turnovers that are questionable whether it should be theirs or not.

TOM PENDERS

Teach the jump stop at all levels. Practice shooting after practice when they are tired. Stay for 10 minutes and take 50 to 100 shots with a coach and a teammate. Just as important is your attitude and how you approach your players. On shooting, allow them to do things that they can do.

(Diagram 1) Ballhandling. Start off dribbling with the left hand along the baseline. At the junction, square the shoulders and spin, and then go with the right hand to the foul line, spin again at each corner. We will use the entire floor. A coach is at mid-court. Make a chest pass to the coach, and the coach will return a bounce pass. When you make the spin dribble at each corner, keep the ball below the waist, and have your shoulders square. This is not a reverse dribble; keep the ball in one hand during the spin. Do this three times.

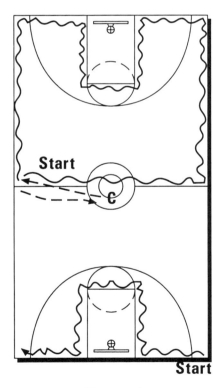

Diagram 1

(Diagram 2) 3/0 full-court. Keep the guards in the middle. First time down make chest passes, jump stop at the foul line and make a bounce pass to one of the outside players for the layup. The other wing gets the rebound, gets it back to the guard and they go the other way. We can do this with a bounce pass also.

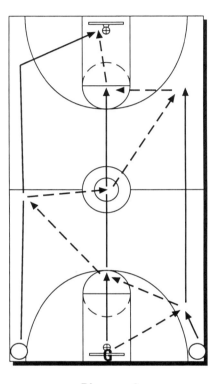

Diagram 2

(Diagram 3) Then do Figure Eights. Pass and go behind the man to whom you passed the ball. Never allow the players to take underhanded layups.

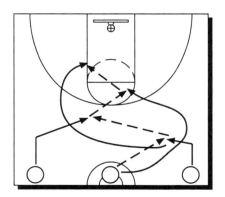

Diagram 3

(Diagram 4) Fast Break Drill. We have two teams, orange and white. It is a 3/2 break. Orange ball at mid-court, two white defenders back. As soon as the ball crosses mid-court, a third white defender comes in, touches mid-court circle and gets back to help on defense. After a turnover or a made basket, the three whites come the other way against two orange defenders with another entering at mid-court. The drill is continuous.

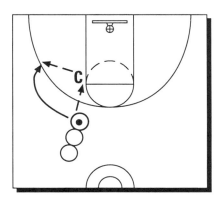

Diagram 5

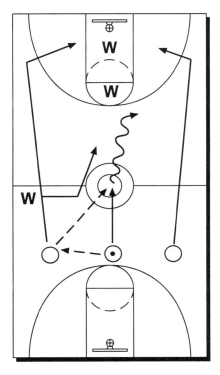

Diagram 4

(Diagram 5) The guards are at the other end of the floor. The coach will tell the guard what dribble move to make or (as shown) call for the ball. The guard breaks and gets the return pass for the shot.

(Diagram 6) We also have paired up shooting drills. He must move after a shot. We do a minimum of 18 minutes of this type of work for our guards. I encourage competition. Maybe four guards vs four guards with spot shooting.

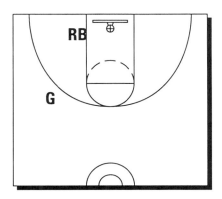

Diagram 6

(Diagram 7) Here is a good transition drill. It is 3/3. Coach passes the ball to a teammate on the baseline. Three offensive men start down the floor. The man guarding the offensive player who received the pass from the coach must hustle and touch the baseline before helping his two teammates play defense.

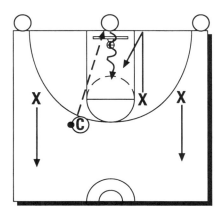

Diagram 7

DAWSON PIKEY

A Fast Break for All People

I coached for 20 years, 19 years with boys at the high school level, and one year with junior college girls. The most enjoyable year was the year I coached girls. I heard a couple of things at this clinic that I sincerely believe. Jane Albright-Dieterle spoke about being yourself. Joe Ciampi talked about the fact that you must believe in the things you do. Most of the things that we did, we did to survive. I coached in an all-white, affluent high school of 650 students, nine through twelve. Ninety to ninety-five percent of our students went on to college so I had some very bright kids, but I did not have very big kids. They didn't jump or shoot very well, nor were they very fast. With that background, you would ask how we could fast break?

I went to a clinic and heard Sonny Allen, who coached at Old Dominion. I took some of his ideas and adapted them to my small kids. I will show you my fast break and then come back and break it into parts. Then, I will show you how we used it to counter pressure. Once we implemented the break, the program got better every year. In our best year, we were 29 and 3 and went to the final four in the state tournament. We were the smallest team in the tournament, got beat by the team that won it and played them a closer game than anyone.

(Diagram 1) For simplicity, I am going to teach this out of a 2-3 zone, but if you ran a man-to-man or another type of zone, you could do the same thing. 1 and 2 are the guards, 5 is the center. The rebounder, 3, brings the ball down quickly, half pivots and starts a power dribble away from the basket. 3 could not take more than three dribbles. Ideally, we wanted 3 to take a line to where the half-court line met the sideline. This would differ depending on where the rebound was, but this was the optimum.

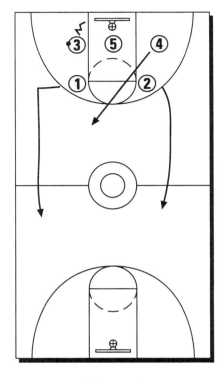

Diagram 1

At the same time, when we saw we were going to get the rebound, we released the weakside guard, 2. We wanted 2 to go all the way to the sideline. We are trying to outnumber the defense. You want to get down the floor first. The person who is farthest away from the board, 4, or 5, in this case 4, came to this position. 4 is in a lane outside of the free-throw lane extended. As we powered out, 3 first looked for the deep pass.

We taught two types of passes, either the two-handed chest pass or a baseball pass on the run. We told 3 to find the basket on the other end. 3's eyes are going to the basket on the other end; the shoulders are square. 3 can make a two-handed chest pass, which is what we did with the girls, or the baseball type pass. Remember that when you are throwing the pass, it cannot be a flat pass. As you make the pass, you must get arch over the middle of the court. The first option is the pass from 3 to 2.

The second option is the pass to 4, the relay man. The third option is to 1. 1 comes straight out at the free-throw line extended and then adjusts down the floor depending on where the dribbler is. 1 is the safety valve. If the dribbler comes toward 1, 1 releases accordingly. We maintain a 15' spacing between 3 and 1.

(Diagram 2)   The pass is not released to the 10-second line, it is not released and "let's see what happens." It is a commitment that 2 is gone. If the pass is intercepted, 2 stays at the other end of the floor. If the opponents scored, we step out and make the long pass and score anyway.

We would play 4-on-4 if intercepted because they would always keep someone back. We felt we didn't lose anything. 4 goes to the ball-side block and looks for the pass from 2. On the pass to 2, 1 releases and runs to rebound. If 2 does not shoot, 1 breaks to the high post for a pass from 2. That's the primary and secondary phases of the break.

(Diagram 3)   3 and 5 are coming as **trailers**. Their positions are dictated by where the defense is rather than ball location.

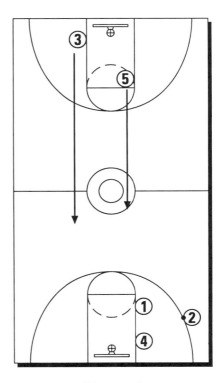

Diagram 3

(Diagram 4)   We want to get into a quick half-court offense before the defense can set up. We have a quick turnover offense, the third phase. If 4 does not get the pass from 2, the ball is reversed. 4 rolls to the other side of the floor. 1 sets a backpick for 5, and 5 goes to the post position on the other side of the floor. 1 would then come to the other side of the floor. The ball went 2-5-3-4-5 or 2-5-3-4-1. This is the initial break off of a missed shot.

(Diagram 5)   Usually the defensive players were in the traffic lane. No matter which level, that's where you find them. It never made sense to me to get the ball to the middle. There is probably nothing about rebounding I haven't tried. The most successful thing was that I quit trying to block off. I would block off chest to chest. We tried everything, even double-teaming on the rebound. I found out that

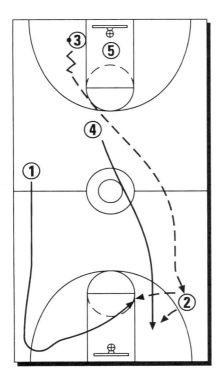

Diagram 2

no matter what I did, five big kids against my five little kids, they would get the ball because officials don't call the foul with the hip.

As an offensive rebounder, you can get your hip on the defense and sort of walk yourself in behind the defense. But, when we started releasing, it relieved pressure because our opponents started rebounding just three people. The first game we used this, no one knew. We had not done this the year before. We were in a tournament, not seeded and we were up 30 points by half.

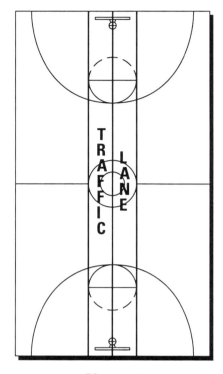

Diagram 5

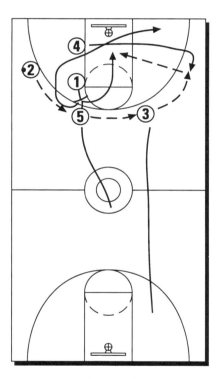

Diagram 4

(Diagram 6)   If 3 cannot pass to 2, the second option is 4. 4 also has a maximum dribble of three, but it might only be one. 4 then passes ahead to 2, or as 1 sees what is happening and breaks down the sideline, 4 can pass to 1.

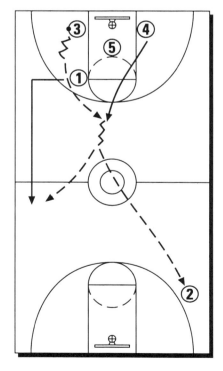

Diagram 6

(Diagram 7) Suppose 4 passes to 1. We then do the opposite. 1 and 2 are both offensive threats. 1 will not pull up and stop. 1 will keep the ball and go as far as he can. At some point, 1 must decide whether he is going to shoot it or pass it. 1 doesn't come down and stop in a non-threatening area. 1 has the ball; 2 will break to the high post and 4 will go to the block on the ball side.

Diagram 8

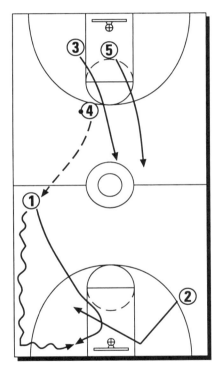

Diagram 7

(Diagram 8) 3 and 5 will be trailers, and we are set up for the turnover.

(Diagram 9) Let's turn it over. The ball will go 1-3-5-4. Meanwhile, 2 will back-screen for 3, who will go to the ball side block. 2 then rolls across the lane to the high-post area. If 4 doesn't have a shot, 4 can pass to either 3 or 2. Stress to your players that the pass from 3 to 5 is not a lateral pass. It is passed back at an angle so that it cannot be intercepted. That's the big picture.

Diagram 9

(Diagram 10) If 3 dribbles out and passes to 1, we have the same thing. We have the same options. If 1 passes to 2, 4 goes ball-side block, and 1 breaks to the high-post area ball side. This is on a missed shot when we got the rebound, and we will do the same thing if it is a made shot. We will also do the same thing off a missed free throw and a made free throw.

I'd like to show you some of the drills that we used. The very first day of our practice, we hoped that they had done something prior to the season. We started working on passing; bounce passing, chest passing, and baseball passing. We would make the sharp 15' passes, then we would widen out to 20' and then 30'.

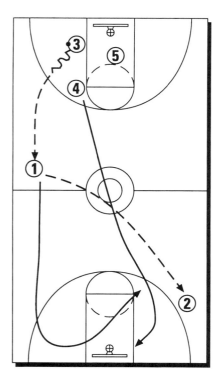

Diagram 10

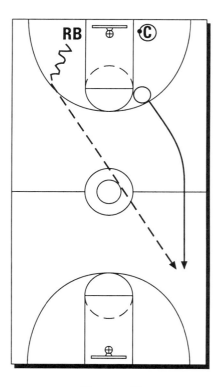

Diagram 11

(Diagram 11) A coach throws the ball off of the board. The rebounder would power out on the dribble, and the other man would release for the pass from the rebounder. Teaching points are the pass and the power dribble being under control. Remember the arch, they cannot throw a bullet pass. Sometimes I would have a manager stand in the middle of the floor.

(Diagram 12) Add another player. The rebounder makes the shorter pass and that player would make the long pass. We want the person who is throwing the longer pass to make the pass from the dribble.

(Diagram 13) Next we would work the drill with three options; 3 rebounds and then passes to 4 who then makes the pass to either 1 or to 2. We would call out which option we wanted, either the pass to 1, 2, or 4.

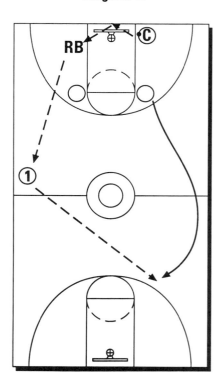

Diagram 12

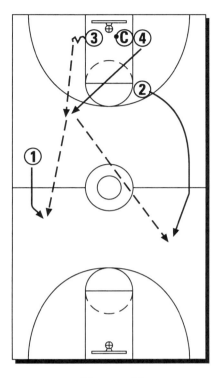

Diagram 13

(Diagram 15)   That got me to the sideline. I wanted the ball on the sideline and my second man on the 2-on-1 situation on the same side of the floor that the ball was on. We are no longer passing the ball through an obstacle. The defensive man must make a decision. Most coaches tell the defensive player to protect the basket first. The defensive player will probably defend the player on the **block**. That gives the player with the ball an open shot.

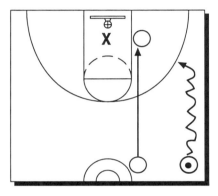

Diagram 15

(Diagram 14)   Add one person on defense. You probably had your two players on a 2-on-1 situation passing the ball back and forth as they were near the middle of the court. The defensive player was usually between the man with the ball and the man who was receiving the ball. The offensive player had to pass the ball by the defensive player. I asked myself, "Why do I want to create an obstacle for the passer?"

(Diagram 16)   We run this drill with one defensive player starting at mid-court. We go 4-on-1. I wanted to make sure that we scored. How do you teach your defensive player to react when it is 3-on-1?

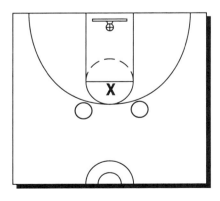

Diagram 14

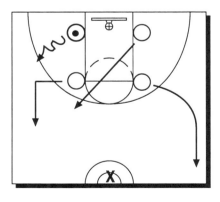

Diagram 16

(Diagram 17) Here's the type of 3-on-1 you are usually facing. I taught the defensive man to challenge the ball and get the man with the ball to stop dribbling, and then react to the pass, and hope that by then you had help.

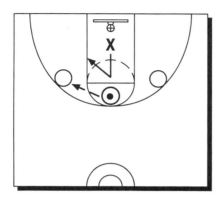

Diagram 17

(Diagram 18) By getting 3-on-1 on the side with the ball in the corner, a player at the block and another at the high post, you probably won't make a pass.

Diagram 18

(Diagram 19) Let's add a second defensive player. Both started at the head of the key, and on the rebound, one defensive player had to touch the end line and then get into the action.

(Diagram 20) Add a third defensive player. We are showing this for clarification only to the right.

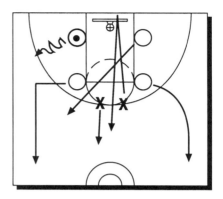

Diagram 19

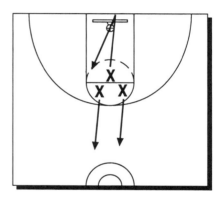

Diagram 20

(Diagram 21) If 3 rebounds, 5 possibly can get to the position shown for 4. If either 4 or 5 can see the other person in front of him, it is the other person's lane. 5 moves to ball side to rebound and would not get to that lane first.

Diagram 21

(Diagram 22)   If 5 rebounds, he powers out taking 3's spot. But since 5 is in the middle of traffic, usually his method of releasing the ball was a pass to 1. Many times, if 5 got the rebound, we didn't have the break. Sometimes 5 might hit 4 at the top of the circle.

Diagram 22

(Diagram 23)   You can run this from a 1-2-2 zone. This shows 4 rebounding. 1 is almost the designated release man.

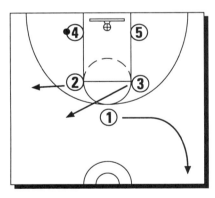

Diagram 23

(Diagram 24)   Suppose the pass is made to 1, and he cannot make the next pass. 4 goes to the low block, 2 releases and then breaks to the high post. 1 dribbles as far down the floor as he can. 3 and 5 will be the trailers.

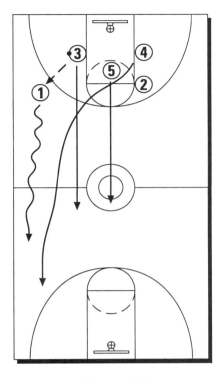

Diagram 24

(Diagram 25)   If 1 cannot get the shot, the ball is reversed to 3 to 5. 2 back-screens for 3 who breaks low. 4 crosses the lane and breaks wide, and 2 then rolls high. The ball goes 1-3-5-4-3 or 1-3-5-4-2.

Diagram 25

(Diagram 26)   If 1 and 4 are both defended and 3 cannot pass to 2 from the power dribble, (3 doesn't dribble because he isn't a good ballhandler) 3 passes back to 5; 2 comes back to relieve the pressure. 1 can release with 2 passing to 1.

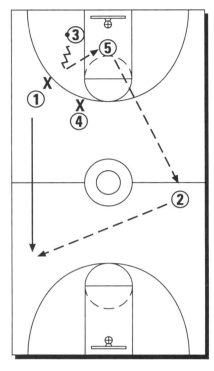

Diagram 26

Diagram 27

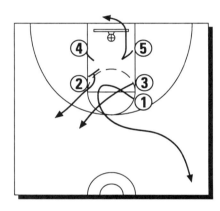

Diagram 28

(Diagram 27) Here is a teaching point. Once the ball comes across the 10-second line, percentage wise, forget the cross-court pass because the defense is back and it is difficult to get the arched pass crosscourt.

(Diagram 28) The break from the made or missed free throw. We want our best passer at 5. We rebound five people because we are small and we make certain we do not give up an offensive rebound. We work at blocking off. 1 blocks the shooter and 1 releases. Off the made shot, 5 takes the ball out of the net, and doesn't let it hit the floor. As 5 goes out-ofbounds, he turns and looks down the floor. The ball is back and ready to be thrown. 2 is the outlet; 3 is the middleman. Nothing has changed. If we are down several points with a few seconds to play, we don't call a special play; we run this, something that we have been running all year. This is our lastsecond play.

(Diagram 29) Break the Press. We line up in a 1-4 vs 1-2-1-1 press.

We run our fast break. 1 and 2 are guards. We spread floor with 3 and 4 at the elbows. 3 breaks up and toward the corner. We fake to 3. 1 is the release man. 4 comes into the hole vacated by 3. 2 jockeys for position in the release area.

(Diagram 30) If 5 passes to 2, 1 releases, 4 the middle man. Remember, we will have someone open. A 1-2-1-1 press must adjust to what we are doing.

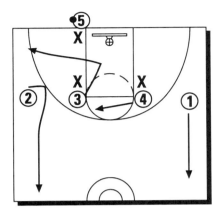

Diagram 29

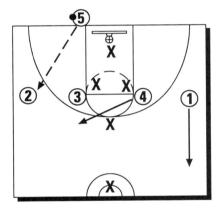

Diagram 30

(Diagram 31) 2-2-1 Press. If 5 passes into the corner because 3 was left open, 3 would make an arching pass to 2 as the trap materialized. We really didn't like the pass made into the corner, but sometimes it happened.

Diagram 31

RENE PORTLAND

Changing Defenses

There are a lot of things we do defensively that makes a team concerned when they play us. I am going to give you some of the things we do that are just a little different. Hopefully, you can take some of these things and use them. We are a good defensive club and it has a lot to do with the heart of your players, but also has something to do with the teaching techniques. We are in very good condition at Penn State. We start Labor Day and it is a lot of running and work. Conditioning is our number one thing in preseason. During the summer, our players are working on their skills; they aren't doing a lot of conditioning. We give our players two things to improve on. We give them a program to do these, and we expect to see improvement when they return to school in the fall.

Your team must be in great condition to be a good defensive team. You must be a great transitional team to be a good defensive team. Don't just teach your kids how to play defense. Teach them the simplest part of offense, and that's transition. If you think about it, if you press, all you are asking for is a layup. Many kids cannot shoot a layup, and what we work on is basic transition skills. So, to be a good defensive team you must work on your transition game and eliminate the role models. We want to keep it basic.

You must make them believe in defense. Talk to them about defensive mentality. This part of practice is hard. When they do a shooting drill, that part is fun. When a defensive drill comes up, you see our coaches turn it up a notch. It starts with the head coach. When it comes to a defensive drill, I no longer stand on the sideline and observe. That's when I throw myself into it. We talk about the easy things of defense; make it quick, make it easy. Talk to your team before the game. We want to set the tempo. We want to score the first basket of every game. We want to score the first basket of the second half. Penn State is hard to play.

I have two books with me all the time. One book is all late situations. We seldom lose a game in a late-game situation. These are out-of-bounds plays and other plays that we have, and we practice two of them every other day. In a late-game situation, I can open the book and they can see what the play is. I'm not drawing something new for them. The other book is the playbook. This has everything that they are taught the entire year broken down for them. This playbook has 56 out-of-bounds plays in it, just last year's plays. We use seven or eight prime time defenses because I want Penn State tough to play.

There are two different philosophies. Do several things perfectly. There are such teams. They are very simple to scout, but they are good. That's one side—I like the other side. And our players like it. They like a lot of material. If we do something different, then you must spend time on us, and you don't have the time to spend on yourself.

Always remember your personnel. Are they quick, athletic? We teach our players defensively to dictate, not react. We move on every pass, not on every catch. That's just a small thing, but you must teach it. When they get tired, they will move on the catch. Man-to-man, we do some different things. If you are scouting us, watch me because I call everything from the sideline.

(Diagram 1) In man defense, anything in the backcourt, we have head on ball, we want the offensive player to zig-zag. Near mid-court, we push to the sideline. At the high school level, you may want to push them to their weak hand. Have head on head. If she changes direction, we don't teach the dropstep, we hop and put the head on the ball. We always keep the same lead foot.

Below the foul line, you can fan or funnel. We push to the sideline and then protect the baseline. We do not give up the baseline. We work hard at protecting the baseline. If the ball is above the foul line, your lead foot is on the help line. If the ball is below the foul line, your inside foot is across the help line. We overextend our help. Let's look at a 2-3 zone with different rules.

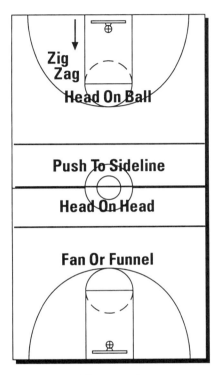

Diagram 1

(Diagram 2) To teach this zone we use six offensive players, A through F. When A has the ball, X1 must establish a side. X1 goes out; X1 and X2 are not in tandem. What that does is to move X2 into the position to split the high post and the elbow. As X1 moves, X3 "cheats." That's the word you use "Who's in cheat?" X3 almost halves the distance.

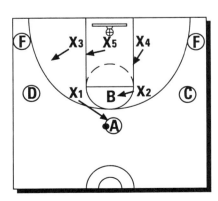

Diagram 2

(Diagram 3) X1 wants A to pass to D. When A passes to D, X3 can get there quickly. X3 could steal. Suppose that the pass is made from A to D. X3 plays D for a second. X1 goes to the elbow to check the high post, and then X1 comes out and plays D and X3 drops to corner. X5 moves over, and X4 is near the off-side mid-post area looking. X2 is at the elbow.

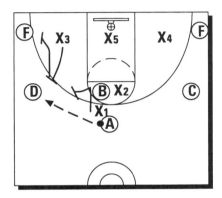

Diagram 3

(Diagram 4) If D passes to E, X3 is on the ball, X2 moves back, X1 moves back to elbow, X4 and X5 remain about the same.

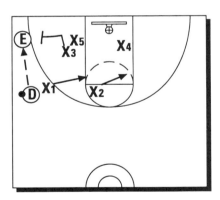

Diagram 4

(Diagram 5) This gives you a box formation.

(Diagram 6) When the ball is passed back to D, X1 takes the ball, X2 takes the high-post area, X4 slides up the lane, X3 stays back.

(Diagram 7) As the ball is reversed to A, X2 runs out in a position to stop reversal and push the ball back to the same side.

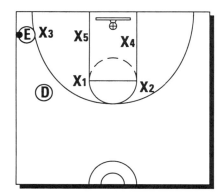

Diagram 5

Diagram 6

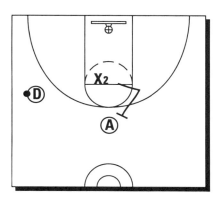

Diagram 7

(Diagram 8) High Post Coverage. X1 has established a side; X3 is in cheat; X2, X5 and X4 have adjusted. When the ball goes to the high post, the rule is; X5 comes up, X1 goes to elbow, X3 drops back.

Diagram 8

(Diagram 9) This means that X5 plays the post and everyone else is in a box.

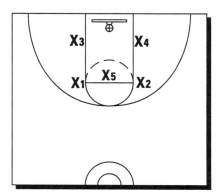

Diagram 9

(Diagram 10) If the pass is made from the high post to corner, X3 takes the ball, X4 comes across to the ball side and X5 rotates to the off side. X1 has high-post responsibility because usually the high post will come ball side. So X3, X4, and X5 rotate.

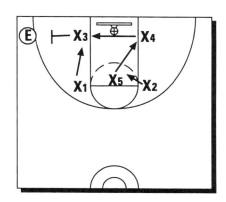

Diagram 10

(Diagram 11) Suppose the ball went from the high post to the other corner. Same rotation.

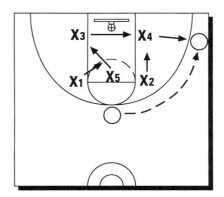

Diagram 11

(Diagram 12) Coach at high post, and pass the ball to the four corners and make X3, X4, and X5 rotate.

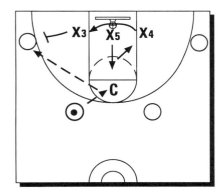

Diagram 12

(Diagram 13) Do the same drill with a low post added.

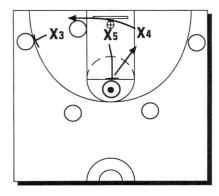

Diagram 13

Question: What technique do you use in defending the low post?

Answer: (Diagram 14) Anytime the ball is below the foul line, we go baseline. I'm not a full-front person. I only do that when we are in foul trouble. If the ball is above the foul line, we play on the highside and go in front. If the ball comes back out, we go around the back. We only go around the front once, and that's with a lot of hand contact with one hand out front all the time.

Diagram 14

Question: If the low post steps out to the short corner, how do you cover it?

Answer: X4 goes with her. But this will depend to a great extent on our scouting. "That's a scout."

Let's trap. (Diagram 15) X1 establishes a side and X3 cheats. Suppose that A passes to B. We automatically trap with X1 and X3. Our guard gives the signal, and we trap on the first pass. We practice this; don't assume they know how to trap. We want the legs overlapped so that the knees are closer. We don't want the dribbler to split the trap.

(Diagram 16) X1 and X3 are trapping near the three-point line. X2 plays the high post. X5 is in the low post. No low post, X5 can cheat. X4 is in the lane.

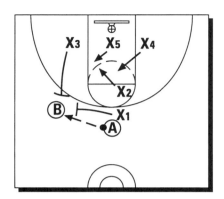

Diagram 15

Diagram 16

(Diagram 17) Suppose that B passes to D. We must move on the pass. X3 and X5 will trap in the corner. Don't give up baseline. X1 drops to the elbow. X2 replaces X4, and X4 plays the low post.

Diagram 17

(Diagram 18) Now you have your biggest player (X5) on the trap. X5 can get there. Teach them to be big.

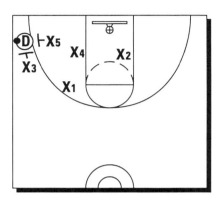

Diagram 18

(Diagram 19) If the ball is passed back out, we don't harass it. X1 plays normal, and everybody goes back to the normal 2-3 zone.

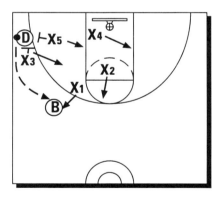

Diagram 19

(Diagram 20) If the ball is reversed, X2 will jump out and try to stop ball reversal. As X2 comes out to play A, X2 is establishing a side, and X4 is our cheat person. As A passes to C, X2 and X4 will trap. X5 will be in the low-post area; X1 goes to high post.

(Diagram 21) If the ball goes to the corner, X4 and X5 trap. X2 is at the high post; X3 takes the low post, and X1 is in the lane. We only trap when the ball goes down, not up.

Diagram 20

Diagram 21

Effective Presses

We have a 1-2-1-1 full-court; we normally do that after foul shots. We also play a 2-2-1, a 1-3-1 half-court and a 1-2-1-1 where we continue to trap. We use them all. We break down one of these presses. You just don't press by having your offensive team try to beat your press. Rarely do we go 5-on-5, we usually do 4-on-4. Teach your X5 to play 2-on-1, etc. When your players learn to work without X5, they get better.

(Diagram 1) Our 1-2-1-1 Press. We trap the first pass. We put X4 in front of the ball because of the size. We have a pressing team from our bench. This gives your starters a chance to rest. The press gives them some playing time, and the starters on the bench would really get into it. We always gave our pressing team four possessions. X1 is at mid-court; X5 is deep. This is one trap.

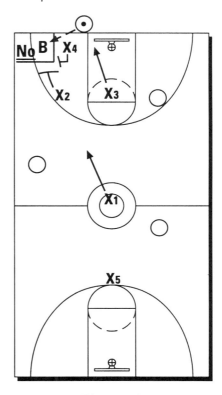

Diagram 1

We don't want to front anyone. As an offensive player, you don't want to go into the corner. But in the heat of the game, they will do it. As the ball is inbounded, X2 and X4 form the trap and X3 automatically goes after the inbounder. X1 takes a chance, and that's "a scout."

(Diagram 2) 2-2-1 Three-Quarter Court. Anytime the ball is on the sideline, you are in a box; anytime the ball is in the middle you are in a diamond. Forget X5; let's work with the other four. X2 and X1 are partners; X3 and X4 are partners.

(Diagram 3) If the ball is here, the press is passive and you are in a box. The ball is returned to the inbounder. Now a diamond is formed. X4 takes the ball. X1, X2, and X3 rotate.

RENE PORTLAND

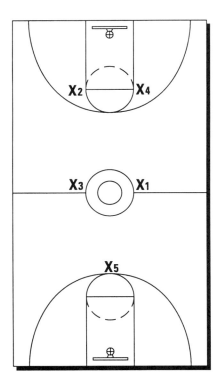

Diagram 2

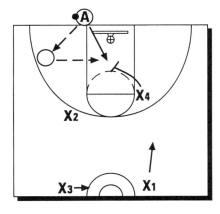

Diagram 3

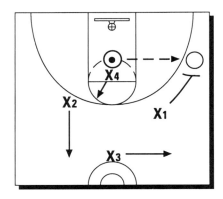

Diagram 4

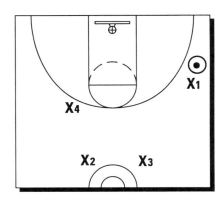

Diagram 5

(Diagram 4) X4 is on the ball, and the ball is thrown to the side. We are now back in a box. X1 comes up; X3 goes over; X2 and X4 drop.

(Diagram 5) We are in this position.

(Diagram 6) If the ball is dribbled, X1 follows the dribble and we are in a diamond, X1 on the ball, X2 is back, X4 drops. If you see a two-guard front, you set up to beat a two-guard press. Then, you will see a one-guard front and things change. When the ball is dribbled, stay with it; when the ball is passed, go to it. Teach this 4-on-4.

Diagram 6

RENE PORTLAND

(Diagram 7) This is a Half-Court 1-3-1. This slows the tempo of the game. X1 and X2 work in unison. They must talk. X4 and X5 start facing in so they can see the entire floor. X2's job is to play the passes between the two guards. You don't really attack, but you slow down the offense. Try to get them to pass. She is saying "stay" so that X1 knows what she is going to do.

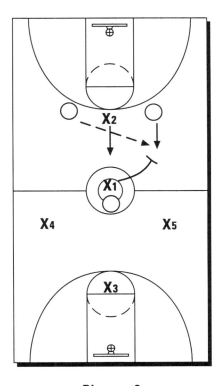

Diagram 8

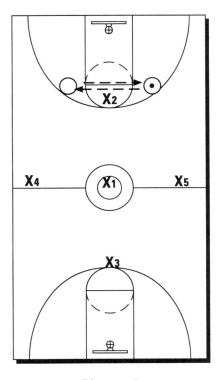

Diagram 7

(Diagram 8) Suppose the pass is made and X2 can't get there. X2 says "switch," and X1 will take the ball and X2 will replace.

(Diagram 9) To break this press, you will put someone in the middle. We drill X1 and X2 on this drill. X1 plays this like post defense.

That's the first drill. X1 can't leave the center person until X2 is in position to defend. X1 must time her movement with X2. This must be practiced. Stay or switch, cover the high post, and keep the ball out of the high post.

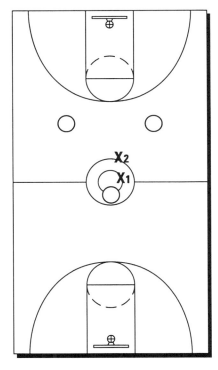

Diagram 9

(Diagram 10) This is the next breakdown drill. Coach passes and the offense dribbles. X4 and X2 will rap.

I don't care where the trap happens as long as it happens. Ideally, the trap should be over half-court so the ball cannot go back. Work hard with X4 and X5 not to give up sideline.

(Diagram 11) As X4 advances to set the trap, X5 is on a diagonal, moving back. X3 is on the line of the ball.

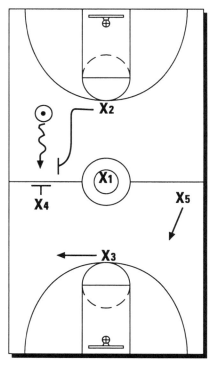

Diagram 11

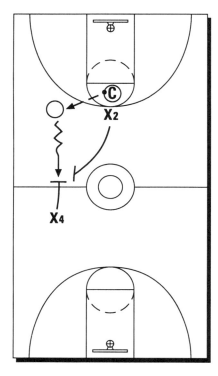

Diagram 10

GEORGE RAVELING

Creating Better Player/Coach Relationships

It is important that you understand that there are really two aspects that you must deal with as a coach. One is the mental and the other is the physical. Most coaches do a good job with the physical, and not many coaches do a good job coaching the mental.

If coaches want to understand how to coach young players today, all you have to do is to look around in society. We live in a different era. I grew up in a household where my mother believed that children should be seen and not heard. It was unthinkable for us to ever sit in a room with adults and enter into the conversation. My mother was the kind of woman who would say, "If I want your opinion, I'll ask for it and I'll tell you what it's going to be." What is becoming increasingly obvious in coaching today is that coaches who are succeeding are the coaches with good people skills.

I think that people who are succeeding in any endeavor in life today are people who have good people skills. I want to cover a variety of things I think might stimulate you to create a more workable atmosphere with your players. At the same time, it could produce winning. We have a unique responsibility. Most of us spend more time with that child than either parent does. We are the last citadel of discipline today. In most corners of society today, discipline has eroded. We must understand that we are teachers, motivators, and leaders. And in a broad sense, most of us are moms and dads to those kids, too. Not long ago, I had one of my grad assistants go back and research this for me. In the 20 years I have been a head coach at the college level, 75% of my players had no father in their home. It is not all about X's and O's. The players have a lot more to do with winning than you do. Most coaches think it is them. It is about loving, teaching, leading, discipline, and if you surrender those rights you have, as a coach, soon you will be out on the street. We have a great opportunity. We can have more influence on society today than anybody else in America with these kids.

The biggest pleasure I have when a kid comes back 10 years later and says, "I understand now. I didn't understand then, but I understand now." Those are greater victories than beating UCLA. You know that you played a positive role in that young person's life. The people who are going to survive in this profession in the next decade are going to be the people who have the best people skills. Kids today are crying for discipline. I believe that kids will go out and bust themselves for you if they believe that you truly care about them, if you really love them and if you are really going to fight for them. I'm always fond of telling my players: "What you do speaks a hell of a lot louder than what you say." That's what they see in us too.

The Tower of Babel

One of the things that we get caught up in coaching is what I call "The Tower of Babel." It is all of the bunch of terms we use. Sometimes I wonder if the players understand these terms? I give my players a little dictionary of terms I use. It is not what I know, but what I can transfer what I know to someone else that is important.

Conflicts

So much of our job today centers around resolving conflicts. They come at us from all directions. These come from girlfriends, the media, drugs, alcohol, academics. There is a spillover of societal problems into the coaching profession. We must deal with them, and the sad part about it is that most of us were never trained. We must educate ourselves about drugs and how to deal with them. We must learn about agents. Each of us must make sure that we keep ourselves informed on issues so that we

GEORGE RAVELING

can give our players better guidance. If they don't get it from us, in many cases, they aren't going to get it.

Three Basics

There are three things necessary in any human relationship: trust, respect, communication. It is not enough for me to tell my players they must trust me, I must also trust them. In any human relationship, success starts with trust. Then we must respect each other. What we expect out of our players, we must be willing to give to them. Never worry about players liking you. You want their respect. If a person respects you, liking you will come very easily. Then there is communication. Lack of communication creates lack of understanding. The player has the right to come in and tell me that he thinks I'm wrong. You must create an atmosphere that will stimulate the young player to come in and talk to you.

Attitude

Let's talk about attitudes. Attitudes are at the heart of success and failure. They are formed by words, what we say to a player. These words will trigger a mental picture and bring about an emotion or feeling. This emotion will be manifested in a positive attitude or negative attitude. I have a positive practice day about once a week. Anytime any coach says anything negative (the manager keeps a record), the coach must put a quarter in the pot. You can find creative ways to correct players without being negative.

Five Reasons Why People Strive for Success

- Ego—like a fast break. If it gets out of control you can get hurt.
- Reward—a scholarship, being drafted in the NBA.
- Peer Pressure
- An obligation to fit the image that others have of you. I have had two seven footers in my coaching career and to this day, I believe that if they were only 6'5", they would have never played basketball. Everybody expected them to play. I don't believe they really wanted to be players. They were trying to live out someone's image of them.
- Parents, relatives and sweethearts put pressure on them to excel.

Five Reasons People Fail

- Peer Pressure—let others run our lives. The choice is, do we run it or does someone else run it? We let other people tell us how to live our lives.
- Blame others for failure. Did you ever meet a self-made failure? It's always somebody else's fault. I keep a little jar on my desk and it says "excuses." When a player comes in and starts giving me excuses, I go get the jar, take the lid off and say, "Speak a little louder so I can catch all of these excuses."
- We underestimate our potential. Most of us are looking for a reason to fail. We spend more time talking to ourselves in the negative than the positive. The real question for you is not what do other people think of you, but what do you think of yourself? If you don't love yourself, how can you love somebody else? But God gave us all the elements of greatness. God doesn't make any failures. People make failures.
- Surrender to fear instead of faith.
- Lack of a goal in life. You must have a goal. No goal, no fun. About nine years ago, I started having a five-minute team talk before practice every day. It rarely has anything to do with basketball. One day it might be about the importance of a smile. One day I will talk about discipline.

GEORGE RAVELING

Discipline

The greatest discipline is self-discipline.

- Do what you are supposed to do.
- When you are supposed to do it.
- As well as you can do it.
- Do it that way all the time.

One of the great things that happened to me was to be an assistant coach in the Olympics in 1984. One of the things Bob Knight told the players was "things that you do well will win for us, and things that you do poorly will get us beat. You don't want to lose, and I don't want to lose; therefore, I must always be critical of things that you do that will get us beat." I always share this with my team. Then I show how it relates to discipline.

The Parato Principle

Take any team and I'll bet you that 80% of the problems are caused by 20% or less of the players, and 80% of your success is caused by 20% of your players. Don't lose your perspective. Gain a balanced perspective.

The Art of Listening

One of the hardest things for a human being to master, particularly for coaches, is to listen. Each year I set a goal of how many books I'm going to read and the last three years, I've tried to take a specific subject and do most of my reading about that subject. The first year, I decided that I was going to read about the art of listening. I wanted to see if I could improve my ability to listen. Experts estimate that most of us spend about 70% of our waking hours in some form of verbal communication. It breaks down to:

- 9% spent in writing.
- 6% spent in reading, and that tells you a lot about our problems.
- 30% spent in talking.
- 40% (almost half) spent listening to something or someone else.

It is important that we learn to listen. A player comes in and says, "Coach, I want to talk to you." That's your first test of whether you listen or not. He has something he wants to tell you, so be quiet and listen. The first thing I do is to make him comfortable, make good eye contact, listen and I try to help him say the things that he doesn't know how to say. The next time a kid does this to you and after he leaves the room, write down the percentage of time you talked and the percentage of time he talked. You may find out you talked more. The person who listens the most gets the most information. The person who talks the most gets the least information.

When a Kid Comes in to Talk, I Listen for Three Things:

- What is he saying.
- What is he not saying. That is the most critical point of listening.
- What he would like to say, but needs help saying.

Ask for feedback. "Let me see if I understand." Sometimes we assume that we understand, but the only way you really know is to ask for feedback. The first sign of intelligence is to admit that you don't know something. There is no shame to say that you don't know. When I teach something on the floor, I think we make a great mistake if we just ask if everybody understands. Then, what happens when we go to implement it? They don't know, and it is your fault. Ask a player to go to the board and explain what you were talking about. Or, we are going out on the floor and I have a player teach it. When you start doing that, you will be amazed at what better focus you get from your players. I do this all the time. I teach something and then ask for feedback. Then I know if they know and it forces them to concentrate.

GEORGE RAVELING

We must constantly look for ways to get our players to concentrate in practice. Performance declines when you don't ask for feedback and when you ask for it, performance improves. Don't settle for kids saying that they understand, make them demonstrate. We can learn a lot from our players if we don't let our ego get in the way. I ask my players a lot of questions. During a time-out, I'll ask them what defense they want to play. I want to find out what they are committed to. What I tell them and what they are committed to are two different things. We must communicate with our players. We don't have to agree with them. But we should be willing to hear their opinions. They can teach us if we are effective listeners, if we are effective motivators, if we are effective salesmen, if we are patient, compassionate and giving, and if we are fun to play for. Sometimes we put on blinders. We don't want to find out these things.

Hear/Listen, Look/See, Play/Participate

We want our players to understand there is a difference between hearing and listening. Everybody in this room can hear me but not everybody is listening. Hearing encompasses a sound wave entering the ear, passing through the brain and exiting the other ear. Listening encompasses the sound wave entering the ear, and being analyzed, digested and stored in the brain. It's the same thing with looking and seeing. If there were a picture of the Mona Lisa hanging here, we could look at that picture, but not all of us could see it. The difference is that when you see something, you see the subtleties that lie beneath the surface. And the same goes for playing and participating. We have many participants but not too many players. You must get your players to understand these differences.

Win/Win

In all human relationships, we end up in one of three situations: Win-win, win-lose, and lose-lose. We deal with these on a daily basis. With a lose-lose situation, I lose, you lose; it is a waste of time. Sometimes it's important to be wrong so someone else can be right. I ask the players what type of uniforms they want. On things that don't make any difference to me, I let the players decide. The worst thing that can happen in a player-coach relationship is that we both lose, or if I lose, I'll make sure that you do, too. The ideal situation is that when a player comes in to see you, both of us feel good when he leaves. That's a win-win situation. You should always leave a person with their dignity after a confrontation.

Feedback

Here are some expressions you can use in dealing with players. The best way is by asking questions. Questions provide the critical feedback necessary to make sure that the two-way communication is on track. "Let me see if I can summarize what your concerns are."

"If I understand you, you are saying....."
"Have I explained this to your satisfaction?"
"How does this sound to you?"

These feedback phrases create good communication with our players. Most of these are applicable to any phase of life. These are just good people skills.

How to Build a Happy Player

- Self evaluation
- Goal setting—before every game each player has a goal card on his stool. It has room for three defensive goals and three offensive goals.
- Planning—I have had every one of my players in over the last two weeks, and we planned out their summer activities. Notice I said WE. And when we were finished, I asked if each felt comfortable with it.
- Achieving—you must show them a method to achieve these things and how it will benefit them.

GEORGE RAVELING

Judging a Player

Judging a Player. Here are a few thoughts on judging players.

- Would I like to play with him? That's one of the first things I ask myself when I start to recruit someone.
- Does he make himself visible? We have a very good player in our league, and I have seen games where he was invisible. Sometimes when the heat is on, players have a strange way of disappearing.
- Does he make others better? That is the essence of it all. Larry Bird made the other players better. Magic made the others better.
- Does he keep things together on the court? Leadership!
- Compare him to other players you have coached. Who does he play like that you coached before?
- Does he like to play, or does he just play?
- Does he play within his game or outside his game?
- Am I impressed with him more because of his mental abilities than his physical skills?

These are the Most Overlooked Responsibilities of a Coach.

- Eliminate excuses. When I hear an excuse, the first thing I do is figure out a way to eliminate the excuse.
- Allow margins for mistakes. You do not have to accept them.
- Recognize a mentally tired team. We know when to practice, but do we know when not to practice? I am amazed on how few coaches really focus on that. Some coaches practice just to practice. I've had days when I've gotten into practice a half hour and it was obvious that they were not ready to go; they were tired. I called them together and said, "Let's end here and pick up tomorrow." There is no way that you will go through a season and get quality practices every day and the reverse is true. We had one day this year when one of my assistants came up to me and said, "Coach, their practice is so good today that it's frightening." I agreed. I called the team over and said it isn't going to get any better; let's go home. Reward your players now and then.
- Eliminate jealousy. We know you can't coach every player the same. Some you kick, some you whack, and some you kiss on the cheek. You have a different standard for your best shooter. Just explain it to them...Coaches spend far too much time on the how of things and very little time on the why of things. I believe that if we explain why, the how becomes very easy.

The Head Coach

- Teacher
- Learner—constantly trying to keep up with the trends in the game and in society. The smartest coaches change before they have to change.
- Facilitator
- Role Model
- Friend—not only their coach, but their friend.

Player-Coach Communication Concepts

- Create a comfortable atmosphere when a player comes to talk to you. If we stay in the office, I will never sit behind the desk. It can become a barrier. I come around and take one of two chairs on the same side of the desk. I want to be close enough to him so that if I reach forward, I can touch him. I make sure we have good eye contact. Many times we will go for a walk, eat lunch, get some coffee.
- Seating arrangements.
- Morning practice (values). For the last 10 years, we have practiced at 6:00 a.m. I can come up with five positive reasons for every negative reason you can name. First, the concentration level is at its highest.

GEORGE RAVELING

- Introduce new items early in practice while the concentration level is good.
- Use of notebooks. I don't know of any other form of teaching in America where we don't require them to take notes. Then we get mad at them when they don't remember. Every player brings his notebook to practice every day.
- Tell and show. Tell them what you are going to tell them. Tell them. Then tell them what you told them.
- Ask for feedback.
- The why is far more important than the how.
- Dealing with "Coach, I want to talk to you."
- Use effective body language, a smile, a slight touch.
- Speak a language that they understand.
- Use his name.

We bring in three people every year to meet with our staff. We had George Allen, the football coach, meet with our team. He passed a paper around the room and every one put down his name in the position in which he was seated at the table. He set it down in front of him and each time that he would address someone, he would look down at that paper and call that person by name. To this day, every time I go to a meeting, I do this for myself.

Random Thoughts Relative to Player-Coach Relations

Coaches must constantly stress to players that drills are not used for conditioning purposes: they are used to refine our offense and defense. You would be surprised how many of your players really don't understand why they do the drills. They just think that it is a part of practice. I always tell them what we are trying to accomplish in each drill. Then I show them how it is related to the whole.

Our physical abilities rarely change, but our mental attitude can change hourly. You can be physically ready to play the game, but not mentally. Teams knowledge of basketball is 5%, knowledge of people is 95%. I got this from Coach Knight and I use this with my players. "We are getting a good physical effort from you, but a poor mental effort, and do you understand the difference?" Talk to the players after practice in the dressing room. Talk to the players who you got on that day. Find something positive to say. "To he who much is given, much is expected."

Get the players to play toward their strengths and away from their weaknesses. That is the secret of coaching. Maximize their abilities and minimize their liabilities. When you build your offense, do you ever ask what your player does best and are their opportunities in this offense for him to do it? What does he do poorly, and am I putting him in a position to have to do that? As a coach, you try to make people specialists.

Players are made in the off-season; teams are made during the season. Everybody practices during the season. The teams that overachieve are the teams who do the little extra things.

Rating My Coach

Most of you won't want to do this. This will scare you. The only way that I can find out if I am doing a good job is to ask somebody. I don't know of any other way. I can't just base it on winning and losing. I tell my players that sometimes you can win and still lose, and sometimes you can lose and still win. So, I ask my players every year. They don't sign their name, all they do is circle numbers. They rate the entire staff every year.

We also give them a practice session evaluation. Evaluate the team's attitude, work habits, enthusiasm, knowledge of the system of play, are the practices too long, teaching methods, staff's attitude, morning practices. We always get a low mark on morning practices. Then the last one, "What areas of the game do you feel that we need to make the most improvement in and why?" When you do these kinds of things, you create a comfort zone for

GEORGE RAVELING

your players. When I ask someone for an opinion, I have paid him a compliment. This makes your players feel like they count. And it gives you some insight where your players are.

"I am"—Statistics

This form will give you the ability to have a better insight into your players. It continues to amaze me at how little some coaches know about their players, The more information I know about my players the better job I can do in assisting them. Many times we may be having a problem with a player because of something that is going on at home. I do this every year for freshmen, and once every two years for the others. As a coach, I must get that kid to buy into what I think is important for the team and yet show him that I can still achieve his goal. But I can't do that if I don't know what his goal is. Good goals are shared goals, goals that the coach and the players make up together. When you finish reading these, you will know your players a lot better than you knew them before, and you will be shocked at some of the information.

Team Evaluation

My perspective of the team and the team's perspective of the team are rarely the same. This is a very good one: The four players you most like to play with. It is interesting. Almost every year, one of the non-starters is high on the list. What is it about this player that makes everyone on the team respect him so much? Then, present these same questions and present them in a negative manner. How about the four players you least like to play with? One year my second leading scorer appeared on everybody's sheet. I had a problem. I hadn't recognized that. I can't call him in and show him. But this tells me I have a problem on my team. You would all like to know this information. How about the two players I trust the least, the most? That gives me insight in selecting captains. I never let my players select the captain. I am looking for someone with leadership skills, not someone who is popular. Most leaders aren't popular. As Satchel Paige said, "If you are getting kicked in the behind, you must be out in front."

Player Self-Evaluation

I have two major meetings, one before the season, one after and I meet with every player once a month, year round. Before the season, we discuss the goals for the season and discuss anything they have on their mind. After the season, we critique each other and talk about the summer plans. It is important that you develop that type of dialogue with them. I fill one of these out also, as do all of my assistant coaches. It's hard to play if you don't know the rules. If a player is not playing because he is a poor defensive player, he needs to know that. When you say that he is a poor defensive player, you have now defined the problem. Now you must come up with the solution.

The Master Coach

- Emotional stability
- Willingness to listen to others
- Orderliness
- Physical endurance
- Need for success
- Ambitious
- Highly-developed consciousness
- Dominant personality
- Low in defensiveness-trusting person
- Low level of anxiety
- Is not an exhibitionist
- Salesman-must sell himself before he can sell the players

I keep this under the glass on my desk, and I keep it there to remind me of how far I must go to become a good coach. Notice that we spent a lot of time discussing the second one.

GEORGE RAVELING

The World's Greatest Defense

- Good officials
- Scheduling (people you can beat)
- Fans (loyal ones)
- Players (talent) (work hard)
- Coach (teacher-salesman)

Most of us work to have a winning team. There is no doubt in my mind that you will win the championship if you get these five. A reporter asked me for the most important things in coaching. I told him; recruiting, scheduling, and coaching. I really believe that. At the end of the year people don't remember who you beat. Schedule someone you can beat. I'll bet you this will happen to you. Someone asks about your record. You say, "26 and 1." I'll bet you that the next statement is "Who did you lose to?"

Question—How Do You Deal with Discipline Problems?

Answer—When I have problems with discipline, I try to deal with them swiftly, fairly, and realistically. I do not make the punishment group punishment. That is difficult, but must be done. One year at Washington State my best player got into serious trouble with five games remaining in the season and we were tied for first place. The school hasn't been to the NCAA Tournament since 1938, and if I put the kid off the team, I penalize him, but I also penalize a lot of innocent people, too. What's the fair way to resolve this? I had four seniors on the team that year and it was the only time that they could say that they had played in the NCAA Tournament. And what about the school? Was there some other way to punish him? Without him, we would not win the last five games. I don't think that's fair to the other kids. Many years ago, I was speaking with Denny Crum and he was the one who helped me get a balanced perspective about discipline. He said, "George, I am never going to lose a national championship over a six-pack of beer." I knew this kid would have to go to summer school. I wrote his mother and said I could not justify paying his tuition in summer school after what he had done. So, it ended up costing his family about $5000. I am overly sensitive about not making it a group punishment.

I served on an ad hoc NCAA committee to review enforcement procedures. One of the things I argued about is this idea of group punishment. One player goes out and accepts money under the table. Then a whole lot of innocent kids get punished. Take the Kansas situation. The kid who got in trouble left. The next year that team is on probation and could not go to the tournament. Not one of those kids on that team had a thing to do with that, but they had to suffer. The other kid transferred to another school. It becomes a group punishment. As a coach, be conscious of that. I know some coaches who, when someone screws up, they make everyone else run and that guy sit there. I'm not that smart. I'm not into that sophisticated stuff.

Coaching beyond the X's and O's

Most of you are accomplished people when it comes to the X's and O's of basketball, and you know how to apply it to your talent. Most people leave coaching because of burn out, not because they are confused or disillusioned because of the X's and O's, but rather by things off of the court.

I'd want to talk to you about coaching beyond the X's and O's, things that will make an impact on the longevity of your career. I'd like to focus in three areas:

- you and the coaching profession (your profile)
- developing and promoting your program
- relationships with players, parents, staff, administration, and media

The successful coach not only anticipates what will or could occur both on and off the court that could impact on a particular season or impact on a coaching life expectancy.

YOU AND THE COACHING PROFESSION (YOUR PROFILE)

- What preparations and approach do you use when interviewing for a coaching position? There are some things you need to focus on immediately. A short phone call will get you confirmation of the job, and you ask the person who is putting things together what they are looking for in a coach. What kind of person do they want to attract? Ask if there is anyone currently on staff at that school who is an applicant for that job. If you are interested, secure two phone endorsements from high-profile people. More than that may be detrimental.

  When you are talking with someone, you must anticipate two scenarios; the questions they are going to ask and prepare answers that profile you as a desirable candidate. Have a list of questions you want to ask because some time during the interview, they will ask if you have any questions. Anticipate they are going to ask you about a teaching philosophy, a coaching philosophy, your offensive and defensive approach, how you are going to motivate players, how you discipline players, how you deal with parents. If you prepare, you will more than likely have acceptable answers, and you will be a better candidate.

- Don't leave your questions to rote memory. Write them down. You must be aware of the school size. Know the situation with regards to the post season route. Which way do you go? You need to know how much input you are going to have in such things as hiring assistants, scheduling, officials and handling the budget. Ask what monies are available for scouting, for attendance at professional clinics and to attend post-season state competitions with staff and players.

  You also want to know if you have any input in conducting off-season programs, the summer camps. Are the gymnasiums available, and are there any charges for these gymnasiums? May I hire people to come in; may I charge a fee? Is the school's philosophy to accept the fee and pay me a salary? After you get the job, make friends with the custodians, cooks, and maintenance people because likely they have been there longer than the people interviewing you and the coach before you.

- Why do you go on the court and coach, and what continues to motivate you? There are probably two common denominators. They are great passion for the game and great competitive spirit. There must be something that sustains us year in and year out for us to continue to coach. What continues to motivate you? Our players don't share the same agenda that you share. You cannot assume the kids are thinking about basketball all of the time. They may be there because of family pressures or their friends are there.

If you are fortunate, you might have one player in any given year that has the same passion you have. If you are aware of that, I think you can be a better motivator and understand what motivates you. Your season has a beginning and an end. You have that freshness of the new start. Regardless of what your record was last year, you are here to prepare yourself so that it might be better next year. That's where the motivation is.

- What is your coaching style? I caution the young coach not to emulate someone else. Don't buy into a personality that is not yours. Your coaching style should be an extension of you.

I think there really are only three coaching styles: a passive style where you show up, scrimmage a little, and go home. Whatever happens, happens. There is a command style. That is the style I started with because it was how I grew up. Crew cuts, no talking on the bus going to or from the game, etc. "My way or the highway," the command style. The third style is the cooperative style. You must get your players to a point where they want to think about X's and O's.

They want to understand what you are doing, what is happening on the floor. You must create that environment. We play a lot of 12-point games, where the first unit must get 12 before the second unit gets four. At the conclusion of such a game, we will bring the units over and ask why weren't we successful? Instead of telling them, you have created a situation where they will critique themselves.

- Coaching organizations and professional memberships. This is important. Get involved in your state association. Within the structure of the organization, you will have opportunities to serve on ad hoc committees, advisory committees. Get to know the power brokers in your state organization and give them the opportunity to know you. Probably, within the state there is a basketball coaches' organization. Again, get involved, volunteer your time and get to know the people who are the movers and shakers in that organization.

- How does the faculty view you as an educator? Most of you are educators in that you have a class (academic) assignment. Can you do anything to improve or enhance that perception from the faculty regarding you as a teacher? Some folks view you the way the media portrays you, as some mentally deficient dumb jock, and that's why you are a coach. Make the other teachers see you as a totally committed individual in the educational process.

- How can you cultivate the alliance with your administration? Your bosses do not like surprises. I don't mean that you must involve your superiors in what takes place in your practice every day. But, there are some things that can occur in your lifetime while you coach that you need to share with superiors.

If you are having trouble with a person on your team and the parent has reared an ugly head, you should share this with your administrator ahead of time. If you have a personal problem, you need to share that, so they know it ahead of time. Your superiors probably function in a social setting in the community and they interact with many people. Keep them informed of your actions and your program so that they can support and defend you, if defense is needed.

MEL ROUSTIO

- Where do you go after games? This seems like an innocent question, but it is a big one. Whether you like it or not, you are a topic of conversation, at least during the season. In any community, there are the haves and the have nots and some folks in between. The one common denominator may be the love of basketball and you are the coach. So, you belong to them.

    I have mentioned to my wife that it is interesting how during the winter months we are invited to all kinds of parties. Come June and July, there are no invitations anywhere. I don't take that personally; I just see it for what it is. I'm a trinket in many circles. If I can be dangled at a party after a game, "the coach was over at our house," I'm not offended by it, just recognize it because coaches can get in situations where someone hears half a conversation and by Monday all kinds of things are being said about what the coach said. The best thing after a game is to change. Don't go to the party every time and don't go to the saloon to have a few beers with the "good old boys" every time. Your best bet is to take your best friend, which is probably your spouse, and go get a sandwich with another couple or members of the staff.

- Do you volunteer your professional services? Offer to help without compensation occasionally. At Jacksonville High School, we help the West Central Illinois Special Olympics Organization by working with the people who will coach in their program. Maybe you can go into the underprivileged areas of your community. I think these things come back ten-fold to you.

- How do you deal with specialization? Specialization is an interesting word to me. On one hand, it conjures up a very positive connotation and on the other hand, it can seem to be a very negative word. This past winter we all sat and marveled at the feats of these Olympic athletes. TV took us back to their hometowns and showed us the commitment they had. We say that's what it takes.

    We have gotten ourselves in a precarious situation. Years ago coaches brought kids in early in the morning to shoot free throws. Then a coach decided he could get ahead if he had his players in the summer. This led to more specialization. That's not all bad. Kids today are by far better because they come from medically stronger families; they benefit from people like you who spend time giving expert coaching. Many of you only coach one sport. In your school, it becomes a mathematical game. Sports are expanding, and there are only so many athletes to go around. Suddenly, coaches are in competition with each other.

- How are you going to posture yourself regarding specialization? You can offer everything you possibly can for off season involvement for kids who have an interest in your sport. On the other hand, make sure that you don't suggest to a kid that he shouldn't play something else. If you can do that, you're clean.

DEVELOPING AND PROMOTING YOUR PROGRAM

- How do you develop "ownership" commitment to your program? Loyalty is a must in your program. Saying it won't make it so. You must have loyal assistants. The only way you can have this is to give them meaningful responsibilities in your program. For example, weight training, direction and promotion of our elementary basketball league. Our junior high coaches are involved in our summer camp and in our games during the season. They all have the opportunity to do very meaningful things in our program so that they can look at it and see their name on it.

- How does your spouse and the spouses of your assistants relate to the program? The most enjoyable fund raiser I have been involved in was a style show that my wife orchestrated for six years. Show me a parent who doesn't want their child to be paraded across the stage in a latest fashion. My wife formed committees, contacted every merchant in town that sold clothing, got players from every level of our program and the cheerleaders involved. We split $1200 between our program and the cheerleader program. We had a full house on a Sunday afternoon. But more importantly, what a wonderful fun thing after a long grueling session. The players loved it.

- How do you subtly, yet effectively, enlist positive media support? We have a daily paper and a weekly paper. They all cover sports. What are you going to do as a coach to enlist positive support?

  First, don't see them as allies. You can't pick fights with the media over issues; you are going to lose. Be honest with them while being protective of your players. At the beginning of the year we had a media/photo day. We help them get started. When they ask you about the season, etc., be totally honest with them, but protect your players. Don't sandbag them and tell them you are going to have a bad season. The veteran basketball fan will see through that and know you are trying to make yourself look good when you have a good one.

  If you think you are going to have a bad season, don't say it. The kids might believe it. Be honest. Point out what you think the team's weaknesses are and what the strengths are. Tell the paper how you are going to play toward the strengths and away from the weaknesses. You don't want the fans to show up and not understand what you are doing.

- What projects can your team be involved in that will benefit your program profile? In Jacksonville, Crimson Basketball and the Muscular Dystrophy Association are almost synonymous. The past twelve years our program has raised $12,000 for MD and banked the same amount with a simple free-throw marathon. All of our players get their charts, sponsor sheets and will get at least 30 pledges for a penny a toss. During the month of June, they will take two days and shoot 500 free throws. We split 50/50 with MD. When our co-captains present the check to MD, it is a positive high profile for our program, and it makes them aware of how to be a giver and not just a taker.

- How can you teach players to be givers in a society that promotes takers? I've really covered this. We use our kids with the Special Olympics and the aforementioned Muscular Dystrophy, just to name two.

- Who is involved in your off-season programs? Our junior high coaches work in the summer camps along with former players, and we have former players, instead of fathers, coach the elementary league teams. Current players serve as officials in the September/October elementary league.

- The best time to promote your program is the night of the game. The National Anthem is an event. We have a class court come out and present the colors; we have all the cheerleader squads, the pom pom squad, and our jazz band plays the anthem. If we just have one parent of every kid in the National Anthem in the stands, we have a break even crowd. I'm suggesting to you to look at what you are doing. Don't be mundane about it. We have had great success in bringing back former teams and honoring them prior to the game. We do that with teams in other sports. We also do the same with former coaches. Use your imagination. These things create a warm feeling in the community.

MEL ROUSTIO

RELATIONSHIPS (ASSISTANTS—PLAYERS—PARENTS)

- Do you understand and appreciate the player–parent relationship? Make no mistake about the interaction between mom and dad and the child at the supper table. The coach, is a frequent topic of conversation. Kids want to please their parents. And parents will do anything in their power (and sometimes beyond) to insure the success and happiness of their kid. You are the culprit when things aren't going right. Now, what can you do to address this situation? Every coach has some sort of preseason meeting with the players and parents. We have an intra-squad game one week before the first game. It is mandatory that every player has at least one parent there. When the game is over, everybody must leave except the parents and the players. We go through a list of things such as practice times, academic requirements, etc. We tell them basketball is not an equal opportunity situation. Some are bigger, stronger, faster, quicker, and as a result, some play a lot, some play a little, some don't play much at all. I want to be sure they don't have virgin ears if I ever have to say it again.

- Now, having said that, how do you deal with the unhappy parent? We tell them at the preseason meeting that any time they want to talk to us on a personal level, please feel free to do so. Here are the guidelines. Call me at school, don't call me at home. I will set up a meeting for you, me, my assistant and your son. Many parents don't want the son to know. I don't coach the parent, I coach the son. There is one rule. We don't talk about anyone else's son. We are going to talk about their son, his skill level, and his role in the program.

- How do you incorporate training rules in your program? I would hope every school represented here has a master training code for all athletes. If you don't, make sure you have one for basketball. Read the policy at your preseason meeting and have both player and parent sign the contract at that meeting. Do you know that you can be sued if you release information about a student without the parent's consent? Your parent must give consent for his child to play. The player's signature indicates he or she heard the training rules and any subsequent punishment to the violations. Then you are home free. Don't give them the card to take home, because their friend will sign it instead of their parents.

- What responsibilities do you have regarding academic success of your players? Every state association has an in-season check process. But when the season is over, it behooves the coach to continue checking, for several reasons. It shows that you are interested in the academic achievement, not just his eligibility status, and to be sure that the kid doesn't drop through the cracks.

- Do you have a college recruitment plan in place for your higher profile players? You should have. If you do, it allows a better relationship between a college recruiter and the parents of the kid that they are recruiting.

- Do you video tape games? Sure you do! Video a couple of practices a week. We tell our kids that we will send a game tape of your choice to the college you want it sent to, but we will send a practice tape of our choice.

- What thoughts have you given to the method of cutting your squad? This is one of the most sensitive areas where a young coach can get burned. Some kids cut themselves by not participating in the off-season. A year end conference with each player to tell them up front what it looks like for them in the coming year is wise. With a marginal player, be sure they know a drastic improvement is needed.. Before we cut, we give the squad a list of the players to rank, including themselves, in terms of their ability. Interestingly enough, the total graph will show that they agree with the coaching staff. Many times the self-evaluation part will show one or two bubbles high, but when you average it all out, it is consistent. Give out the results but don't show who ranked who.

- How do you communicate in pre-game and post-game interviews? Always remember that your players and their families are going to read your comments about their child. Be honest, but be protective of your players. Don't accentuate negative things at the end of a game, missed free throws, turnovers, etc. Chances are they occurred throughout the contest. In the pre-game interview, talk about your program. Talk about where you are and where you are going. Talk to the media about performance objectives. If you have performance goals and you work to achieve those, wins will take care of themselves, talent being equal. Educate the media on these goals in the pre- and post-game interviews. You need to talk with your players because the media wants to get quotes. We want our players to come directly to the dressing room after the game. Don't stop to see the parents, the girlfriend, and by all means don't talk to anyone who has a pencil in their hand. After five minutes, we allow the press into the locker room, and we educate the players to never say anything negative about an opponent or the opposing coach. We always want our players to say positive things about their teammates and accentuate team performance objectives.

Tiger Fast Break

Until you establish a philosophy, you really can't do much. When we come to clinics, we want to see some X's and O's, but we all know most of that. What is crucial is how we implement it into our system. Many coaches will look at their players and say, "How can we run?" You may have short slow players. Whatever type of players you have, if you want to implement the fast break into your system, you can. It's just a matter of where you want to put them. We have players at Missouri who are not very tall. Our tallest player is 6'2". We don't have great athletes; hard workers, yes;but not great athletes.

The first thing we do is start with our weight program. If your players can jump, run, move, are strong, they can move and have a good range of motion, you are going to have a better athlete. If you can get your players involved in a weight program, even one or two days a week, it is going to help them. Also, we do everything quick. We time everything. In a fast break, you must make decisions and you must make them quickly. So, from day one, I want them making decisions under pressure. And that's exactly what a fast break is.

We start with conditioning. We started out by having the guards run the distances in a certain time, the forwards had their time and the posts theirs. One of my post players came to me and said, "Coach, we're only 6' 1", why can we run with the others?" And it came to me that when you start labeling your players, you are saying to them that some are slower. Now we don't have different times. We want our guards to be the best; they must be out front. We do speed work in our conditioning. We do a six-minute mile, but after that, 220 is our longest distance. We do short distance work, time world, and sprints. You must get them in the proper mentality. If you are going to put in a fast-break offense and your defense is a set zone, I think the transition is so hard from the fast break to a stand-up zone or a set offense. We run directly from the fast break into a secondary offense or a motion or a flex offense. You have your movement going before the defense sets. Defense, we like to play man press, up-tempo.

Everything in our program is one big philosophy. That doesn't mean that we don't play some match-ups, we don't ever play some zone. But it's difficult to have one philosophy on one end of the floor and another philosophy on the other end. Do your players like to run? We try to do as much running as we can, making it fun. We do as much as we can on the court with the ball. I don't just sprint. I want them making decisions. We do other types of running. We do cross training, parachute work, anything that you can use that doesn't seem like running to them. We play frisbee in post season. We do a lot of juggling for hand-eye coordination. If you have a player who has poor hand-eye coordination, poor hands, get them three tennis balls. They love it. How many of your athletes have proper technique in running? The first thing we do is to spend some time with the track coach to go over the mechanics of running.

We go over eight basic skills with our players:

- Running—what is the proper running position— stride, arms, breathing, leaning, the whole synopsis of what we want them to do.

- Jumping—arms, leg position, stride, the proper technique. Some players don't know how to jump. We do plyometrics; we do a lot with boxes. Get your shop to make them.

- Pivoting—especially in a fast break: offense.

- Passing—We spend a lot of time with that. They must make decisions when they pass.

- Rebounding—Have them take a ball, hold the

arms straight up and have them pass it back and forth going up and down the floor. How long can they do that? They will not be able to do it for a minute. How much work can they do with outlet passing and rebounding if they can't hold up their arms for a minute? So, we try to spend some time developing upper body strength.

- Catching—Hands up. We never drop the hands. We do not drop the hands after we make a pass. The hands stay up, thumbs up. The hands are always in the ready position.

- Dribbling—Who can handle the ball? We want the guards to be the best ballhandler. But, we let our forwards and post handle the ball if it is the last resort. When we fill lanes, we don't assign lanes. When we started this, we assigned lanes, but the players seemed to have an excuse why they couldn't get there so we just started filling lanes by positions.

- Shooting—get the shot that you want to use out of the break; right- and left-handed layups, power layups, free-throw line, backboard shot. Those are your main shots off the break. Those are the four main shots we want off the break. These eight basic skills are everything we implement from day one. If you have a player who can do these eight things, you have a player.

During practice we chart everything, makes and misses. At the end of practice, we know how many layups you made and how many you missed. I think an athlete needs to know what they are doing good and what they are doing bad. I ask a player in the gym how many shots she took and how many she made and she doesn't know. How does she know that she is getting any better? We have more of a controlled break with all five people running. We want everyone filling lanes. We don't want anyone lying back. We put the 4 and 5 players in the drills.

(Diagram 1) Our first pass goes to the outlet side, and then into the middle. It may go back to the outlet and back to the middle again. When the middle person gets to the free-throw line, she throws the ball off the glass. 4 must come in and tip it back on the glass, and 5 then puts it in. So, 4 and 5 are trailers, and make sure they are in the fast-break drills. We have five players running, and we want to get the ball up the floor as quickly as possible.

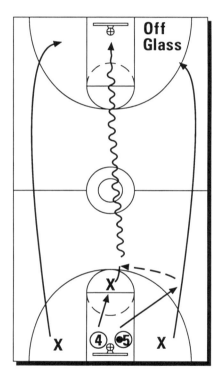

Diagram 1

(Diagram 2) If the outlet pass is made here, we want to get the ball into the middle as quickly as possible. When this happens, it is the key for the other people to fill the lanes. We say that nothing happens between the tops of the circles. You should be able to cover this distance in three seconds. You don't want to waste this time.

JO ANN RUTHERFORD

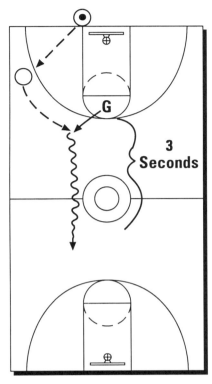

Diagram 2

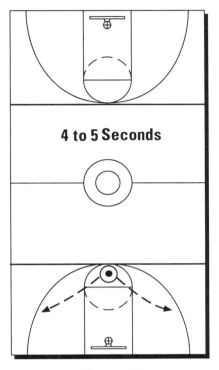

Diagram 3

(Diagram 3) The next distance is to the top of the free-throw line where the guard stops. The ball should be passed to the wing position in 4 or 5 seconds overall. We never make a blind pass and once within the scoring area, the player in the middle becomes the key. You must have a guard who makes good decisions.

(Diagram 4) How do we decide who fills? The shot is missed and rebounded. The rebounder always fills the opposite lane. The outlet makes the pass to the center and fills the other outside lane. The guard is in the middle. 4 and 5 fill in between. What if the guard gets the rebound? Same thing. Guard outlets and the other person fills the middle. Most of the time your guard will have the ball.

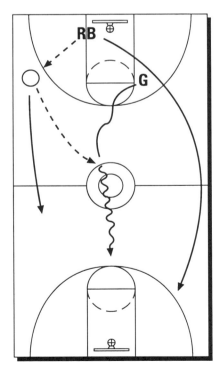

Diagram 4

JO ANN RUTHERFORD

You must have talking guards. The guard must be the leader, directing the players. I like a verbal team. Something else. If you start getting a lot of turnovers, don't panic. Don't give up the break. Keep working with it.

Question — We have a lot of trouble with the second pass, with the turnover with the guard moving away. What do you do about that?

Answer—(Diagram 5) You must always teach your guard to cut to the ball and make sure that there is no defensive player between the outlet and the guard. The guard must cut in front of the defense and go to the ball. That is her responsibility. And if the defense is cheating, she must fake and go long. She must read this. Sometimes she must come all the way to the sideline to get the pass. If she does, then someone else will fill middle.

The outlet must have her hand up, make a V-cut, and call for the ball. She must be moving to help the rebounder and make sure that your rebounder turns the right way. If she is on the right side of the basket, she turns right; if she is on the left side of the basket, she turns left. She doesn't pass across the court. If the ball comes off in the middle, she can go to either side. We do everything full-court. We do some 3-on-2, 2-on-1, 4-on-2 situations where they must know where the defense is. This is decision-making.

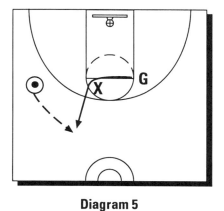

Diagram 5

(Diagram 6) I'll use three people, not 4 and 5. I'll set three defensive players near mid-court. The ball is thrown off the glass, rebounded and the outlet pass made. Then, the three offensive players will go full-court against these three.

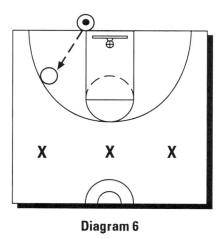

Diagram 6

(Diagram 7) The next time one defense is up, two are back.

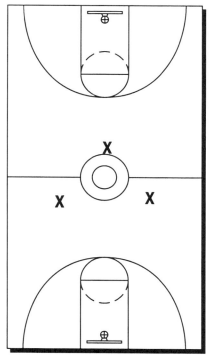

Diagram 7

(Diagram 8) Next, three will be up. We will vary the situations so the offensive team running must react to them. Even if we see a half-court defense, we will not give up the break.

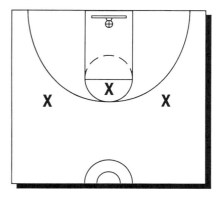

Diagram 8

(Diagram 9) Suppose we don't have the break. 4 and 5 are trailers. We are 5-on-3, but no break. The ball is passed to the wing. 5 goes to the block on the ball side. If she doesn't get the ball, she clears. 4 follows.

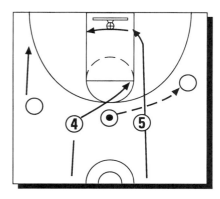

Diagram 9

(Diagram 10) If 4 doesn't get the ball, she screens away for 5. We want to get as close to the basket as we can and get the high-percentage shot.

Diagram 10

Rebounding

If you can't control the boards, you are not going to run. I used to think you had to be tall to be a rebounder, but if you ever work with stats, you will find that sometimes you have some small player getting the rebounds. My whole philosophy has changed on rebounding. I don't care how slow you are, how tall you are, you are going to rebound. How much time do you spend rebounding in your practice? Think about it. It is an assumed thing that you think your players can do and they can't. Fifty percent of the shots are missed, on the average, so you have a one out of two chance of getting the ball. We have always led the Big Eight in rebounding and have always been in the top 90 in the NCAA in rebounding. This year we were fifth in the nation. It comes down to the time you spend.

We start with how much we want the ball. First of all, what type of hands do your players have? Women have very weak wrists and fingers. We spend time with tennis ball gripping, anything that will give them strong hands. We have a drill where we give a player the ball and they hold it about waist high, and other players try to take the ball away from them. No one takes it away!

JO ANN RUTHERFORD

Take pride in the rebounding. We start our rebounding with foot position, a basic thing. We want the feet shoulder width apart, the knees flexed, the elbows out, eyes on the rim. How can you rebound when your hands are down? Jumping. Don't rely on jumping alone. If you don't block out, they go around, or come over the back and get the ball. Work on footwork, knees, and eyes focused on the basket. What type of approach do you have? We want them going to the basket where the ball is. Rebound with two hands. We say if you can get one hand on it, you can get it. Don't slap at it. If you can touch it, you can pull it down. Bring it to your chest, no lower. I like the overhead two-handed pass for the outlet pass. Some use the baseball pass for the outlet. We catch and turn at the same time. We don't come down and then turn. The outlet better be giving me the hand and yelling and moving. You need timing between the rebounder and the outlet. That's the key. Rebounding is aggressive; it's contact, so we do some contact drills.

(Diagram 1) For footwork, we have three players at a basket, two on one side, one on the other. Put the ball up and off the glass to the other side. Then change sides. Each person does the same, keep it going. This is good for foot movement. Rebounding depends on good foot movement. We spend time daily studying where will the shot come off? If she shoots a shot with arch, it will probably come off on the other side. If she shoots a flat shot, it will probably come back to her. If we know where the shot will come off, we have an advantage. How do they think about that? Conditioning, every day. When the ball is shot, we yell "Shot." First we think, "Where will the shot come off?"

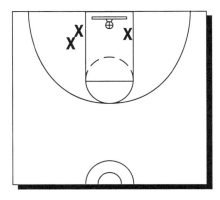

Diagram 1

Blocking out. Need good footwork. Hands up, pivot, either reverse or front. But you must step into the offensive player, turn, put your butt on their thigh, feel with one hand, and have the other hand up. Don't hold, but definitely touch with the one hand down. If you don't make contact, they are gone. The feet must continually be moving up and down. How many times do you try to block out and a quick player slides by? Keep the feet moving. It takes all five to block out. If there is a person getting beat, why are they getting beat?

(Diagram 2) We call this Circle Up. Just put the ball on the glass and block out. Then, after we block out and rebound, we run the break. If you are in a zone, find the nearest person to you, in your area. When the shot goes up, we block out the people on the perimeter. You take them wherever they are.

Offensively, we teach them to step around. One thing drives me crazy. We have inside position on a free throw and we don't get it. It's because you didn't make contact. It should never happen. When we play defense, the opponent is going to get one shot, not two. We keep rebounds in practice and the winner gets a reward. Rebounding is a mind set. If you are going to run, 70% of your fast break comes from missed field goals. Count them. I'll guarantee it. We also run on missed free throws, loose balls, and jump balls. I can't stress enough to keep the feet continually moving. I am either going to the basket or moving to keep contact.

(Diagram 3) Here is a block-out drill, very simple. 3-on-3 and the coach shoots. Block-out, rebound, and fill the lanes. Next, we give the offensive commands, one or two steps to the right, or to the left. Also, since we are the Tigers from Missouri, when we bring the ball down to the chest, we have to growl. We do this with the freshmen. You need to have some fun, too. Make it competitive as it is in the game. Reward the defense. I never reward the offense; that takes care of itself. Don't let the offensive team get more than one shot in practice.

(Diagram 4) The outlet is the key. If the ball comes off on the left, you must outlet on the left. Some people pass across the court. We don't allow that. You must outlet on the same side as you rebound. Pressure the rebounder in practice. If you don't get the outlet pass out and then make the pass to the guard, you don't have a break.

(Diagram 5) We spend a lot of time on the outlet pass, the outlet player making a V-cut and moving to get the pass, and the guard cutting in front of the defensive person to the ball. Always come to the ball. Then fill the lanes.

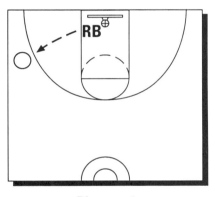

Diagram 4

Diagram 2

Diagram 3

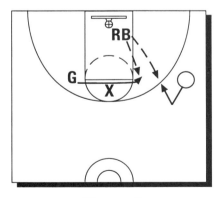

Diagram 5

One of the problems is how do you get your big people to rebound? They are not aggressive; strength is a factor. When some jump, you can't get a piece of paper between their feet and the floor.

Size doesn't make any difference. Keep your feet moving, get in position by knowing where the ball is coming off, and make contact. Challenge your worst players to become rebounders. Here is something that will help your offensive rebounding. Make the shooters retrieve their own shot. We have too many retrievers today. Many players always shoot in pairs with one shooting and the other retrieving. Make the shooter rebound any missed shot.

Question: You mentioned rebounding when the opponent shoots a free throw. Do you have any specific moves you do at this time?

Answer: We always place our players as close to the hash marks as we can, as close to the player that they will block out if they can. We don't go to the basket. We put our hips in the direction of the person we are going to block out. On offense, sometimes we switch and go across the lane. This makes the defense go across the lane with you. Many times we just try to roll inside. We have a guard back when the other team shoots, but we have one person assigned to the shooter so she doesn't get her own shot.

Question: If you are fronting the post, do you get help or do you have your player fight through?

Answer: We get help from the off-side. My philosophy is that once the ball gets inside, it is two points. The guard comes down to screen off the weakside and everyone rotates.

Once you get the rebounding mind set in your system, it will remain because the players will instill it in the players coming in.

Twelve Rules for a Zone Offense

The zone offense isn't pretty. You never draw it up, nobody likes their zone offense. So, let's develop a little philosophy here. You must decide where you want to attack that zone. Do you want to attack on the strongside? I doubt very seriously that there are many people who want to attack on the strongside. Why? Because you are going to shoot too soon. My preference would be to attack the backside. If I had a preference beyond that, I would attack the backside block. Why? Because I would prefer to attack the zone from the inside out as opposed to the outside in. Because that big guy can throw over the zone, skip the ball for you, throw diagonal passes, attack the zone on a diagonal and you can be a lot more successful going with the inside out attack. Now, I am going to set my offense to get the rebound.

Every night you strive, pray, and hope to shoot 50%. Anytime you've shot less than 50%, you've missed more than half of your shots. Why don't you design the offense to get the rebound, knowing your opponent will miss more than 50% of their shots most nights. Next thing you must decide is whether to move with the ball, to move people, or are you going to do a combination? If you do a strong evaluation of your people, you will find out that some kids can shoot on the move, some kids can't. So, why should you set up shots for them to catch the ball and shoot it on the move?

You might be better off to stand them in the gaps on the perimeter and use them as catch and shoot players. Don't design your offense on who can cut pretty, design it on whether your players are catch and shoot players or whether they can catch the ball on the move and shoot it. Probably you want a combination of both. The last thing, before we get into the rules, guard against being pretty. Don't make that thing flow so that it looks good on paper.

Evaluate it on the number of open shots you get and on the number of second shots that you can get. Then set up your zone offense and depend on your offensive rebounding to help you.

Here are the rules. At this point, I am going to take 12 rules, then at the end we will draw a zone offense with those 12 rules in it. If you have an offense with these 12 rules in it, you have an effective zone offense; you have done your job. Another question is, are you going to attack for three? Some coaches have had a hard time deciding whether they are going to be the same type of coach they were before the three-point shot or after. Shoot the three! And teach your kids to rebound long rebounds.

Rule 1: Penetrate the Gaps. Do you penetrate the gaps with the dribble? (These are in no particular order.) In the NBA today, 90% of the offense is penetrate the gaps and pitch. Get two people on the ball and throw the ball to the open man.

(Diagram 1) Here is a two-guard front zone. I am going to attack this middle gap with the dribble. You must make a serious coaching decision on how you attack the gap. Do you attack the center of the gap? Do you drive at the inside shoulder of one of the defenders? Two things are important. To distort the gap, I would penetrate toward the inside shoulder of one of the defenders. I will go into the gap with a saddle-dribble type of technique. I will turn sideways. The reason is that I don't open my body so both defenders have a chance to deflect. Set your offense to cut down on the number of turnovers. If I attack the inside shoulder, I fully occupy one of the defenders and draw the other over several steps opening up a wing pass or a post pass. If you go up the center of the gap, you leave yourself nothing to throw to except the wings.

Rule 2: Screening the zone. If I had my choice of zone offense and only could pick one, I would attack every zone out of a 1-4, or a 1-2-2, regardless of whether it was a one- or two-guard front. I would set the offense and attempt to flow into the gaps instead of having a different offense for every defense.

(Diagram 2) The decision you must make is are you going to screen the strongside of the lone for a shot, or are you going to screen the weakside of the zone for a shot? In every chance I have, I would screen the weakside of the zone. Anytime you attack the strongside, they have more defenders in the area than you have offensive people. So you want to screen the backside, throw and cut through.

Diagram 3

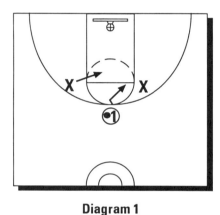

Diagram 1

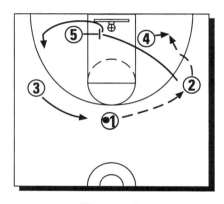

Diagram 4

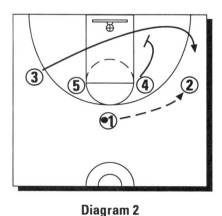

Diagram 2

(Diagram 3) 1 passes to 2; 3 cuts through. 1 cuts through and out. 5 screens the backside of the zone.

(Diagram 4) As he picks the backside, we fill each of these positions with someone. Keep in mind that this is not a play. Never look at the player that you are going to throw the ball to.

(Diagram 5) Always look at the screener. Tell your players to set the pick and run to the ball. We are looking to hit the screener because we want to attack from the inside out. Get the ball to the picker.

Rule 3: The Dribble Rule. Remember this is not an offense, this is a rule. If you have a dribble rule, you must have a straight rule and a modified rule.

(Diagram 6) My straight rule is, if I dribble toward you, you will run away from me. If I am behind the ball, I follow the ball. That sinks the backside of the zone, and 3 will get a quick shot from the reversal. That's a good three-point shot. Does your dribble rule have 2 to clear all the way through and that 1, 2, and 3 replace each other? How far do you want your people spaced? Don't always go with that 15' to 18' spacing that someone told you, because your kids may not be able to throw anything longer than a 15' pass. You determine your spacing based on the ability of your kids to throw a quick hard pass back across the zone.

Rule 4: Flashes, that's different from cuts. Flashes are short, quick bursts up into the center, the heart of the defense from behind the zone

Diagram 5

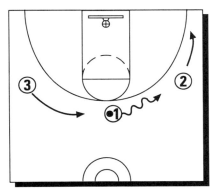

Diagram 6

(Diagram 7) I would prefer that those short quick flashes be done on a diagonal. I want to get you thinking. Build your own offense. Some have these cuts all the way through the zone into the gap areas. I don't like that.

Rule 5: Cutters, different from flashers.

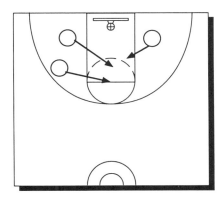

Diagram 7

(Diagram 8) Cutters are going from one side of the court to the other; down and out. Do you have cutters through the zone? If so, I make the decision based on which way I want my cutters to go. If I were using cutters, I would go from strongside to weakside as opposed to the opposite. Why? There are less defenders on the weakside, and rapid ball reversal will get you a quick shot on the backside of the zone with less defenders. So, go from strong to weak.

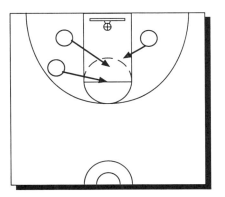

Diagram 8

Rule 6: Jump passes.

(Diagram 9) I mentioned the word "stationary." Do you stand your people in the gaps? You can let all of the movement be done by the inside people. This was started by Cal Luther. Cal Luther throws jump passes. He would penetrate the gap, jump in the air above the zone and made the jump pass to the perimeter men. Never do it against a man defense.

Consider a jump pass in your perimeter stand.

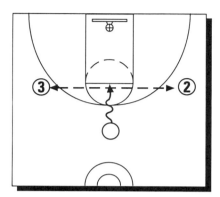

Diagram 9

Rule 7: The Step Out.

(Diagram 10) This is one of the important rules. If you play against a zone, you may be playing against a match-up zone most of the time. Did you ever hear anyone ask, "What are your fears in basketball?" The fears are attacking the press, attacking a match-up, and gimmick defenses. They want you to play a straight man or a regular zone. If you are going to play against match-ups, you must do something like this. You must step people from inside the zone to the outside to give you four on the perimeter. Make sure that you have four on the perimeter if you attack a match-up, it is the most difficult match there is. This is especially true if a player steps out from inside the zone.

Diagram 10

Rule 8: Post Crosses. "Post X s"

(Diagram 11) Let me say this again, this is not an offense. 1 passes to 2. 5 flashes to the elbow. The ball is reversed from 2 to 1 to 3. 5 slides down to the block and 4 comes off 5's rear end. Cross them off of each other's rear end. What does that do? That pinches the zone and opens up the perimeter shot.

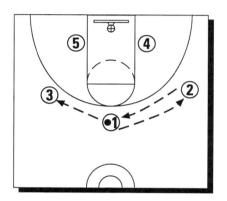

Diagram 11

Rule 9: Fill the vacuum.

(Diagram 12) We can fill the vacuum off of the dribble or the pass. 1 dribbles toward 2, who cuts through and 3 follows. That's filling the vacuum on the perimeter.

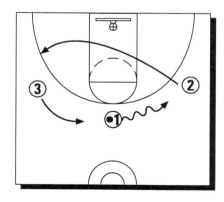

Diagram 12

(Diagram 13) You also fill it on the inside. 1 passes to 2; 4 slides down, and 5 fills the hole.

Rule 10: Denny Crum attacks a zone as well as anybody.

(Diagram 14) But when you first see him, it doesn't look like he's doing anything. He stands his biggest player behind the zone (5). He plays 4 in the gap and the shooters on the perimeter. He is now second or third in the country in three-point shooting, not the number attempted but the percentage. He stands his big man there. Give him the ball there and he is up looking over the zone. He is throwing skip-passes across the zone, hitting cutters going down the middle, hitting players filling behind the cutters. So he attacks with a standing player behind the zone, a big man. No matter what type of zone you are playing, who is going to block out big 5? No one can block him out if he runs in to rebound, runs inside and seals. If you are shooting 3's, he will run longer to rebound. Long rebounds are his.

(Diagram 15) We just showed it with 5. This is 2 skip-passing to 3. This is the fastest way to move a ball against a zone. When you attack a zone, and the ball hits your hand, where do you put it? Do you put it in the triple threat; do you chin it; do you put it above your head? You must develop a passing philosophy. Teach every player to fake a shot, fake a pass, fake a drive. During a game, do all of the combinations of these, depending on the abilities of your team. Which way would you do it? I know I would fake the shot first. If the ball hits my hands, I am not going to hold the ball low. I want it up in shooting position. I would only have the shot fake and the pass fake because I want to be able to skip it every time to get it back across the zone.

Diagram 13

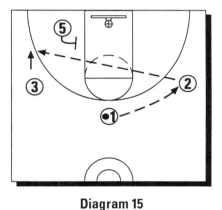

Diagram 15

Rule 12: Diagonals.

(Diagram 16) Make a pass to 5 in the short corner and have him pass to 2. That is a diagonal. Work on diagonals. I can make a diagonal pass to 3.

Diagram 14

Rule 11: Skip-passes.

Diagram 16

The Zone Offense

We would prefer to line up in a 1-2-2 or a 1-4. Let's use a 1-2-2.

(Diagram 1) First move. 1 passes to 2. 5 flashes to high-post area. 4 holds for two seconds and then goes to the short corner. Anytime the ball goes to one of the inside people, we have a high-post rule and a low-post rule. If the pass goes to the high post, it is the high-post rule, etc.

The rest of the offense is based on perimeter play. We want to get the ball inside any time we can. We are going to do the perimeter rule first. 1 takes two steps in the direction that he passes.

Diagram 1

(Diagram 2) We want 2, 3, and 5 in a line. That will make the defensive guard drop down to guard 5. 1 will get the return pass from 2 who dribbles away hard.

(Diagram 3) When 1 dribbles away, we are in a modified dribble rule at this time. 3 runs to an opening and sets up for a catch and shoot situation. Next rule, 5 steps out from inside. Now we have 4 on the perimeter.

Diagram 2

Diagram 3

(Diagram 4) The reason for the dribble was to pull the defense over. 1 now passes back to 5.

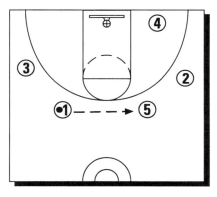

Diagram 4

(Diagram 5) The ball is in the hands of 5. 4 is in the short corner, 3 is in the dead corner.

As the ball starts toward 5, action begins by the other people. 3 runs the baseline to get inside rebounding position. 4 pins the deepest defender in the zone, he screens. 2 sets up for a shot depending on which way the defender tries to move. If the lowest defender in the zone goes around the bottom, he slides high. Normally they will go over the top, and 2 slides low. If he stays behind, he is ready for the 3-point shot. Make sure that your two best shooters are 2 and 3. After 4 sets the pick, he steps to the ball.

Diagram 5

(Diagram 6) 4 can catch the ball in the seam of the zone. But, suppose that 5 passed to 2. The only time he would throw to 2 is if 2 is open for the 3-point shot. As 5 passes to 2, he cuts into the heart of the zone. 1 fills that area for another 3-point possibility because the defender will either be fronting the high post or moving with the cutter.

(Diagram 7) 2 has the ball. 4 has picked and posted. 5 has cut inside. 3 is in position to rebound the backside, 1 is in a position to shoot a 3-point shot. If 2 shoots the ball, 3, 4, and 5 have the rebounding triangle. Who gets the long rebound? 2 moves to the elbow, 1 moves for the long rebound but really thinking "back." You need to be able to do this too. Let's go back a time. 4 screens that low man on the zone. When 4 picks, my first move is to take two steps to the ball. If the ball is passed to 2, 4 screens the defensive post man. Now 4 is in a position to score with the pass coming in on the baseline side. He has sealed the middle defender on the zone.

Diagram 6

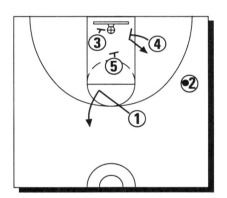

Diagram 7

(Diagram 8) Let's go to the backside. Remember we have designed the offense to get the rebound. Make sure that when you are working on an offensive rebound vs. a zone, you are attempting a lot of long 3-point shots. The ball is going to bounce longer. 2 passes to 1, 1 reverses the ball to 3. This is the only time we make a long, extended pass. Now we use a post X. 5 breaks down to the block, preferably about the block. 4 cuts off of his rear end to the open area. There's your X move.

(Diagram 9) 5 holds for a 2-second count, and goes to the short corner. Never throw the ball to a man cutting to the short corner. Make sure that he is in the corner with his feet facing mid-court before you throw the pass. Now you have a man behind the zone. Make the man behind the zone work both sides of the floor. 1 fills behind the pass.

Diagram 8

Diagram 9

(Diagram 10) When 3 passes to 1, 1 dribbles away extremely fast toward the other side. 4 steps out from inside the zone.

(Diagram 11) 3 is setting to shoot. 5 is in the short corner; 4 has stepped out on the perimeter; 1 has the ball; 2 ran to the corner when 1 dribbled toward him. 2 is a threat to shoot the three-point shot. The zone is now spread. 1 passes back to 4, and everybody goes into action. 2 runs the baseline to rebound on the inside. 2 cuts around and under and comes back inside. 5 picks the only player who can cover 3. 3 will slide low, or slide high, or step up, catch and shoot. When 4 passes the ball, 4 cuts back inside looking for the return pass. 1 fills right behind 4 for the attempted three-point shot. I have a 6'9" Russian playing for me, and all he does is step out and shoot 3's. He can't make a layup, but can shoot from the outside.

Diagram 10

Diagram 11

(Diagram 12) Here is 4. We tell him to drive the ball to the goal. That's where the penetrate and pitch comes from. In European basketball, they always fill the area from which they have penetrated. 1 fills behind 4 as 4 has taken the defenders with him. 4 turns and passes back, and 1 shoots the three-point shot. There is the gapping rule.

(Diagram 13) We work these types of drills. 2 has the ball; 4 is on the block. 2 drives to the baseline; 4 loops out.

Diagram 12

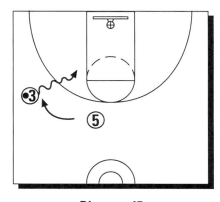

Diagram 15

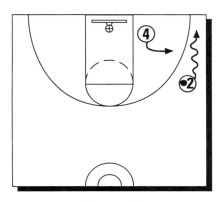

Diagram 13

(Diagram 14) If 2 drives out, 4 loops toward the baseline into an open area.

(Diagram 15) If you are on the perimeter and make a penetrating move, we fill behind on the loop.

Diagram 14

(Diagram 16) Here is the inside part now. This is the high-post rule. 1 passes to 2. 5 flashes to the high post. 4 holds for two seconds and goes to the short corner. Suppose 2 passed to 5.

(Diagram 17) When the ball goes to the high-post man, the low-post man crosses the basket in front of, or behind the defender, whichever is open. The wings slide into an open spot. High-post rule: look low, look weakside, look strong. Why weakside? Because there are less defenders over there. That is a skip-pass. 3 will be more open than anyone. Here is another part of this. Let's say that 5 passes to 3. 4 is crossing the lane; 1 is filling the top area, and 2 slides. Say that you passed the ball to 3. The rule is, anytime a skip-pass occurs, don't cross. That's too slow. Come straight to the ball as quickly as you possibly can. You are into your offense. If the ball is thrown to 4 in the short corner, here is the rule. High-post man dives at the basket. Wings slide into an opening. If the pass is made to a wing, both post men go to the ball.

Diagram 16

Diagram 18

Diagram 17

Diagram 19

(Diagram 18) Suppose that 5 passes back to 1 and 1 starts dribbling away. 5 steps out.

(Diagram 19) After that has occurred several times, the guard on that side will come out with 5 and try to steal the ball. Anytime that occurs, the skip-pass is open and you get the better 3's on the skip-pass. 1 immediately looks for the skip. This offense was designed to get the rebound and was designed for three-point shooters. This offense was designed to step out on the perimeter so you can play against match-ups. What hurts a match-up more than anything else? Screening the match-up. Teach your people to react to the screen by coming to the ball, by fading off the screen, by curling off the screen. The fade is the best way to shoot, not coming to the ball, but fading away.

Shooting

The most neglected phase in the game of basketball is the teaching of shooting. Why? Many coaches don't know anything about it. Let's say that you want to help them with their shooting. The first thing that is going to happen when you try to change their shot is that it won't feel good to them and they can't score. They can't shoot a lick when you change their shot. When you try to teach someone to shoot, you tell them that it isn't going to feel good, and they are not going to have immediate success. You are going to have to shoot for a week, shooting a hundred shots a day before you start to feel a groove and start to achieve some success.

SONNY SMITH

Here's the problem. I'd rather have a player with his form messed up than have his head messed up. So, you must get it done in the summertime, out of season. If you teach shooting, you teach it two ways. You teach them how to judge. Judge means how far to shoot it, how high to shoot it, and when to shoot it. That's judgment. The next thing you teach them is alignment. You must get everything lined up properly toward the goal.

While you are teaching, remember that judgment and alignment are in no way related. You can't teach them both at the same time. You must teach one area at a time. Then you must teach one area of an area. The first thing we are going to do is to teach alignment. This is jump shot, set shot, catch and shoot, on the run, whatever. You must pick out the pans of the body that are most involved in shooting and you must line them up with the basket.

If I am a right-handed shooter, my left leg doesn't have a lot to do with my shooting. It is a balance foot. My right leg does. I want to point my right foot at the center of the goal. The hand has a tendency to follow the foot. It swings freer following the foot than any other way. Try it. Turn your foot out and try it. You will feel the tightness. Next, the knees. You bend your knees just enough so you can slide a coin under your heel. The farther away you are from the goal, the less you bend. The closer you get to the goal, the more you bend because you are going for an explosion to get up over people. When you teach them that, you also eliminate the bad shot.

We now come to the elbow. Normally, there will be an elbow problem if they are young people. Here's why. The best players at younger ages usually aren't the best players later on because they screw up their shot. They will take the most shots, take them farther away, and when they get farther away, they will bring their arm back to throw the ball and the elbow comes out when they need the strength. Take the elbow and line it up with the toe. Now you have everything going in a straight line toward the basket.

There are several elbow positions. The low elbow position is when the elbow is even with the arm pit. When the elbow is as high as the chin, that is the medium elbow position, still in line with the toe. Your high school players should be at least that high. In college or late high school you need a high elbow lift, and get it up even with your nose or even your eyes. Any are good as long as it is lined up with the toe. Now the wrist. Tell the player that sometime during the shot, the wrist must be parallel with the floor. If it's not parallel with the floor, my wrist is half cocked and I get no arch on the ball. I shoot the ball at the basket.

You can't score shooting at the basket. When I bring the ball into a cocked position, now the ball is going to leave the hand going up and when it gets to the goal, it is coming straight down. If you cock it behind your head, you will shoot it short until you learn to compensate by straining your muscles. About this arch. If the ball is coming with little or no arch, it will only go through the back of the basket. So, you are shooting at a half a goal. If that ball is coming straight down, there is more room. Get two balls and you can push two balls through the rim at the same time. Teach your people not to shoot at half a goal. Tell them to push up and through the ball. That is the teaching technique for releasing the shot.

Did you ever see a player walk out on a court and shoot without dribbling? Never. When I dribble it, here's what happens. I catch the ball in the center because I can dribble it better. Watch what happens when I take the ball up to shoot it with my hand in the center of the ball. Look at the elbow, it is out, not in alignment. The index finger is more involved in shooting than any other. Take the index finger and line it up with the valve core. It doesn't have to touch it, but must be somewhere near the valve core. Spread the other fingers until they start to feel tight and quit. When you do that, stop. Bring the ball straight up and the elbow will be in line with the toe. This grip is tricky. Don't spread your hand as far as you can.

SONNY SMITH

Notice that my palm is not on the ball, but neither are my shooting pads. You can see all the way to the fingers. If I stop spreading my fingers when they start to feel tight, my palm is not on the ball, but the shooting pads are. Here's a little trick that is really important. Put your thumb straight up with the wrist cocked. Now snap your wrist and look only at your thumb. The thumb kicks in a little. Take the top joint of your thumb and cock your wrist back with the top joint of the thumb on the ball. Now snap your wrist forward and the thumb goes straight down. The ball rolls backward. You don't get a sideward roll. Now, that is the total alignment; toe, knee, hip, elbow, wrist, grip.

The left hand doesn't have a thing to do with alignment. It has to do with balance. There are two parts that have to do with balance. One is your left foot, put it as wide as your shoulders, toe to instep. The left hand is the balance hand. The left hand is not a part of shooting. Spread it comfortably and put it on the side of the ball. If you put it on the side of the ball, there is nothing in front of my vision. Now put the hand on the bottom of the ball. Big vision problems. Take your shooting finger on your shooting hand and hold it out in front of your shooting eye. Look straight ahead with both eyes. You will notice that you can judge distance with your left eye, but can't with your right eye. Now, make that finger the size of a wrist and look out there. You are a one-eyed shooter; that's all you are. I have shown you alignment.

Now let's talk about judgment. Here's what judgment is; knowing how high to push it, how far to push it, and when to push it. Your balance hand and balance foot has something to do with judgment because it gave me vision when it was on the side of the ball.

How far to push it? You must tell the player where to aim. Do you aim at the front, the back, or the center? Put your player in his favorite shooting spot, like a free throw. Have him shoot one hundred shots. Have somebody record his shots. Have a hundred circles on a paper. Each time he shoots it you put an X where it hits. Use one circle for every shot. When he finishes, look at the pattern. If more misses are on the back of the rim, tell him to aim at the front of the rim. If more shots miss by hitting the front of the rim, tell him to aim at the back of the rim. What if more shots hit on the side? His judgment is perfect; he has an alignment problem.

We have now covered how far to push it. Now we work on how high to push it. Tell him he has three choices. He has a low arc, a medium arc, and a high arc. If he has a low arc, he is shooting at a half a goal, and can only go through the back of the basket. Eliminate that choice immediately. Have him choose the medium arc because it takes more muscular strength to shoot it high. It will still be coming straight down when it gets to the basket

When to push it. When you are more open than anyone else on the court and someone else closer to the goal is not more open than you. But the most important thing about when to shoot it is when you are in your shooting range, in your comfort range. Here's how you teach range. Start the player at a 3' range and bank the ball in. Back off two steps and bank the ball in. When they can bank the ball in comfortably, they are in range. When it gets to the point where he must lunge toward the goal to bank it in, he is out of his range. Don't let him shoot at the rim. Make him shoot bank shots. Remember, shoot up and through the ball. When you follow through, point your index and middle fingers toward the goal.

BOB SUNDVOLD

Practice Preparation

One of the reasons you attend clinics is to refresh yourself on things you know, but could be overlooking. Your season is just over, and a lot is still fresh in your mind. A great thing about our profession is that we continually try to improve ourselves and each other.

We think when we put on a whistle and the coaching shirt the players are automatically going to listen to us. Why should you be heard by your players? I was at a USA Coaches Clinic several years ago when Debbie Holley spoke on this topic. Think about it. In college, I've recruited my players, so I naturally assume I have sold them that maybe I can coach and the school is a good place to be. But, they may not be sure and you must sell them. The first thing I ask myself is, "Do I care?" Do I care about the person? Not the player, the person.

Are the things I am doing in the best interest of that person? How do you expect someone to listen to your game plan when they don't take your advice about going to class and being on time?

Players of the nineties are growing up on TV and computer games. You don't have competition any more. There is a reset button. If a kid is disappointed with how he's doing, the easy way is to reset and start over. They are more attuned to what's going on with the video game and on TV and competition is nowhere to be found. You must be prepared for this. You must create competition.

The players will be satisfied with whatever you tolerate. If you let them play sloppy, they will. If you let them take bad shots, they will. If you don't let them do it, your players will do that, too. If you don't tolerate mistakes, your players will be happy to do that because they really want to win.

What you are doing now is the key. You are starting an overview for next season, a master plan. Decide now what you want to do next year. Make a master plan for the year and go through everything from stance to drills.

Once we get into the season, I record what days I did the drills. For example, the 4-man shell drill. I have listed floor position, off the ball, ball side, inside cut, screen away, vertical or horizontal screen, help and recover on the dribble, baseline drive, post defense, etc.

You have a new team in your conference, a new coach moving in. Where's he from? What did he do at his last job? Do you have anyone who stands out that must be covered early? Practices are for coaches; games are for players. You may be thinking about a game in late March and are preparing for it in November. Players are thinking about finishing practice. Prepare to add a play or two in February, maybe add a defense. You can't do the same thing in February that you do in November.

Think about utilization of staff and facilities. How can you maximize teaching and learning and minimize the time? Our maximum practice time is two hours and fifteen minutes. How many managers will I have? How many assistant coaches will I have? How many volunteers will I have?

Thirty minutes prior to the start of your practice is the most important time for you as a coach in setting your frame of mind for how you are going to teach. Do you want to just "get through" a practice? Don't have an early morning 8:00 am Saturday practice. Your players aren't going to go to bed early to get ready for that practice. By the time practice is over, you'll be mad.

Set up a practice so it is the best two hours of that player's day and the best two hours of your day. I write up the practices the night before, often immediately after practice. I share this with my staff the next day. I get feedback from them so when we go on the floor, we have a definite plan. Our drills are short. Individual drills are four to five minutes and a team drill is 10 to 12 minutes. We use transition in our drills. If you are working on rebounding, take it to the other end. By mid-season, it drops to an hour and a half and at the end of the year, we drop to 45 minutes. Keep the players fresh and enthused.

This is my version:

We take a day off during the middle of the week and practice on Sunday. We have a lot of out-of-state kids, and they don't have much to do on weekends when the in-state players go home. If a player isn't on time and doesn't get finished with stations, he remains after practice to finish. We seldom have a post practice for an individual. Players look at it as punishment. If we keep someone, it is only for offense, usually shooting. We always stay if a player asks for help.

CENTRAL MISSOURI STATE UNIVERSITY

Practice #: Day: Date:

Emphasis of the Day:

Thought for the Day:

Stations
    A:
    B:
    C:
    D:

Time   Subjects
2:15 pm   Defense
3:15pm   Offense
4:15pm   Whatever...

Stations is pre-practice time. The emphasis of the day could be getting back on defense or contesting shots. Our pre-practice changes. For example, we could have form shooting. How many times do your players get to come on the floor and shoot twenty 6' shots, just like you teach in summer camp? A station could be rope jumping. Another could be six trips up and down the floor dribbling for a layup, crossover moves, etc. A station could be working on stepping through a double-team, working against a trap.

A Zone Defense for a Man-to-Man Coach

There are coaches playing zone today part of the time that, a few years ago, you would never see playing it. It comes as a surprise and change. Coaches want to change the momentum. People use their defense as a weapon; they use it to score. Team depth: nine to ten players being used in a game. There is a trend for quickness over size. The skill level of many players today is such that they don't need a lot of offense to get a shot.

I never played zone. In 13 years as an assistant, we used a 1-2-2 zone occasionally. We called it a plunger defense. The point would drop all the way to the baseline, he would plunge to the baseline.

When you are a man-to-man coach, you get such an ego that every shot made against your zone is magnified. It feels like the opponent scores every time.

We wanted to change momentum and tempo and get the opponents out of their offense. We wanted to change the defensive pressure, the spots on the floor where we were applying pressure, and we wanted to be able to play our best players, quickness over size. So, I started using this zone.

Here are the advantages of this zone. It gives you good man pressure on the ball. It also has a built-in helpside defense, again man-to-man principles. It plays like man-to-man, but it looks zone and forces your opponent to go to the zone offense which is easier to defend. This zone also defends the three-point line better than conventional zones. This is crucial.

Here are the rules of this 1-1-3 zone:

- (Diagram 1) We stop the ball. Start the point guard near mid-court and make the offense declare a side.
- Pressure the ball. Those who don't pressure the ball very well in man-to-man because they fear being beat when you go into this zone, will become great at pressuring the ball. They don't feel the responsibility like in a man-to-man.

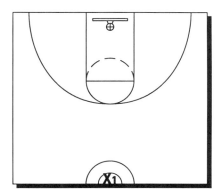

Diagram 1

- (Diagram 2) Deny lead and penetrating passes. Play the forward just like in a man-to-man. Front the post. The low post and the high post are the key areas in which to deny the passes.
- We must run to coverage areas. In man-to-man, we talk about sliding. In this zone, you must run.
- Trap all dribble penetration.
- Rebound all five men.

Diagram 2

(Diagram 3)   Here's the alignment. Our point guard comes as far up the floor as he wants to go to contain the man. When the ball is being dribbled by the point guard, X2 stays between the ball and the basket. X2 denies the high-post pass. If the ball gets by X1, X2 is the trapper. As soon as the side is declared, (this time to the right), X3 steps out and contests the wing pass. X5 steps to the ball side, denying any pass to the low post. X4 is the hoop man, he drops.

to the "half-guard position." We want X2 to stay with the high post. X5 takes the low post, plays on top; X4 is the weakside help. The ball is on the wing. In our man-to-man, we turned everything to the baseline. In our zone, we still want things to go to the baseline. We do not want ball reversal. We want the ball to go into the corner because that is the easiest shift for us to make. We take away the reverse pass by X3 overplaying and pushing the wing to the sideline.

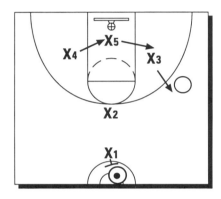

Diagram 3

Diagram 5

(Diagram 4)   You need pressure because you can see what would happen if the ball is passed across court to the opposite wing area. They would have an open shot. You cannot allow the point guard to make the easy pass.

(Diagram 6)   When the ball goes to the corner, X5 comes out under control with hands up. X3 makes the run. X3 takes two hard steps to see what's going on, and then goes to the basket. X4 comes baseline side to front the low post. X2 remains in front of the high post. There is always an illusion of an open man. When the ball is in the corner, X1 will take away the reversal pass to the wing.

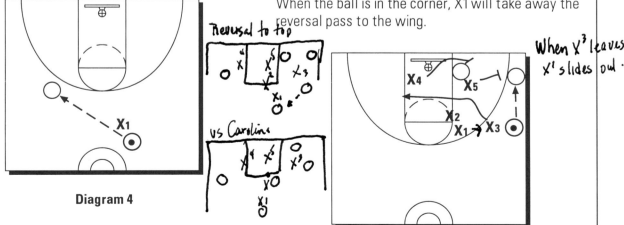

Diagram 4

Diagram 6

(Diagram 5)   When the ball is passed to the wing, X3 defends the wing. X2 is in the high post; X1 drops

BOB SUNDVOLD

(Diagram 7) X1 is in deny position. He wants to steal the pass or if X5 dribbles the ball, X1 can trap with X5. With X3 on the backside, you stress the rebound. X3 must close-out. box If X3 runs hard from the original position, he will get a lot of deflections because of passes out of the corner.

(Diagram 8) If the ball comes out of the corner and X1 didn't deny soon enough, when the ball is reversed, X1 and X2 exchange assignments. X2 plays the ball, and X1 becomes the down guard.

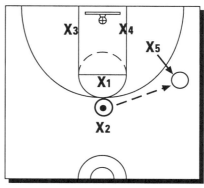

Diagram 9

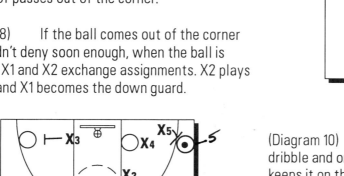

Diagram 7

When X1 connects to the wing, X2 takes point on reversal; X1

(Diagram 10) Pressure by X2 will make the guard dribble and once the ball crosses the center line, X2 keeps it on that side. That allows X3 to play denial on the wing; X4 comes to the post; X5 sprints to the hole. You must run to the coverage areas. X3 must sprint out to the wing.

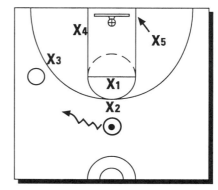

Diagram 10

Diagram 8

(Diagram 9) X5 comes to the "modified position" because if the ball comes back, X5 must come out and pressure the ball. X4 is at the low post; X3 is in the hole. X2's job is to make it as hard as possible to reverse the ball.

(Diagram 11) Against a two-guard front, X1 takes the ball, X2 will step out just like man-to-man. X5 will play ball side on the high post. X3 and X4 are on the wings until a side is declared and then one will play denial and the other will go to the hole.

(Diagram 12) If the pass goes into the high post, X5 is there. X3 and X4 go to the block areas. X1 and X2 go to the elbows. When the ball goes to the high post and the post catches it, if he turns to either side, one of our guards will trap him.

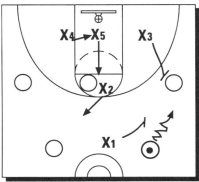

Diagram 11

Diagram 12

(Diagram 13) Suppose that with the two-guard offense the guard passes to the wing. It is just like the one-guard defense. X4 plays the ball. X1 will take the high post; X2 will drop to the half position. X5 drops to the low-post area; X3 goes to the hole, and we are in the regular defense.

Diagram 13

(Diagram 14) We can trap with this. We can't have the ball in either the high-or low-post areas. Other areas detrimental against the zone are the short corners. That is an automatic trap area. X3 is guarding the ball; X5 is fronting the low post. On any pass to the baseline, X3 starts for the basket for two hard steps and if he sees the ball in the short corner, he traps with X5. X4 slides over to play the low post, and X2 drops to the weakside.

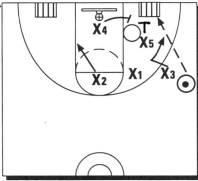

Diagram 14

(Diagram 15) You can trap the ball in the corner. If the postman ever leaves to trap, X4 will cover, X2 drops, and X1 plays centerfield.

Diagram 15

(Diagram 16) Trap the dribble penetration. If X1 gets beat, X2 will trap. X3 turns; X5 fronts, and X4 is in the hole. X1 can play on the side and entice the player into that trap.

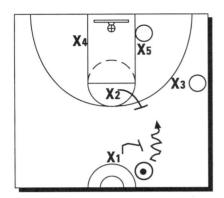

Diagram 16

(Diagram 17)   If the wing dribbles, X1 is in the half-position and will trap.

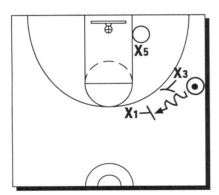

Diagram 17

(Diagram 18)   X3 can play on the side and encourage the dribble toward the baseline. X5 leaves to trap, and X1 covers the post. X4 stays at the basket; X2 is at the high post.

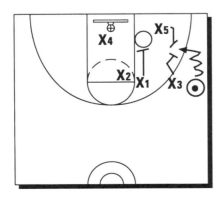

Diagram 18

(Diagram 19)   Suppose the ball is in the corner, X5 is too slow and the man dribbles around him on the baseline. X4 is fronting the low post. X4 comes to trap; X2 will drop to cover the post.

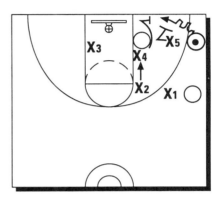

Diagram 19

(Diagram 20)   If the ball is dribbled high out of the corner, X5 and X1 will trap, X4 stays on the low post, X2 at the high post. Here are the drills.

Diagram 20

(Diagram 21)   "2 on 4." This is for the two guards. Declare a side, play the post, etc.

(Diagram 22)   The ball is reversed so that X1 and X2 exchange assignments.

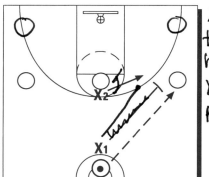

Diagram 21

X1 drops to the half guard
X2 has the post.

(Diagram 24) Big Man Drill, "3 on 7." The offense is stationary. X3, X4, and X5 work on area coverage and moving to the proper positions. The ball is passed to wing. X3 takes the ball; X5 fronts post; X4 is in the hole.

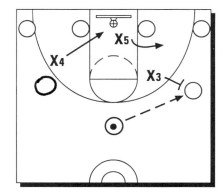

Diagram 24

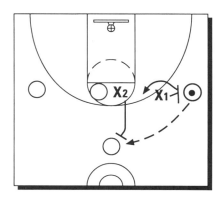

Diagram 22

(Diagram 25) The ball goes to the corner; X5 takes the ball; X4 comes baseline side, fronts the low post, and X3 takes two hard steps and sprints to the hole.

(Diagram 23) Rebounding is done from the same drill. Pass to the wing who shoots. X4 guards the shooter. X1 drops to the half position; X2 is guarding the high post. X2 runs to the position shown; X1 gets in the way of the high post. X2 must really be conscious of weakside rebounding because X3 is in the hole.

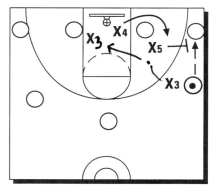

Diagram 25

(Diagram 26) The ball comes out of the corner into the guard position, but we don't have any guards in this drill. X5 comes to the half-way position so that when the ball is reversed back, X5 is in position to play the wing. X5's position is called the modified position.

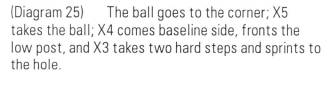

Diagram 23

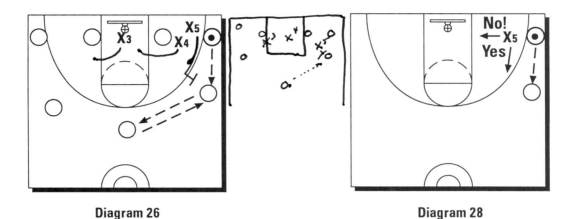

Diagram 26 **Diagram 28**

(Diagram 27) When the ball goes back into the corner, X4 takes the corner, X3 goes to the baseline to front the low post, X5 will take two hard steps and run to the hole.

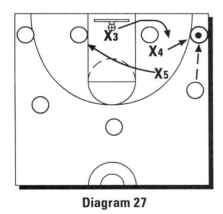

Diagram 27

(Diagram 28) If 5 is in the corner, X5 must not drop to the basket on the reversal of the ball. X5 must come to the modified position.

(Diagram 29) If the ball is reversed on the dribble, X3 must come out to take the ball, X4 slides across and X5 goes to the hole.

(Diagram 30) If the ball goes to the corner, X4 takes the ball, X5 fronts the low post and X3 takes two hard steps and runs to the hole.

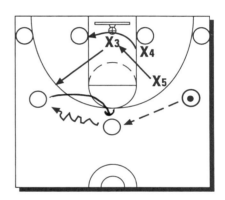

Diagram 29

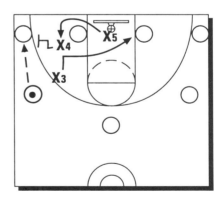

Diagram 30

(Diagram 31) "5 on 8." Every spot is covered by an offensive player. We pass on the whistle. The offense cannot move.

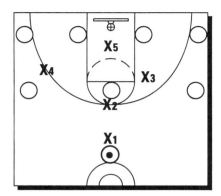

Diagram 31

(Diagram 32) We run this a little full-court. X1 takes the ball at 3/4 court and declares a side. X2 takes the middle, and X3 denies the pass on ball side. X4 and X5 must be alert. I like the shifts of this zone.

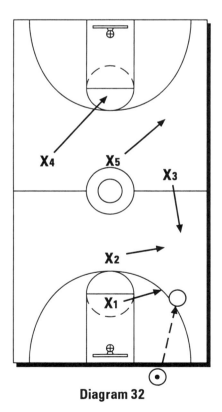

Diagram 32

(Diagram 33) If the ball goes up the side, X5 comes out, and X4 goes to the basket. X3 deflects crosscourt passes as he runs to the weakside.

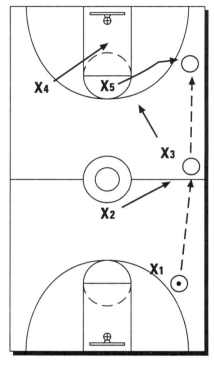

Diagram 33

ROY WILLIAMS

Teaching the "3"

The two best things Coach Smith told me during the 10 years I worked with him were: 1) be yourself, and 2) don't be stuck with one style or philosophy. Make your style and philosophy fit your players. We change each year. We use some plays every year, but change the position of the players.

(Diagram 1) Here is a good out-of-bounds play. 3 has the ball out-of-bounds. 4 and 5 double-screen for 2, who is our best player. Against a man-to-man, X4 and X5 are on the inside. The only way 2 can be covered is that X5 can switch out to 2. We tell 2 to read X2, get him low enough to rub off on the screen.

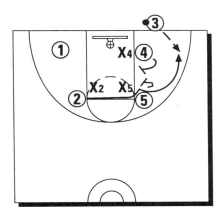

Diagram 1

(Diagram 2) They may switch, but if they do, 1 steps hard to the ball and 1 sets a screen for 5 who comes down the lane. If they switched with X2 and X5, you have a smaller person guarding 5.

You must understand my philosophy on the three-point shot. In my first five years at Kansas, 51.5% was the lowest field goal percentage we had. In that five-year period, we were first out of 298 Division I teams. This past year we were 47.2% which is a heck of a drop. That was the lowest. In 1990, we were 53.5% and led the nation in field goal percentage and shot more three-pointers in the Big Eight than any other team. Three of our kids had the green light to shoot the three. They could shoot the "3" any time as long as there was more than one defensive player back. This year we shot 47.2% and that's not good.

We had to find a way to win games. In the past, we outscored people. This year the other team had three defensive people in the lane because we could not shoot as well. We had less than five backdoor layups for the entire season. We had fewer drives to the basket than we ever had and that's because three players were not guarded when they went outside of the three-point line. That made it difficult for us to score a lot of points, especially with the elimination of the five-second dribbling rule. That took away our pressure on the wings. We didn't get as many steals, therefore we didn't get as much scoring from our defense.

We decided we were going to win this year with the defensive field goal percentage, and our rebounding. We were 7th out of 298 with defensive field goal percentage, 38.6%. Your job is to find a way to win.

Diagram 2

(Diagram 3)   This is against a zone to get a three-point shot. 3 takes it out. Every play we have is designed to get a layup with an option for the three-point shot. We wanted the ball to go inside first. It is a high-percentage shot and at the end of the game, we don't want to be playing against your five best players. By taking the ball inside first, I have a chance to get you in foul trouble and by the end of the game, one or two of your best players may be fouled out.

This is called "#2." 4 sets a screen for 5. 5 comes down the lane. We will always take the layup if he is open, but if he isn't, he goes to the corner. 4, after the screen, will roll into the lane. 1 will screen for 2.

zone, whoever comes out. So, the ball went from 3-5-2-1-2.

Diagram 4

Diagram 3

Diagram 5

(Diagram 4)   3 passes to 5, and steps in. 5 can pass to 3. Here 5 passes to 2 as 4 moves into the high post. 2 passes to 1. 4 must come across below the foul line, right about where the old dotted line was. We want 4 to occupy X4. 3 screens for 5 to go behind for the lob. You don't need anyone who can dunk. 5 can go up, catch the ball, then power the ball back up. It may be better because 5 has a better chance of being fouled.

Diagram 5)   When that happens, 3 steps out into this area. Now, I am going to decide which man to screen because we are sending 2 behind that screen for the crosscourt pass from 1. 2 has a three-point shot. 3 screens either the top or bottom man of that

(Diagram 6)   Against a Man Defense. "Double." 2 takes it out. 3 either comes around or has 4 and 5 set the double-screen. 4 then screens again for 5. 1 fakes inside and then steps wide.

(Diagram 7)   3 is near the corner; 5 is on the perimeter; 4 at the top of the key. The ball goes from 2-3-5-4. 4 fakes hard to 1 because we want the defense to shift. 3 and 5 set a double-screen, and 2 comes off for the three-point shot.

(Diagram 8)   Against a zone, we cross-screen. 3 screens high; 5 screens low, and 2 comes off for the shot. The cross-screen gives us a better angle.

Diagram 6

Diagram 7

Diagram 8

(Diagram 9)   1 is in the low-post area, and 1 screens for 5; 2 lobs to 5. You can use "double" against a zone or man.

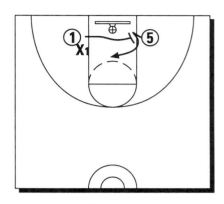

Diagram 9

(Diagram 10)   "Penetration." 1 can pass to either side, usually away from your best shooter. 1 passes to 3, and there is a quick exchange between 1 and 2. When 3 catches the ball, he kills a little time to wait for 2 to get to the top of the key. 3 penetrates toward the middle, not the baseline. 4 screens anyone in the middle of the zone. Or, if there is not a middle man, 4 will screen all the way across the zone. 5 goes behind, curls and looks for the pass from 3. 5 must go to the baseline side and get inside the weakside forward.

Diagram 10

(Diagram 11)   At the same time, 1 comes back and screens for 2 who moves for the three-point shot.

(Diagram 12)   This is against a man-to-man. We put 4 and 5 at the elbows and initiate our offense by hitting either. I don't think 4 or 5 will get out and pressure as much as 2 or 3, so I know we can get our offense started. If 4 and 5 are pressured, 2 and 3 come up. 4 and 5 are interchangeable. They have three ways they can get open. They can bump, cross, or 4 can screen for 5 and then cross. Let's say that they go at this team, but the other team does not let them get the ball. In that case, 2 and 3 will come up the lane hard. They have the same options; bump, cross, or screen.

who flares for the possible pass from 1. We then have somebody in position to shoot the three-point shot from either side. 4's thought is that one of his teammates is going to shoot and he should get inside position. If you ask me, our best shot is the layup, and then having the backboard covered when someone shoots. We don't like surprises. I'll stop practice and ask how many liked a shot. Sometimes I do that on a good shot. I want to be sure that everyone understands what is a good shot.

Diagram 11

Diagram 13

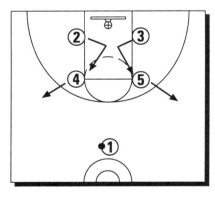

Diagram 12

Diagram 14

(Diagram 13) "Post Option." Let's say we hit 3. 5 goes backdoor. 3's first look is to 5, a two-handed bounce pass. If 5 doesn't get it, he swivels back and gets the defender on his back. 4 is thinking rebound. 2 screens for 1 who goes to the weakside. 3 has the ball.

(Diagram 14) 3 can pass to 1 for the three-point shot. As soon as 3 passes to 1, 3 sets a screen for 2,

(Diagram 15) Secondary Break. The only time we run the secondary break is when there are more than two defenders back. If there are two or less, we want a quick shot and that should be our primary break. If there are more than two, we take the ball to the baseline and flatten out the defense. We want to attack before you can get to the man you are supposed to be guarding. 3 looks in to 5. 3 passes to 1 who looks in to 5. 1 passes to 4 who looks in to 5 and then reverses the ball to 2. 2 looks into 5 as 5 works across the lane. As 4 passes to 2, 3 moves in and then comes high and sets a back-screen for 4 to go for the lob.

Diagram 15

(Diagram 16)   If 4 didn't get the lob, he continues across and screens for 5 as 2 passes to 3. 5 must go the baseline side and wants to get inside the baseline defense. 4 or 5 is open much of the time. A teaching point is that when 3 sets the screen, 3 just turns for the ball. 3 does not go out wider. We want 3 as tight as he can be. We go from this into motion.

Diagram 16

(Diagram 17)   "Secondary Break for a 3." We must call this. This is a good shot near the end of the game. 1 will penetrate and pass out to 3. 4 goes to the block; 5 stops at the top of the key.

Diagram 17

(Diagram 18)   3 will pass to 1 or skip-pass to 5. 5 fakes to 2; 3 comes up and screens for 1, and 5 passes to 1 near the corner.

Diagram 18

(Diagram 19)   "Reverse for 3." Same situation. 3 has the ball who passes to 1 to 5. 5 makes the fake to 2 as 4 comes up the lane. 4 will then turn and set a double-screen with 1. 3 comes off the double-screen for the shot. So, the ball goes from 3-1-5-3. This can also be run against the zone.

(Diagram 20)   "Isolation." 1 chooses a side, and 5 head hunts on the opposite side. 1 passes back to 3 for the three-point shot. Remember, we are running hard with our biggest player setting the screen.

(Diagram 21)   In our secondary break against a zone, the only difference is that the screener for the lob will screen anyone in the middle of the zone from the side. The lob must go inside to anybody in that back zone. I said 3 doesn't come out after setting the back-screen vs the man defense. Against a zone, 3 will have to come out higher. Other than that, they are the same. We want to run the secondary break after a make or a miss so quickly you cannot get set up to guard the man you are supposed to be guarding. Three different times this year the other team scored and four seconds later, we scored at the other end.

Diagram 19

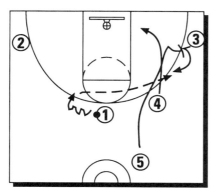

Diagram 20

Let me give you the free-lance rules that tie in with the secondary break. If we don't get the primary or secondary break, we go into our free-lance offense vs a set defense. We have three rules. 1) 3 passes unless there is a layup. 2) Change sides of the floor. 3) Give the defense a chance to make a mistake.

Think about the teams in your league. You know after two passes how strong it is; after four passes it's not quite as strong; after six passes it's not strong at all. Now, if there are two or fewer back vs the break, we are going to try to get a shot in two or fewer passes. We want to get the ball inside and when you change sides of the floor, it kills the pivot defense.

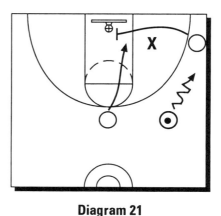

Diagram 21

Field Goal Percentage Defense

We had to make a decision on how we were going to win games this year and our field goal percentage defense was 38.6%. The best way for us to win this year was for us to stop you from scoring and for us to minimize your second shot opportunities. Because of the dribbling rule, we couldn't get out and pressure the wings and get the steals. The best defensive principle is "hand up on shot." Take your best player, put him at the three-point line and have him shoot 100 shots. Then have him shoot 100 with you in front of him, just putting a hand up. They won't shoot as well. How many times have you seen kids reach in at their gut? That doesn't bother players at our level at all. We work on this several ways.

(Diagram 1) "Close-out and Challenge." The defense sprints out and breaks down the last step and a half and gets in the defensive stance, but he must challenge the shot. The shooter can shoot off the pass or take one hard dribble either way and shoot. If the defense can, we want the defensive man to go up with him. If not, stay on the ground, but get your hands up.

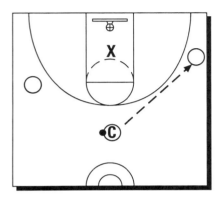

Diagram 1

(Diagram 2) "Support and Challenge." The coach drives. The defensive player must stop the dribble. The coach passes out to shooter and the defense must close-out as before.

Diagram 2

(Diagram 3) Inside, the defense is in the middle. The offensive man is on opposite block. The dribbler attacks and tries for the layup. X5 works on blocking shots. X5 faces out. The left arm is up, and the right arm is out forward.

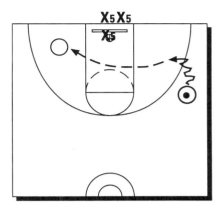

Diagram 3

(Diagram 4) "Pivot Defense." If you get on the block, or below, we completely front you. We face the ball. We have one hand at our side, the other hand up. We want to lean back into you. So, if you leave, we know it. If you are one stride off the block, we will play you with the hand around in front. If the ball is above the free-throw line extended, that is a great position. If the ball is below the free-throw line extended, that's still a good position. But, when the ball gets below the line that the pivot player is on, then that's a tough spot.

Diagram 4

(Diagram 5) Suppose we have one hand in front, and they try to throw the bounce pass to your inside hand, what do I do? We say, "Don't go fishing for it and miss it." We don't go over the top. We go behind you and "wall it." Now at least you must shoot over us. Get both hands up, and get the hands back.

Diagram 5

Exaggerate hands back. If you are able to go over the top and get around on the other side, you are going to beat that team anyway. But the good teams will ride you out and make the lob pass. By doing it that way, we push you lower to the baseline. Now, when you turn, the backboard isn't there.

(Diagram 6) This is the middle and this is the sideline. We think there is a great difference in where you have the ball. If you have the ball in the middle, we are a little more conservative with you. If you have it on the sideline, we are going to do everything we possibly can to keep it over there, and we are going to try to run you where we have help.

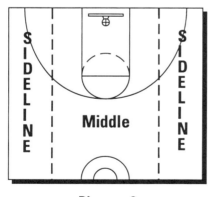

Diagram 6

(Diagram 7) We want the feet perpendicular to the sideline. We want to cut off a yard in either direction. We don't let you drive that yard. We do not let you drive to the middle of the court. We are going to stop any pass to the top of the key, and we are going to deny anything to the low post. We are going to keep you on the sideline when you get over there. When you are offense, would you rather have the ball in the middle of the court or on the sideline?

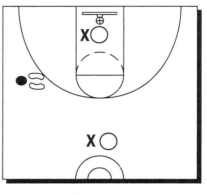

Diagram 7

(Diagram 8) When we say head-up, we mean this. We don't want you between the man and the basket. We are running the ball into an area where we have help.

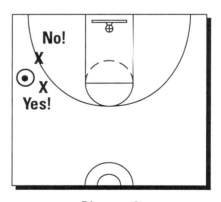

Diagram 8

Diagram 9) If the defensive help comes from the weakside, we want him to come soon enough to stop him outside the lane.

(Diagram 10) If the help is on the strongside, and X4 is fronting, wait until the last instant to help. We don't want X4 to leave because X3 can't get there. If you can do these things, you will keep the field goal percentage down. We tell our players we want as much pressure as you possibly can apply, but we can't afford to get beat down the gut. If you can't handle it, you must drop off another half step. Each player must understand his limitations.

Our first objective on defense is to steal the ball. Our second objective is to let you take an outside shot over our hands and for us to get the rebound. Our third objective is to not let you do what you do every day in practice. If we come up against a very set team, they are going to have a tough time with this. We try to stay with our philosophy. We spend about 10 minutes showing what a team did against us last time. We are going to teach our defensive principles and that should take care of it. If not, we will find another principle and work on that. If we get ready to play somebody that runs a certain thing, we will emphasize that defensive principle.

Diagram 9

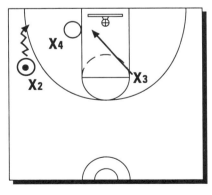

Diagram 10

Question: How do you guard a player who can't shoot? Answer: We don't.

(Diagram 11)   When we had Michael Jordan at UNC we played him there. He had to know where his man was, and he couldn't get a layup. But, you are talking about the greatest athlete I've ever seen. Jordan could guard the other four people. We gave him the other team's worst player. If you have one person who understands your defense better than anyone else, play him as a rover. Jam up the inside.

If we aren't playing a rover, we are getting after everybody. We don't want them to run their offense. I don't want them to do what they practice everyday. If we are better than you are, we are going to scramble, trap, pick you up full-court, and try to make as many possessions as we can. If you are better than we are, we are going to try to make as few possessions as we can. If we are about the same, we are going to play our regular game and hope that it's our night. With teams that are about the same, we will give them personnel. We will list the penetrators and the shooters. We will differentiate between people. I think you can do that. We did that at the high school level. You must make some decisions. Is that man going to hurt you more putting the ball on the floor or shooting from the outside? We still try to create tempo. Our game doesn't change, but you must emphasize different things.

Diagram 11

Question: If you are denial on the wing and there is penetration, what drill do you use to teach that?

Answer: (Diagram 12) Support at the point where you can still see your man and the ball. X2 must stop the dribbler and then get move on the pass. You expect the drive, but close-out so that if he goes up with the shot, you can get a hand up.

Diagram 12

(Diagram 13) This is my favorite defensive drill. We let them make the first guard-to-guard pass. And we let them make nothing after that. When 1 has the ball, X4 is in denial, and X5 is off his man. When 1 passes to 2, X5 must sprint out to the denial spot and X4 moves to the help spot.

Diagram 13

Question: When the ball is on the wing, do you deny the pass back to the point?

Answer: Yes. We try to do two things.

(Diagram 14) We have the imaginary line of ball. We want to be close to, or below, the line of the ball. We don't deny, unless it is "dribble used."

Diagram 14

(Diagram 15) Now, if the man is close, then we will deny because I do not want the ball to change sides of the floor.

Diagram 15